Global KATA

Success Through the Lean Business System Reference Model™

Terence T. Burton

New York   Chicago   San Francisco
Athens   London   Madrid   Mexico City
Milan   New Delhi   Singapore
Sydney   Toronto

1234567890   DOC/DOC   121098765

ISBN: 978-0-07-184315-7
MHID: 0-07-184315-9

e-ISBN: 978-0-07-184433-8
e-MHID: 0-07-184433-3

Library of Congress Cataloging-in-Publication Data

Burton, Terence T., 1950-
  Global kata : success through the lean business system reference model / by Terry Burton.
    pages cm
  ISBN 978-0-07-184315-7 (alk. paper) — ISBN 0-07-184315-9 (alk. paper) 1. Industrial efficiency. 2. Lean manufacturing. 3. Organizational effectiveness. 4. Organizational change. 5. Leadership. I. Title.
  T58.8.B87 2015
  658.4'013—dc23

                                                                    2015016385

McGraw-Hill Education books are available at special quantity discounts to use as premiums and sales promotions, or for use in corporate training programs. To contact a representative, please visit the Contact Us page at www.mhprofessional.com.

CONTENTS

PREFACE

There have been hundreds of books written about Lean and specific topics of continuous improvement. I have lost count, but I know that I have read most of them. All these books provide useful information about continuous improvement principles and tools for the production floor. The need for culture change is discussed, but the approaches all seem to point back to using tools and improving production processes as a basis. The tools side of improvement is visible; therefore, it is easy to learn and unfortunately easy to mimic the improvement activities of other organizations. The behavioral alignment and cultural development side of improvement is invisible; executives have put off this side of improvement because it is too slow, it takes too much time and effort, and the human element is complex. For decades most organizations have cycled their way through numerous fad improvement programs with a documented failure rate of over 80 percent. Over this period many organizations have acquired varying degrees of knowledge of Lean manufacturing tools, principles, and terminology and have also achieved varying degrees of success. Most initiatives become derailed because of the lack of longer-term leadership commitment and the permanent architecture to establish a formal, adaptive, systematic, and sustainable *management process* of continuous and sustainable improvement. During this same period Toyota is the only organization that I am aware of that has focused on a single approach to improvement: the Toyota Way and the Toyota Production System (TPS). Toyota's unmatched success is also the result of paying attention to both the *visible* (principles, tools, best practices) and *invisible* (kata) side of continuous improvement.

We began construction of a Lean Business System Reference Model just before the 2008 meltdown to help clients (and ourselves) through a new paradigm of Lean driven by accelerated business and economic requirements, emerging technology, and a heightened focus on management infrastructure and behavioral and cultural development needs. Over time we have built out the reference model by integrating new thinking, client implementation experiences, benchmarking, enabling technology, and proven best practice information strictly for internal use in our current client engagements. Because it is a reference model, it is a continuous work in progress and is never complete. However, the reference model approach has evolved into a very useful framework and guide for implementing a culturally grounded Lean Business System in any country or operating environment.

Because there is so much confusion about designing, architecting, and implementing a *for-real,* enterprisewide Lean Business System, we decided to share new knowledge through this book and provide guidance by making the Lean Business System Reference Model™ available to a much larger audience. A major objective of the reference model and this book is to guide organizations away from the superficial mimicking and success-limiting scope of Lean manufacturing principles and tools from other successful organizations and to think, innovate, expand boundaries, develop the right improvement Kata culture, and become the next global Toyota organization *in their own way.*

Global KATA: Success Through the Lean Business System Reference Model™ is our playbook for evolving Lean to a holistic, enterprisewide Lean Business System. This book sheds new light on the future of Lean and the next generation of adaptive systematic improvement. The reference model is not a replacement for the Toyota Production System (TPS); in fact it is an endorsement of its greatness. Toyota is without a doubt, the industry benchmark poster child of enterprisewide adaptive systematic improvement.

Global Kata Versus Toyota Kata

What is the difference between Toyota Kata and global Kata? Toyota Kata is discussed with reference to the Toyota Production System (TPS) and is focused on meticulous coaching and nurturing patterns of behaviors and thinking (kata) in *production*. In this setting, processes are typically more defined, standardized, and visible (via our senses) by specifications, routings, operator and equipment work instructions, maintenance schedules, production boards, and so on. Global Kata is a broader interpretation of Kata based on the *visible* and *invisible* aspects of how organizations define, create, nurture, and reinforce patterns of behavior and attribute codes in their enterprisewide culture. *Visible* includes the principles, methodologies, and best practices; *invisible* includes patterns of behavior and cultural attributes *plus* other untried, unknown, and undiscovered opportunities (which are also invisible). There is an unlimited amount of unknown and undiscovered improvement opportunities in the broader and more complex interconnected network of professional knowledge-based transactional processes. These opportunities too are invisible and cannot be harvested with a narrow *production* tools and principles focus. Here is the big differentiator: the visible and invisible complexity of improvement increases with the level of globalization and the human professional and technology content of processes, but so does the incremental value contribution of improvement. The challenge is that organizations cannot uncover and harvest these opportunities with a limited Lean *manufacturing* tools mindset and a single production model for patterns of behavior and cultural attributes. Global Kata nurtures and reinforces the desired patterns of behavior or Kata across the global enterprise but also recognizes and adjusts to local cultural norms and customs. Kata is different in every organization and in every geography. The objectives of improvement may be uniform, but *how* it is achieved and sustained around the world is influenced by idiosyncrasies between cultures.

For the 80 percent + of organizations that wish they could accelerate their Lean program, are exhausted from mimicking the Toyota Production System (TPS), are confused about how to apply Lean to nonmanufacturing areas, have hit the wall with their Lean program, are thinking about initiating a Lean program, think that Lean is not applicable to their different and unique environments, have their Lean program on hold because of more pressing business issues, or have been sitting passively while asking "What's next after Lean?," this book is the new evolution and higher-order benchmark of Lean success. The elements of our Lean Business System Reference Model are closely aligned to Toyota's companywide business philosophy but go even further by integrating improvement plus emerging technology. Additionally, the dynamics of global competition and emerging technology have mandated all organizations to rethink Lean and *improve how they improve*. The Lean Business System Reference Model also incorporates design guidelines and best practices for architecting a more laser-targeted, accelerated deployment, and rapid results model of improvement while building the right patterns of behavior (Kata) and cultural standards of excellence.

The Urgent Need for This Book

Let's step back and take a candid look at the current state of Lean in most organizations:

▲ The Toyota Production System (TPS) is solid, but its interpretation and deployment by most organizations have been too narrow and superficial. Continuous improvement looks simple, but it is not easy. For decades, this has been the story with continuous improvement: a *tools* focus and *imitation-like* approaches. It has not worked, yet organizations remain on the same improvement treadmill. Organizations will never become the next Toyota by mimicking or copying and pasting (a misinterpretation of) the tools side of TPS into their own organizations. There is so much more to Toyota's DNA than *visible* manufacturing principles and tools. Toyota has been operating in an enterprisewide "Toyota Business System" environment for decades. Throughout the book we may make references to the limitations of TPS, but we are referring to these superficial interpretations and deployments of TPS in other organizations with a tools focus, imitation approaches, and a downplaying of cultural development.

▲ Toyota Kata is so much more than a production worker and a coach and a target value in a Toyota factory. At Toyota, Kata is not limited to the production system; Kata is an enterprisewide pattern of behaviors and a cultural standard of excellence and perfection in everything that Toyota does as a global corporation. In other organizations all global leaders, executives, and managers *mentor* and *coach* their organizations and create patterns of behavior: good Kata and bad Kata—relative to Lean and relative to all other business activities. Kata is always an enterprisewide work in progress and never a steady-state practice. In the case of Toyota's long-term success, this fact is not recognized to the extent that it deserves when one limits the discussion of Kata to the narrow interpretations of the Toyota Production System or Lean *manufacturing*, backed up by production tools and examples.

▲ Today, too many organizations are struggling with the conflicts between economic uncertainty, short-term financial performance, and keeping their Lean and continuous improvement activities alive. Many have failed at Lean because of their hasty TPS mimicking approaches and a fanatical focus on tools. Others have abandoned structured and disciplined improvement altogether. The economic uncertainties over the past several years have shifted executive priorities and put a damper on Lean. It is time for a new Lean paradigm that harvests the full potential of opportunities in our challenging global economy. Organizations can certainly benefit from a more holistic and higher-impact framework for strategic and sustainable improvement and a guide for the journey.

No organization outside of Toyota has been able to leverage improvement as a competitive weapon as systematically, as timely, as effectively, as continuously, and as autonomously as Toyota. Why is this so? The main reason is that organizations globally have been attempting to mimic Toyota's success based on what they see and interpret while overlooking the deep values, spirit, behaviors, and cultural foundation that make adaptive systematic improvement at Toyota successful. Many organizations are perplexed by mimicking Toyota and other successful organizations while achieving questionable results. They have hit the wall without real improvement because they are still in a mode of *copy and imitate* rather than leading, adapting, and architecting their own culturally grounded systematic process of improvement. Many organizations are weary of the long parade of fad improvement programs over the past three decades and risk severe unintended consequences by choosing to remain in their improvement-impaired state. There is a simple lesson in all of this: As long as organizations continue to cosmetically photocopy the best practices of others, they will always be followers. The goal of global Kata is to help organizations turn this situation around. Photocopying the best practices of Toyota and other great organizations is easy; but it is not Lean *thinking* and it is not adaptive, systematic, continuous, and autonomous improvement. Global Kata is about going beyond seeing and *observing* things from a different perspective; it's about organizations giving deeper thought into Lean and the tremendous untapped opportunities of adaptive systematic improvement across the entire global enterprise.

What else is happening? Developments in the global industrialized world combined with a rapid evolution in emerging technology has occurred at a faster rate than most organizations can adapt their Lean and continuous improvement strategies. Technology is also morphing the concept of *process* away from physical content and more toward human, knowledge, and technology content. Look at the physical content (e.g., production, equipment) versus the professional, knowledge-based content in most organizations. Now ask where the root causes of many manufacturing problems originate. The majority of sources include the complex network of transactional processes: sales, order entry, configuration management, sales and operations planning (S&OP) and the global supply chain, new product development, customer service, quality, regulatory and compliance, warranty and repair, engineering, human resources, outsourcing decisions, product management, R&D, purchasing and supplier selection, IT, poor customer and supplier planning systems, finance, leadership, and many interactive combinations of all of the above. There are so many unknown and untapped opportunities for improvement in the professional, knowledge-based, transactional process space. Porting over a narrow set of production principles and tools to the office is not the way to harvest these grand-scale opportunities.

Navigating Through Global Kata and the Lean Business System Reference Model

Throughout the book you will read about the principle of *structured means and deliberate actions*. This is a critical design criterion for a holistic Lean Business System. Accordingly, the book is organized using the same principle to create a logical understanding of the Lean Business System Reference Model, and achieve the "global Kata" status of Toyota and a few other great organizations.

Chapter 1 provides a historical perspective of Lean and continuous improvement. This chapter underscores that many of the basic fundamentals and core principles of a *for-real* Lean Business System have been around for many, many decades. Executives, practitioners, and their organizations can gain valuable insights about the future of Lean by paying close attention to the lessons learned through history.

Chapter 2 provides an overview of the Lean Business System Reference Model and its architecture guidelines, subprocesses, and principles. These architecture subprocesses include:

▲ Operating strategy, vision, leadership, governance, and interventions

▲ Living improvement strategy

▲ Deployment planning, prioritization, alignment, and control

▲ Change awareness, communication, management, and reinforcement

▲ Infrastructure and talent development via center of excellence

▲ Execution, ownership, and sustainability

▲ Performance reporting and measurement

The purpose of the Lean Business System Reference Model is to provide a working framework for thinking deeper about both the visible and the invisible (Kata) sides of Lean and adaptive systematic improvement. The reference model is a pragmatic and useful guide that is always in a work-in-progress state and continuously under development. Implementing a Lean Business System in a particular organization requires an adaptive design and integration of all critical success factors. Keep in mind that it is a GPS that leads to a truer and much more potent true north, but executives and their organizations must do all the driving to get there.

Chapters 3 through 8 provide a detailed description of each of the subprocesses of the Lean Business System Reference Model, including design and implementation guidance, frameworks, templates, systematic architecture, examples, performance criteria, and proven best practices. These chapters provide extensive guidance for a higher-order, enterprisewide process of adaptive systematic improvement by introducing new Lean principles about leadership, evolving technology, innovation, transactional processes, and behavioral alignment and cultural development. The reference model guides the reader through the right structured means and deliberate actions to create the right improvement Kata thinking *throughout* any organization and in any country. Collectively, the architecture and best practices provide a new journey to a higher level of enterprise excellence and superior performance, enabling all organizations to evolve to a higher-order XYZ business system *in their own way.*

Chapter 9 provides guidance on how to adapt the Lean Business System Reference Model to organization-centric business requirements and cultural development needs of a particular organization. Throughout the book we talk about adaptive systematic improvement, and the words *adaptive* and *systematic* are hands-down requirements for success. We have also provided detailed guidance on integrating local cultural values, creative improvement methodologies, core business process opportunities, and technology into a Lean Business System.

Chapter 10 provides final guidance for designing, architecting, and implementing an enterprisewide Lean Business System. A few topics discussed include finding the Kata in the self, going beyond learning to see to *learning to observe,* hitozukuri and Kata Harada, agile holacracy organizations, and chronic disruption as the new healthy norm.

The *appendix* provides several examples and experiences about improving the complex interconnected network of core transactional processes. The Lean Business System Reference Model also incorporates four extensive assessments that have been created from these higher-complexity and higher-value experiences, benchmarking and best practices data, and the entire content of this book. They include:

1. Adaptive Leadership Assessment

2. Architecture and Operating Practices Assessment

3. Organizational Design and Dynamics Assessment

4. Improvement Kata Assessment

These detailed assessments serve as immediate design and architecture guidelines for an XYZ Business System, or to evaluate the performance and effectiveness of an existing XYZ Business System relative to gaps between current performance, desired performance, and best-in-class performance.

Most of the recent Lean books that precede *Global KATA: Success Through the Lean Business System Reference Model*™ have been written in a reporter documentary style about the Toyota Production System with a focus on manufacturing and tools. The primary intent of this book is to elevate Lean to a higher-order adaptive systematic process of improvement and to provide detailed guidance for organizations in the design, architecture, implementation, and growth momentum for *their own* organization-centric, enterprisewide, and culturally grounded Lean Business System. This is certainly not the cure all and end all for an organization's total competitive challenges. However, the spillover from the improvement Kata side of a Lean Business System has a tremendous impact on the entire scope of enterprise strategy, execution, and superior market performance.

Get in It to Win It

Come on, world. We can do much better than this with improvement! Have an objective look around your organization. There is a high presence of Lean *skulduggery* in many organizations. Everyone claims to be doing Lean, Six Sigma, TPS, or their own improvement business system. It is visible through the mimicking of tools and principles, the symbolic storyboards, or the beautification rituals, but it is disconnected and questionable in terms of real incremental value, profitability, growth, cultural development, and sustainable success. Some of this is definitely due to poor deployment planning and execution, and an underestimation and oversimplification of what it takes to achieve sustainable Lean or XYZ Business System success—and that is the past. The largest Lean game changers are due to innovation in global industry and enterprise structures, evolving technology, and the urgent need to increase human capital development. Remaining on the same traditional Lean manufacturing path while these new global challenges are evolving at warp speed is the equivalent of insanity: doing the same things and expecting different results. Think about stopping the budgeting and monthly financials process: All hell would break loose, right? Now think about stopping the Lean initiative: It might go totally unnoticed in many organizations. Recognizing this fact is tough, but it is necessary to get on the path of a higher paradigm of Lean and superior, best-in-class industry performance.

Toyota is a great organization, but it does not hold a monopoly on the next generation of Lean. Even Toyota knows this; they are on an aggressive pursuit to rediscover a new, higher-order business model as we speak, which will incorporate several features discussed in the content of this book. The Toyota Way is a great benchmark, but does not provide all the answers to every organization's evolving business requirements and cultural development needs. The *right stuff* is a choice that resides within the souls and resolve of all organizations. It's time to dial strategic improvement into the future with a higher-order and higher-yielding evolution of a true holistic Lean Business System *in your own way.* All organizations are in an economic war of global competitiveness—a war of *improve or fail* that has more far-reaching risks and consequences and upside potential than in any other time in the history of improvement. The behaviors, choices, and actions that leaders and organizations exhibit today and over the next decade will have a significant impact on the freedoms and quality of life of future generations.

Organizations must learn how to design and build this new core competency of adaptive systematic improvement into their organizations because the future is all about keeping up with the speed of change. Architecting a systematic process takes knowledge and experience, patience, and time—and it is never completed. Executives and their organizations may view this as a simple effort, but there is a high degree of leadership, technical details, and cultural development that goes into designing and implementing this overarching systematic process, subprocesses, code of conduct, and permanent competency development. This next evolution of improvement includes more permanence and significant value contribution opportunities for organizations. However, it requires much more than memorizing and regurgitating improvement terminology, renaming your existing Lean manufacturing program, or superficial imitations of Lean production systems, Lean management or business systems (in name only) from other organizations. *Global KATA: Success Through the Lean Business System Reference Model™* provides the guidance to the next generation of Lean as a true, enterprisewide and culturally grounded Lean Business System.

Terence T. Burton
President and Chief Executive Officer
The Center for Excellence in Operations, Inc. (CEO)
Bedford, New Hampshire

ACKNOWLEDGMENTS

Throughout my career I have benefited from dozens of authors' works on the topics of the Toyota Production System (TPS), Toyota Kata, Kaizen, Lean, and Six Sigma as well as continuous improvement in general. Collectively these books have had a tremendous impact on people and organizations pursuing their own improvement initiatives. I have read almost all of them over the years, and I am constantly searching for ways to further the profession and *improve how we improve*. Now it is my turn to reciprocate with my collection of knowledge, experiences, and wisdom—again. The inspiration for this book comes not only from my passion for strategic and operational improvement, but also from the urgent need to guide organizations to the next evolution of Lean in this highly competitive global economy.

First, I thank my family and friends who tolerated the *monklike* dedication and passion that it takes to create a respectable book. This was a very aggressive project with a self-compressed takt time. I must admit that a few *Trappist dubbels* (beer) along the way contributed positively to the monklike Kata progress. Writing a book is a huge professional commitment and a bold personal contract to provide new value to the world. It represents one's voice to the masses about a topic of both expertise and need. Although one attempts to write as much as possible during hotel stays, limo rides, room service dinners, and airline flights, most of the time and effort eat into a huge chunk of one's personal life. Nevertheless, the sacrifice is far outweighed by the ability to provide new knowledge, share experiences, and mentor and develop talent in other people around the globe.

Next, I cannot possibly thank everyone who has influenced my career journey and my ability to create this book because the Acknowledgments section would be larger than the book itself. After working with over 300 clients around the globe, I am truly blessed by having dealt with so many great people and organizations. These experiences include diverse industry environments, a universe of business challenges, different cultures and international locations, executives with a spectrum of leadership styles, and people working on different improvement initiatives in their respective teams. Management consulting is not always the glamorous life that everyone perceives it to be, but it definitely enables one to accumulate a large collection of learning experiences and vast wisdom of improvement. For me personally, the greatest rewards are the collaborative learning experiences, the shared victories, and the impact one can have on people's professional and personal lives. Together we have taught each other over and over that there is nothing greater in business and in life than the self-realization of overcoming a challenge that initially was thought to be impossible. I sincerely thank clients with whom I have worked on their strategic improvement journeys. I thank each and all of them from the bottom of my heart for their dedicated efforts, the mindsets to never give up, the emotional experiences and realization of mutual success, and the many lasting friendships that have resulted over the years.

Next I thank the thousands of authors, universities, professional societies, industry and trade associations and their associated publications, and other knowledge sources for the opportunity to learn and benefit from continuous talent development. We are all fortunate to have access to this great learning and talent development infrastructure, and technology continues to make this access easier, faster, and more widespread. This book is another addition to this great learning infrastructure and the opportunity to give back and share the collected experiences and wisdom that has been bestowed upon me by thousands of wonderful people.

Finally, a special thanks to all those at McGraw-Hill who played an active role in bringing this book to market: Knox Huston, my sponsoring editor; Scott Kurtz, production editor; and others TK. My McGraw-Hill experience was another great Lean experience: It is a great publishing organization that understands how to put continuous improvement, Kata, and technology into action. I enjoyed working with McGraw-Hill with its Lean, nimble publishing process, and its superior quality and velocity-conscious best practices. Thanks to McGraw-Hill, bringing this new book to market has been a pleasurable experience.

CHAPTER 1

The Long Evolution of Lean

It's time for a new generation of Lean and continuous improvement in general. The need for improvement and the new opportunities for improvement continue to evolve at a much faster rate than most organizations can understand and take advantage of. In fact, there are more opportunities for improvement today and into the future than there have been in the history of improvement. Most organizations have more opportunities for improvement today than they did when they began their Lean and Six Sigma journeys a decade ago. The largest opportunities are the ones that are yet to be discovered.

Exposing Your Lean Soul

What is the soul of an organization? It is the nonmaterial essence, animating principle, and moral purpose of the total organization's existence. It is embodied in the mission, vision, purpose, and culture of how organizations work—or do not work so well. Organizations that strive to become superior global industry performers must step back and recognize the changing global industry and technology dynamics, and they must comprehend their gaps in current business improvement strategies, plans, and Lean approaches—or lack thereof. In effect, it requires confronting and exposing one's soul about Lean beliefs, strategies, approaches, and performance. It also requires a recognition of the external factors driving the need to change organizations' souls of Lean. They need to understand, appreciate, and recommit to Lean and continuous improvement as a never-ending evolutionary process, just as it has been for centuries. They also need to trade in the limited short-term, tools-based approaches of Lean *manufacturing* and view Lean as a more holistic, culturally specific standard of excellence throughout the entire enterprise (and extended enterprise). Finally, they need to shift paradigms about their Lean beliefs, strategies, and approaches in order to achieve superior global industry performance. In my previous book, I used a term *improvement excellence*™, which is the organization's capacity to learn, adapt, and *improve how it improves.* This chapter puts decades of Lean and continuous improvement on the chopping block and under the microscope. This is sure to create a tough emotional challenge to everything one might believe about Lean and continuous improvement. However, *improving how you improve* is the first step toward evolving to a better and culturally grounded systematic process of Lean and permanent continuous improvement.

First Question

Have most organizations failed at Lean? Don't get annoyed, but consider the well-documented history of failed fad improvement programs in Western organizations. The historical failure rate has been running above 80 percent, and the recent Lean and Six Sigma initiatives have followed in the footsteps of this disturbing, decades-long pattern of failure. Congratulations if your organization is a long-term 20 percenter. For the 80 percenters, it just means a need to rethink your journey. Have Western organizations achieved short-term gains in productivity and performance? Absolutely, in all organizations! Inefficient organizations can and have benefitted from Lean manufacturing tools and principles embedded in the Toyota Production System (TPS). Were they utilized to their full potential for improvement? Absolutely not in all organizations!

During this time Toyota and a few other organizations have leapfrogged Western organizations by evolving their improvement efforts to *continuous,* permanent, and superior levels of industry performance. Over the years the same reasons have been used to conveniently explain away the Western failures: lack of leadership commitment, poor implementation strategy, scope and magnitude issues, wrong projects, insufficient education, conflicts with other day-to-day priorities, wrong metrics, serious customer issues, lack of executive and process owner support, employee nonacceptance, short-term financial focus, Japan versus U.S. culture, complexity and differences of the business, lack of time to improve and perform regular real jobs, workforce skill limits, and several others. Recognize that these reasons have been stated for decades, for dozens of different improvement initiatives under different banners and slogans, with the same birth-death cycles of improvement. Over time, the perception-based root causes become *excuses*. If we continue on the same path, accept these excuses, and in essence, view Western culture as a detriment to failure—we achieve the same results. We discuss this in more detail later in this chapter.

Second Question

Are the above reasons for failure the true root cause(s)? The above reasons are symptomatic of a much larger, long-term issue with Lean and continuous improvement initiatives in organizations. If we are willing to listen to history in this case, it will tell us a lot about where we need to go in the future. The real difference in long-term performance is the result of two major strategic factors:

1. *Nonadaptive, nonsystematic improvement.* Organizations have spent the majority of their time on the latest tools, principles, and jargon of continuous improvement. Today many organizations have the knowledge of Lean manufacturing tools and principles right, but historically they have not invested in the longer-term leadership commitment and architecture to establish a formal, adaptive, systematic, and sustainable *management process* of improvement. This missing organizational DNA is the superglue that holds this great foundation of knowledge in place and enables people and organizations to continuously *improve how they improve* through structured means and the right deliberate actions. Hence, tools and principles by themselves eventually lose popularity and traction in favor of the next fad program.

2. *Culture and values.* This is a topic that Western executives appreciate but fail to continually transform into competitive advantage. Herein lies the failure to recognize the power of our great Western culture and leverage our values to *innovate, lead, and nurture improvement* rather than *copy the improvements of others.* Culture has been the vulture eating the Lean lunches of organizations for decades because it is easier to copy than it is to lead, innovate, mentor and coach, develop talent, build a permanent adaptive systematic management process, and continually transform culture.

Toyota's organizational DNA and culture were created by Japanese ingenuity over a 70-year period and are still going strong. The production system is really a deeply embedded management system of adaptive systematic improvement throughout the entire corporation. Toyota has aggressively implemented fundamental industrial engineering, Lean, and Six Sigma since the end of World War II, without any fancy labels, belts, or program jargon. Toyota is undoubtedly the grand master of Lean and continuous improvement. It arrived at this status without banners, slogans, and a string of failed fad improvement programs. It arrived there out of necessity through brilliant leadership and a systematic and culturally grounded process of improvement. Western organizations should continue to learn from Toyota's success, but they must create *their own* business needs-driven and culturally powered systematic process of improvement. Merely asking employees to use a few new *visible* tools, templates, and methodologies and instantly act like Toyota equals cultural rejection.

Here Is the Bottom Line

The United States remains the number one global competitor in the world. What *is* occurring for certain is that its lead in global competitiveness is shrinking and in jeopardy of being overcome by other industrialized regions of the globe. This is a global challenge, not a U.S. challenge. Failure at Lean and other strategic improvement initiatives is a matter of perspective and temporary because true improvement is always *continuous*. No organization is perfect or best in class at everything, and certainly not forever. Best in class is a moving target, and it is within reach for any organization that chooses to go for it. The 80 percent failure studies dwell on the negatives and regurgitate the same intellectual reasons for failure. Improvement and success or failure are temporal relationships that do not matter in a single instant. Being one of the 20 percent successes or 80 percent failures today is irrelevant to the future because improvement is a never-ending race without a finish line. Failure is only failure when executives choose to throttle down or stop improvement and institutionalize waste as a norm. It may not be evident, but a *close enough is good enough* mindset in organizations is the equivalent of falling behind. Like it or not, we all live in an *improve or die* world. Best-in-class organizations continually learn from their successes and failures and get back in the race with better strategies and approaches. In it to win it! *Improve how they improve!* Improvement is all about always staying ahead and not falling behind in the race. Falling behind is not necessarily a kiss of death because improvement is always renewable and breakthroughs in improvement are always possible with the right leadership, creativity, and innovation. An organization's place in this never-ending race is a controllable leadership choice. Organizations are always slipping off, or climbing their way up the leaderboard of best-in-class performers. In several industries, the time it takes to go from a trivial follower to a market leader could be only months!

Overall, the progress with Lean *manufacturing* and other initiatives in most organizations has been very respectable. However, it has definitely been below the capability of what was and is still possible when cultural ingenuity fully rises to the occasion. Hundreds of great organizations have demonstrated this ingenuity in their Lean and general continuous improvement initiatives. Future Lean and continuous improvement are all about learning, adapting, custom-architecting, and *living* improvement—lead and powered by an organization's cultural beliefs and values. The challenging journey of how to evolve Lean to a higher-order, adaptive, systematic, and sustainable process of improvement is the purpose of this book.

Culture Rocks!

My long career in continuous improvement has taken me far beyond the specific methodologies and tools and into the unknown wilderness of successful Lean leadership and cultural transformation. For over three decades I have worked with hundreds of diverse organizations and thousands of CEOs and their executive teams across the Americas, Europe, and Asia. Not surprisingly, I have found myself in the middle of a very talented population of executives, managers, and associates with different backgrounds, experiences and cultural influences, corporate beliefs, operating styles, egos, and many other cultural and personality traits. In the United States alone there are significant cultural differences in organizations in different states and regions. This incredible learning experience has taught me that transforming culture is as difficult as hell and a full-time continuous leadership effort. Culture is the brain, nervous system, and backbone of continuous improvement. The term *culture change* is actually a misnomer; the most successful organizations treat it as a continuous evolutionary process, a constant adaptive process of rediscovery, renewal, and enlightenment.

Leading executives and organizations through this evolutionary process is a very emotional and humbling cohesion-building and constancy-of-purpose experience. These executive teams and their organizations were both serious and committed to discovering their improvement model. They revealed their souls of improvement, thumped their chests for their successes, confronted their weaknesses, and recognized the need for a more sustainable model of improvement. For me, leading organizations and their teams of people to improve and benefit personally, professionally, and financially is the ultimate experience of success. It is the impossible and very emotional mega-leadership learning and development exercise where the results are often as amazing as Moses parting the Red Sea! Their experiences have taught me the importance of leadership and the ability to sculpt the right success-enabling behaviors and culture (Kata). Culture matters! The culture within your own country, locale, and organization matters! The successes referred to above are successes because the people in the organizations made the deliberate effort to link adaptive systematic improvement to *their* culture and not a knockoff of some other company's culture. History demonstrates that Western executives and their people have not been able to create and sustain this cultural evolution with many other issues on their organizational plates. Overloaded plates and the gross multitasking of people tend to drive an oversimplification and underestimation of what it takes for success—a "hurry up and finish improvement" mindset and hence, they undermine and lead to the birth-death life cycles of improvement.

The objective of this book is to share my deep passion and interest in these topics, and build recognition and awareness in the Western world (and globally) that we are in the infancy stages of Lean in terms of what is possible. This book has been a multiyear project, integrating years of benchmarking and best practices, decades of implementation experiences, and direct interactions with thousands of executives around the globe. I am blessed to work every day with clients who expand our shared competencies and understanding of integrating cultural values into a systematic process of improvement. There is nothing wrong with any other culture. Culture is the foundation of excellence, and it can evolve to become the best culture for creating a superior systematic process of improvement.

Let's make sure that my message is clear: *The Western world is in the infancy stages of Lean in terms of what is possible. The majority of all global organizations are in the infancy stages of Lean in terms of what is possible.* The concepts, principles, and best practices guidance throughout this book are universal to all global organizations.

Think about the Western culture we all live in. For example, in the United States there is Wall Street, a short-term focus on financial metrics and performance, immediate reasoning leadership, change, speed, ambiguity, complexity, financial independence, professional success, materialism, open thinking, elbow room, freedom of actions, and many other factors of our culture are not going away. Nevertheless, think about all the great cultural personalities that exist in our U.S. corporations, our small and midsized publicly and privately owned companies. Each of these organizations also has its own micropersonalities and codes of conduct. Despite our dawdling economy and other political issues, these values enable us to enjoy freedoms and a high standard of living. This is who we are, what we are all about. This is what makes America great! America's native attributes born out of diversity are not so much cultural as they are great natural human values and beliefs. All societies would adopt these values if they were free to experience the greatness of American values. Culture rocks! So how does all of this relate to Lean and continuous improvement? The underpinnings of Western and other global culture and specific organizational values have been missing in Lean and general continuous improvement initiatives. For three decades, organizations have been attempting to replicate specific improvement methodologies and tools rebranded and repackaged from the East, backed by a *wish and hope* approach for improvement and cultural change. Organizations cannot copy and paste culture; they must nurture and develop the right enabling patterns of behavior and cultural attributes of excellence. Many organizations have discussed their cultural attributes as barriers to success rather than enablers of success. Benchmarking and learning from the successes of other organizations is a good practice, but superficial imitations will never achieve best practices. It's time for all global organizations to adapt and architect *their own* systematic and permanent process of continuous improvement that is culturally grounded to *their own* cultural values. There is no single cultural model of universal success. Executives and their people have been pummeled long enough by the anemic global economy, global competition, and a hollowing out of their industrial bases by China and other countries. Leadership and cultural attributes represent the new requirements to build a superior adaptive systematic process of improvement. It is time for all organizations to step up their Lean game and regain a superior competitive position in the global economy with *their own* style of cultural beliefs and values. This book provides direction for this renewed journey of improvement to a brighter future.

The Evolution of Improvement

Continuous improvement has been around for a millennia, since the beginning of time. Also, there are hundreds of thousands of people who have made significant contributions to improvement, from the ancient Egyptians to the people in organizations giving it their all today. If we go back to 2500 BC, the people building the colossal pyramids along the Nile were using division of labor, standardization, gemba walks, pull systems, one-piece flow, teaming, collaboration, visual management, quality at the source, and many other fundamentals of Lean. People, innovation, and culture drove the development of the methods and tools that made this possible. The Romans continued the legacy of earlier generations with new and improved materials, equipment, and work systems. They constructed landmark architectures and weapon systems that were way ahead of their time, deploying engineering principles that are still in use today. The point here is that Lean and continuous improvement are not new. Generations of societies from the Stone Age to the present have applied improvement fundamentals to further their standard of living. One could easily develop an encyclopedia of continuous improvement, but that is not the intent.

The purpose of this section is to illustrate the ever-evolving generations of improvement and the continuous adaptation and architecting of improvement to the times. It is impossible to mention every contributor and detail regarding the history of improvement. We outline the more modern and documented generations of improvement up to the present time and include some of the key contributors and milestones that evolved to get us to where we are today. For example, Frederick W. Taylor, the father of scientific management, was known as the Isaac Newton of the science of work. He adapted the science of improvement and accomplished great things in his time. Today, he would be perplexed if he walked into the twenty-first century and noticed the small influence of labor, the massive organizational and technological advances, factories replaced by broader and more complex supply chains, people replaced by technology, and the short life spans of his "one best way" philosophy. What worked well in his time is not what works well in current times, but the overarching philosophy of continuously making things better through adaptive thinking and creative problem solving remains the same. Throughout history, the various approaches and methodologies of improvement achieved great success in the respective competitive conditions that prevailed in their times.

The same holds true today: What worked well for Lean *manufacturing* in 1995 is not the same right strategy for the future of improvement. Why? Because in the global economy the world spins faster and faster, driving higher-order improvements that enable organizations to remain in the game. The history of improvement is long and certainly not boring, especially if you have a deep inner passion for excellence and an interest in taking Lean to the next levels of achievement. In fact, it provides valuable insights about how to evolve next-generation Lean and continuous improvement in organizations in order to achieve superior global competitiveness. An open mind will benefit from these long lessons about improvement from the past and help you discover the critical success factors for the future.

The remainder of this section sheds light on the long history—and continuous evolution of improvement. This history has been embedded in several industrial revolutions. For centuries—and in particular, the past three decades—the science of improvement has been called by many names, many brands, many labels. This has created a significant amount of confusion over Lean and general continuous improvement and what it takes to achieve lasting success. This section illustrates the continuous evolution of improvement where the heroes of their time adapted, architected, and time-tested improvement to specific business needs and cultural values. Not coincidently, they were able to adapt improvement and leverage leadership, culture, strategy, architecture, execution, and organizational learning into breakthroughs in global performance. Success was and continues to be the adaptation and innovation of improvement to the challenges and cultural values of particular points in time. This history is extremely important because it reveals many timeless fundamentals of improvement that are critical to the future of global competitiveness.

Figure 1.1 outlines the generations of improvement.

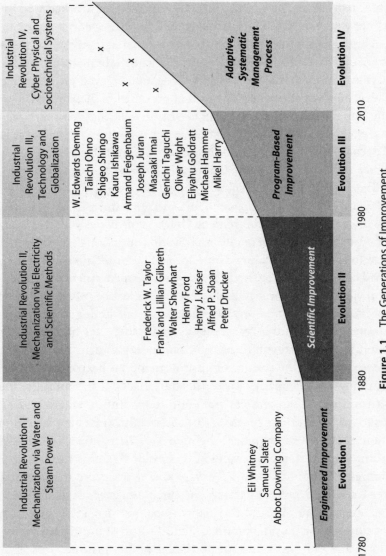

Figure 1.1 The Generations of Improvement
Copyright © 2014, The Center for Excellence in Operations, Inc.

As the chart indicates, the Western world has passed through three major evolutions of continuous improvement and is on the cusp of a new evolution with far-reaching rewards for success. Today, Western organizations are at a tipping point with Lean and continuous improvement in general. The new evolution that is upon us requires adaptive thinking to the challenges at hand—just as it has in the prior evolutions of improvement. The purpose of this history lesson is to underscore that adaptive thinking always creates success at a philosophical level. The details of architecture and culture are the real game breakers of improvement. Keep in mind that it is impossible to give credit to every hero in every evolution in this book. Each evolution includes a few milestones that highlight the improvements of its era.

The First Stage of Evolution: Engineered Improvement

The first stage of the evolution of improvement occurred from the 1780s to the 1880s, fueled by the Industrial Revolutions in Europe and the United States. This is the *engineered improvement* stage of evolution, where inventors achieved significant gains in productivity by harnessing the power of water and steam and standardization. Additional elements of this stage of evolution were organizational strategies to increase productivity. Manufacturing began with handmade "outwork systems" (craft manufacturing) whereby small parts of a larger production process were carried out in numerous individual homes. These strategies worked well for shoe and boot making. However, the major organizational breakthrough was the "factory system" where manufacturing was performed on a large scale in a single centralized location with mechanized equipment. New Englanders are very familiar with the huge historical textile mill landmarks, some of which employed as many as 12,000 men, women, and children.

Some of the improvement highlights and influences of this evolution included:

▲ Eli Whitney, inventor of the cotton gin in 1794.

▲ Samuel Slater, father of the American factory system, built a large textile mill in the early 1800s in Rhode Island that greatly increased the speed with which cotton thread could be spun into yarn.

▲ Abbott Downing Company was a Concord, New Hampshire, manufacturer of stage coaches for Wells Fargo and many other customers across the country. It developed a Lean progressive assembly operation in which interchangeable parts, standardized patterns and templates for woodworking, millwork, upholstery, and finish painting were used.

There are many more influences that could be mentioned here. These influences did not have formal improvement tools, but they had an overabundance of Yankee ingenuity which spread as American ingenuity like wildfire across our great country. During this stage of evolution, New England became a manufacturing powerhouse along rivers like the Housatonic, Quinebaug, Shetucket, Blackstone, Merrimack, Nashua, Cocheco, Saco, Androscoggin, Kennebec, and Winooski. These structures were *built to last*. Today, many of these historical brick textile mills are still occupied as stunning, rich heritage office, retail, educational, medical, and condominium spaces with large windows, exposed beams, and plank maple flooring. These magnificent buildings are a testimony to their *constancy of purpose*—a phrase first used by England's Prime Minister Benjamin Disraeli in the 1800s. On the downside of this evolution was the beginning of worker exploitation concerning problems with wages, safety, and other working conditions. This eventually led to strikes and organized labor later in history. By 1886 Samuel Gompers had founded the American Federation of Labor (AFL).

America wasn't discovered; it was built. At the end of the Civil War, the United States was seen as a failing experiment in democracy; a nation fraying from the inside and at war with itself. Just 50 years later, the United States was the greatest superpower the world had ever seen. The latter part of this evolution is known as the Gilded Age. This landmark transition was due in no small part to a group of business-savvy, innovative young men: John D. Rockefeller, Cornelius Vanderbilt, Andrew Carnegie, Henry Ford, J. P. Morgan, John Jacob Astor, and Thomas Edison. These men constructed a bold vision for a modern America and transformed the greatest industries of our time, including oil, railroads, steel, shipping, automobiles, electricity, real estate, and finance.

The Second Stage of Evolution: Scientific Improvement

The second stage of evolution of improvement occurred during the period of 1880 to 1980 with a large spike in industrial efficiency at the beginning of the twentieth century. This is the birth of scientific management and the discipline of industrial engineering, division of labor, progressive assembly lines, standard methods, and waste reduction. Yes, waste reduction—scientific management focused on eliminating the same eight wastes—transportation, inventory, motion, waiting, overproduction, overprocessing, defects, and skills (TIMWOODS)—that are part of present-day Lean, but the methods were via time and motion studies to improve industrial efficiency.

Some of the improvement highlights and influences of this stage of evolution include:

▲ Frederick W. Taylor, the father of scientific management.

▲ Frank and Lillian Gilbreth developed a system of subdividing worker motions into 18 kinds of elemental motions used in the study of motion economy in the workplace (called *therbligs*—Gilbreth spelled backwards, more or less).

▲ Walter Shewhart is known as the father of statistical quality control. While working at Western Electric Company, Shewhart framed the problem in terms of assignable-cause and chance-cause variation and introduced the control chart as a tool for distinguishing between the two. Shewhart furthered statistical quality and engineering techniques and developed the plan-do-check-act (PDCA) which was popularized by W. Edwards Deming.

▲ Henry Ford, who introduced mass production of cars, adopted Taylor's methods but took them further with the use of machines to replace some of the tasks performed by workers. Ford is one of the originators of Lean, progressive, continuous-flow manufacturing.

▲ Henry J. Kaiser built Liberty ships fast to support America's World War II efforts. Kaiser adapted mixed model and modularized mass production techniques to shipbuilding, and reduced build times from 230 days to an average of 45 days and ultimately to less than three weeks.

▲ Alfred P. Sloan, chairman and CEO of General Motors (GM) from 1923 to 1956, applied what we call *group technology* and *cellular thinking* to organizations. He decentralized GM into independent market/product business units. His actions standardized entrepreneurial thinking and quantitative management by the facts by keeping risk-taking alive within a hierarchical, rule-bound, massive, decentralized corporation focused on financial performance.

▲ Peter Drucker was a Renaissance man and guru's guru of management. In the 1950s he was promoting the notion that workers should be treated as assets, not as liabilities to be eliminated. Drucker was promoting the vast contribution of professional knowledge workers long before anyone knew or understood how human capital would trump physical assets as the essential capital of the global economy.

Many Western organizations with an appreciation for industrial and systems engineering were also involved in many of the manufacturing improvements under our current umbrella of Lean such as rate-based and short interval scheduling, assembly-line balancing, two-bin replenishment systems, more efficient equipment and plant layout, motion and time studies, predetermined time standards, quick setups, preventive maintenance, downtime reduction, quality improvement, and continuous flow that supposedly originated in Japan. This occurred in an era when there were no buzzwords other than the standard industrial engineering (IE) terminology, workplace improvement methodologies, and body of knowledge. Western IE efforts tended to be adversarial, exclusionary, and reactionary rather than prevention-based, with a major focus on cost cutting and maintaining the punitive, incentive-based piece-rate pay systems left over from the Taylor philosophy of manufacturing. The leaders and practitioners of this evolution were undoubtedly the most influential forces of the Toyota Production System (TPS).

During the earlier stages of this evolution of improvement in Japan, Sakichi Toyoda (the father of the Japanese industrial revolution and founder of Toyota Industries Co., Ltd.) was busy in the Toyoda Automatic Loom Works plant in the 1920s inventing numerous weaving devices including an automatic power loom that stops itself when problems occur. Today this concept is part of the Toyota Production System as *Jidoka* (autonomous automation). Toyoda also developed the concept of the "5 whys" which is commonly used in improvement activities today. World War II ended shortly before a scheduled Allied bombing run on the Toyota factories, but the company was on the brink of bankruptcy because of all of Japan's other extreme economic difficulties.

During the latter stage of this evolution of improvement (the post-World War II era), Japan recognized that its recovery was highly dependent upon continuous improvement methodologies of the West. Dr. Deming and his expertise on statistical quality improvement, and Taiichi Ohno with his industrial and systems engineering background and visionary thinking from Toyota took center stage in business improvement. During this same period there were many other contributors to what we now label Lean. This included folks like Kauru Ishikawa, Armand Feigenbaum, Shigeo Shingo, Joseph Juran, Masaaki Imai, and others who are noted in the next stage of evolution of improvement.

Rather than listening to the wisdom of Deming and other U.S. manufacturing gurus, we exported quality and continuous improvement to Japan which was faced with post-war reconstruction issues related to manufacturing. Post-war Japan was severely constrained in terms of space, resources, time, cost, and their perceived low quality by the East. At Toyota, for example, there was a concern with quality and inventory levels, and the costs and space consumption associated with each. Emulating exactly what U.S. companies were doing was essentially not doable and unaffordable. This era was the birth of what was later to become popularized as the Toyota Production System. Much of the TPS is Taiichi Ohno's evolution of basic industrial and systems engineering improvements aimed at the unique inventory, quality, space and natural resource limitations in post-war Japan. Recognize that the foundation of his work was people, innovation, and culture. Development and implementation of the TPS was a lot of work. Relentless, never-ending work. Work that went unnoticed by the Western world until it revolutionized global manufacturing by 1980. Toyota, Honda, Nippon, Sony, Mitsubishi, Canon, Hitachi, Kawasaki, Komatsu, and many other Eastern corporations mastered continuous improvement under the radar screen for years.

The Third Stage of Evolution: Technology and Globalization

Thirty years ago organizations in the United States became painfully aware of the importance of quality improvement, and executives were scratching their heads as they watched the 1980 NBC documentary, "If Japan Can, Why Can't We?" This was a mammoth wake-up call for business improvement. We watched Japan's success at reducing setups, defects, cycle times, costs, and inventories based on improvement techniques introduced by Taylor, the Gilbreths, Ford, Shewhart, and Deming in the early 1900s. Suddenly there was a high degree of U.S. interest in improvement. This third stage of evolution is program-based improvement. This part of the evolution began in 1980 and has lost momentum with the 2008 economic meltdown. During this same period the Western high-technology industry and industrial globalization evolved. Improvement was initially motivated by the stiff competition from the Japanese automotive, consumer electronics, steel, machine tool, and several other industries.

Some of the improvement highlights and influences of this evolution include:

▲ W. Edwards Deming is the father of the global quality revolution and the national folk hero in Japan, where he was influential in the development of the quality culture and the spectacular rise of Japanese industry after World War II. In the United States, he is known primarily for his "system of profound knowledge" which incorporates Deming's 14 points—14 key principles for managers to follow to transform business effectiveness. The points were first presented in his book *Out of the Crisis.*

▲ Taiichi Ohno was the inventor of the Toyota Production System which incorporates many of the manufacturing philosophies of what we know as Lean manufacturing. Ohno and Toyota evolved Western IE fundamentals to breakthrough levels of application and results.

▲ Shigeo Shingo was a Japanese industrial engineer and consultant most well known for his famous SMED system (single minute exchange of dies) which revolutionized setup reduction and mistake-proofing equipment. He is also known for writing about, and introducing the Western world to the Toyota Production System and the Shingo Prize, the premier award for operations excellence which was created in 1988 at Utah State University.

▲ Kauru Ishikawa introduced the concept of quality circles in 1962 in conjunction with the Japanese Union of Scientists and Engineers (JUSE). He is best known in North America for the Ishikawa or cause-and-effect diagram (also known as the fishbone diagram—see this link for additional information: http://asq.org/learn-about-quality

/cause-analysis-tools/overview/fishbone.html) that is incorporated into Lean and Six Sigma and used in the analysis of industrial processes.

▲ Joseph Juran taught courses in quality control and ran round-table seminars for executives around the world. In 1951 he published a book, *Quality Control Handbook*, which attracted the attention of the Japanese Union of Scientists and Engineers, which invited him to Japan to consult with many companies.

▲ Masaaki Imai popularized the methodology of Kaizen in his famous books, *Kaizen* and *Gemba Kaizen*. The origins of Kaizen come from post–World War II reconstruction efforts when Allied forces sent engineers to Japan to teach a course titled "Improvement in 4 Steps" (*Kaizen eno Yon Dankai*). They also installed an improvement program in Japanese companies called the Training Within Industry Program (TWI).

▲ Oliver Wight was a thought leader and educator in the evolution of material requirements planning (MRP) into MRP II, which has become the standard enterprise requirements planning (ERP) and IT architectures in organizations today.

▲ Eliyahu Goldratt is the father of the *theory of constraints* (TOC) and is credited with building awareness of constraints in manufacturing and how it negatively affects total system throughput, cost, and cycle time. His book *The Goal* became a standard manufacturing read and a great success.

▲ Michael Hammer was the proponent of a process-oriented view of business management. His book *Reengineering the Corporation* promoted a simple but academic approach to radical improvement: *Simplify, automate, or obliterate.*

▲ Bill Smith is known as the father of Six Sigma. Developed at Motorola in 1986, Six Sigma is a set of statistical engineering techniques and tools for process improvement. In the 1990s Motorola further developed Six Sigma by introducing a special infrastructure of people within the organization ("champions," "black belts," "green belts," "yellow belts," etc.) who are experts in these methods. Companies such as GE, Motorola, Caterpillar, JPMorgan Chase, Honeywell, Ford, Raytheon, and many others have achieved incredible success with Six Sigma.

There are many influencers that we could add to our wall of fame for this stage of the evolution: James Womack, Norman Bodek, Mikel Harry, Armand Feigenbaum, Seiichi Nakajima, Romey Everdell, Nick Edwards, Dorian Shainin, Genichi Taguchi, Richard Schroeder, Joseph Orlicky, George Plossl, Steve Zinkgraf, and hundreds of other passionate practitioners.

In case you were not around or not paying attention, there is a disturbing trend in this last evolution of Western improvement. History is informative, but it is much more useful if we can learn from it to our advantage for the future. A deeper dive into the *why why why, why, why* in all of this is very revealing in terms of how Western organizations must *improve how they improve*.

Figure 1.2 is an exploded view of our program-based improvement evolution. During this stage of evolution of improvement, organizations went through a lengthy succession of different discrete improvement programs like Deming's PDCA and quality circles, total quality management (TQM), just-in-time (JIT), enterprise resource planning (ERP), reengineering, Kaizen, Lean, Six Sigma, Lean Six Sigma, and dozens more. Each of these improvement initiatives had their moments of popularity and sporadic successes followed by their discrete birth-death life cycles. For the first

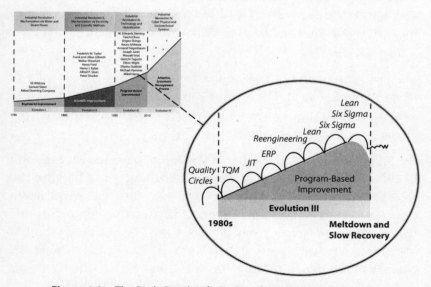

Figure 1.2 The Birth-Death Life Cycles of Western Improvement

time, many manufacturing and service organizations viewed their hourly employees as valued partners in improvement. Through these experiences of each successive program, organizations became increasingly skilled in the methodologies and tools of improvement with good results—for a while. One executive shared his perspective on improvement with me recently:

> American executives never took the time to understand the essence of Deming's PDCA cycle. They were hasty and jumped on the long bandwagon of improvement programs. What happened? The P was oversimplified, the D was too long and scattered all over the organization, and the C and A were nonexistent. There was never any system to the Western way of improvement.

The degree of success and the length of the life cycles of improvement varied from organization to organization. These life cycles have been disrupted over time by multiple leadership changes with leaders with different agendas, and other opportunities for improvement through globalization, technology, outsourcing, customer relationship management, automation and robotics, and other popularized business movements. These birth-death patterns have arisen by organizations' missing the integrated system, the human spirit, and the soul of improvement. Organizations have inoculated themselves from continuous improvement through a long string of failed fad programs and an oversimplified mimicking of improvement tools. Every organization claims to have its mumbo jumbo incantations of a Lean program, but the substance and results are just not present. Keeping this alive and unchanged also inoculates organizations from continuous improvement. Lean becomes a meaningless ritual, a non-value-added, "Yep we're already doing Lean" activity. I walked into a company lobby one day and observed its Lean mission poster and a performance chart that had not been updated for months. When no one was looking, I wrote on the chart, "Please update me." I returned a week later and there was a new version of the same outdated chart without my comment. Today, very few Western organizations can claim a successful and sustainable run at continuous improvement that compares to Toyota's constancy of purpose and success. By the way, Toyota is the only organization in the world that has been on a uniform, evolving journey of continuous improvement with a single strategy and purpose.

The root causes of these birth-death cycles of improvement are a function of Western executive behaviors, choices, and actions:

▲ When things are great, improvement is the first casualty because it is perceived to be no longer necessary. The high-technology industry is a good example of this period. Double digit revenue growth and margins produced enormous profits while hiding the sins of waste. Everyone's focus was on top-line growth and not waste reduction. In this mode, improvement programs become insignificant, check-the-box activities.

▲ When things are bad, improvement is the first casualty because people are directed into instant firefighting and symptomatic problem solving and do not have the commitment and time to improve with structured and disciplined approaches. This mode sends a strong message that improvement is no longer important.

▲ Between these two extremes, improvement has been supported by temporary and wavering commitments, token agreements, follow-the-leader fad programs, massive training, and more going-through-the-motions of improvement. Over time, executives and their organizations ride through many of these cycles, creating a *separation disorder of improvement* culture: People view improvement as an "in addition to" program rather than "an important and expected part of" their daily work.

From post–World War II to the late 1970s U.S. manufacturing became complacent. U.S. organizations stopped taking the deep disciplines of improvement seriously—the same disciplines that had enabled the United States to prevail in World War II. During this period a phenomenal rate of growth occurred in corporate and personal wealth, primarily from the emergence of high-technology industry. The top-line revenue growth and high margins of corporations took care of covering other problems, and waste became an expected, institutionalized cost of doing business. The same opportunities for improvement being aggressively pursued by Japanese manufacturers were present in Western organizations, but industrial engineering departments were diminished to an insignificant function or eliminated in order to reduce overhead spending. Many were decentralized to functional engineering support and management positions where their previous emphasis quickly became overrun by day-to-day crises. The purpose and sense of urgency to improve were secondary priorities. America was the dominant global superpower with very little competition. Shutting down lines to fix problems or running out of inventory or a shortage of employees was taboo. America ran with a "buffered waste" model of production. Why was there a need to change the business model? America's success bred a false overconfidence in future success.

At the same time, Japan was evolving Western quality and continuous improvement methodologies to rebuild itself. It pursued continuous improvement like a religious movement and *mottainai*—the Japanese term conveying a sense of regret concerning waste.

World War II left Japan a country of rubble and ashes that could not manufacture anything, and its people were starving. Whatever could be made and exported from Japan was perceived to be low-quality junk by Western standards. The purpose and sense of urgency to improve was extreme and visible in daily life. Out of necessity the Japanese eliminated waste and maximized the value-added content of work. Japanese executives and their borrowed gurus implemented continuous quality and process improvement as a universal philosophy and cultural standard of excellence. Through the combination of economic interventionism of the Japanese government, a renewed national pride, and U.S. support to rebuilding their manufacturing infrastructure, Japan quickly rebuilt its manufacturing base under the radar of foreign competitors, and catapulted itself into the world's second largest economy (after the United States) by the 1980s.

The result of this evolution of improvement was sheer Western panic. The Japanese miracle delivered the wake-up call by gaining market share over U.S. competitors. Loyal Ford customers were now driving a Toyota, Honda, or Nissan. Tradespeople were upgrading their Black and Decker, Sears, and DeWalt power tools for Ryobi, Hitachi, and Makita. Music enthusiasts were upgrading from their Fisher, Marantz, and Realistic stereo receivers to Sony, Panasonic, and Pioneer. Photographic enthusiasts were drawn to the quality and simplicity of Canon, Olympus, Minolta, and Pentax automatic cameras. Owners of Admiral, RCA, and Zenith televisions replaced them with Sony, Sharp, Mitsubishi, and Toshiba brands. Caterpillar versus Komatsu. New Holland versus Kubota. And the list went on and on. Suddenly there were several executive field trips to Japan to tour factories and learn about Japanese manufacturing techniques. Executives observed the physical mechanics and learned the terminology of Japan's manufacturing improvements without realizing their origins. They did not realize that what they were observing for the most part was a higher-order paradigm of fundamental industrial engineering operating at its max. Translated books about single-point improvement tools—e.g., kanban, cellular manufacturing, one-piece flow, SMED (single-minute exchange of die), pull scheduling, TPM (total productive maintenance), Kaizen, 5S (sort, set in order, shine, standardize, sustain), etc.—and a dozen more books about Toyota, Honda, and other successes were published. Consultants popped up everywhere offering training on the various du jour programs and their associated jargon, methodologies, and tools. Western organizations implemented continuous quality and process improvement with a more hasty and cursory, program-by-program approach because this is what people observed on the surface when they visited Japanese plants. They could neither see nor appreciate the deep cultural foundation that Toyota and other companies created to power their efforts. Nor did Western organizations have the patience to develop the behavioral and cultural attributes to keep the *continuous* in continuous improvement.

Learning about the methodologies and tools is quick and easy; the perceived simplicity lead many Western executives to believe that their organizations could offset Japan's 35-year evolution of continuous improvement by fast implementations of the same methodologies and tools. Western organizations simply emulated Japan's manufacturing excellence successes with a focus on the methodologies and tools themselves. In 1980 Western organizations were eager to catch up and were not willing to work at it for the next 35 years.

Collectively, these various improvement programs have served as drivers to clean up many inefficient Western manufacturing environments related to quality, excess inventory, space, and delivery performance. Many American companies that were direct competitors of Japanese manufacturers have reinvented themselves and have made a great comeback during this evolution, with their hard work being answered by the next challenge of outsourcing. The stream of new references continues: *The Toyota Way* by Jeffrey Liker (2004), *Toyota Culture* by Jeffrey Liker and Michael Hoseus (2005), and *Toyota Kata* by Mike Rother (2009). These books continue to play back Japan's history of improvement. Like Six Sigma and *belts,* Kata is nothing more than an advanced martial arts spin on Deming's PDCA (plan-do-check-act) cycle. We reference Toyota throughout this book because it is the grand master of continuous improvement. Toyota is not the sole inventor of the topic of improvement, but it is without a doubt the innovator and sustaining practitioner of improvement. Toyota has a running 70-year track record of continuous improvement that overshadows the Western rate of progress with no end in sight. Today many executives are waiting for the next magic improvement bullet or have decided to improve through emerging technology or via outsourcing manufacturing, design, software development, customer service, and other strategic functions to China and other third-world countries.

Improvement Lessons Learned from History

The history of improvement reveals a portion of the path to future success with improvement. History reveals that many of the basic fundamentals are timeless—and are never mastered to their fullest potential. History provides a slice, albeit a very important slice, of the future of improvement. History provides some of the enduring design guidelines for architecting the next generation of Lean and continuous improvement. To be successful with the next generations of Lean and continuous improvement, organizations must architect a new systematic process of improvement that also factors in emerging and future business requirements. Although the world of business is evolving at warp speed, several fundamentals of improvement success remain the same.

Ten Timeless Fundamentals of Improvement

Let's talk specifics and list the individual lessons about improvement that are presented in this chapter. These serve as fundamental and timeless design criteria for the future of improvement.

1. *Improvement is and always has been purpose- and needs-driven.* It is the leaders' role to keep the mission, vision, purpose, and recognition of needs in front of their organizations. It is also their role to create the motivation and sense of urgency required to change through continuous communication and reinforcement. This is Deming's "constancy of purpose," a point that organizations must master in the future.

2. *Improvement is first and foremost a philosophy and an operating culture.* Throughout history improvement has evolved as a result of creativity and innovation—and not the means (e.g., methodologies and tools) of improvement. Tools do not create this operating philosophy; people do. These fundamentals of continuous improvement are like gospel; they do not change. This is why many successful executives make analogies between continuous improvement and religion.

3. *Continuous improvement (regardless of the label) is a continuous, full-time effort.* Whether it is Taylor's scientific methods, Deming's PDCA, Six Sigma's DMAIC (define-measure-analyze-improve-control), or Toyota's Kata—these are all continuous structured cycles of improvement. The intent of these structured problem-solving models has always been to foster a culture of relentless, never-ending improvement. This is achieved by 100 percent leadership commitment, 100 percent organizational acceptance as the standard code of conduct, 100 percent engagement 100 percent of the time, and 100 percent of an organization's capacity for ingenuity, creativity, innovation, and talent development. This is the big differentiator of improvement between Toyota and Western organizations.

4. *The most successful developments in improvement include leadership, science, technology, and intellectual capital working together toward a unified goal.* Stated another way, improvement is a cohesive, systematic sociotechnical management system. Improvement is suboptimized when these critical success factors are separated (e.g., improvement just through leadership mantras, just through tools, just through technology, just through teams, just through other single-point approaches). History demonstrates that the influencers of every evolution of improvement have been on a continuous journey of *improving how they improve*. Improvement is a state in time; what makes it successful is its continuous nature.

5. *The Western world and namely the United States were home to the prime inventors, authors, and practitioners of continuous improvement as we know it today.* The respective scientific and engineering methodologies and tools of improvement (the means) have remained basically the same for the past century. The origins, background, and

fundamental methodologies of Lean and continuous quality and process improvement have a long history of development and evolution within the industrial, mechanical, manufacturing, and systems engineering disciplines. Toyota has kept culturally and architecturally in tune with this evolution of improvement.

6. *What we refer to as Lean and TPS (the Toyota Production System) were really invented in the Western world as long as a century ago or more.* The difference in recent times is that Toyota evolved and actually implemented these concepts as *the* operating and cultural foundation for doing business, while Western organizations have emulated the specific methodologies and tools through a number of fad programs (TQM, JIT, TPM, SMED, Lean, etc.). Toyota's improvement efforts have been truly continuous as an operating philosophy and system.

7. *In retrospect, the repeatable, short-lived program-based improvement approaches of Western organizations have been wishful thinking.* Many organizations have put their employees through dozens of confusing, fad improvement programs and their associated arsenal of tools and terminology. It is impossible for organizations to create a permanent cultural standard of excellence with these superficial approaches to improvement.

8. *Improvement requires an exploratory mindset and culture*—one that constantly learns and becomes comfortable with complexity and uncertainty, which opens up the mind's eye to new challenges and opportunities. Lean and continuous improvement are a mindset, not a toolset. The right methodologies and tools under the broader topic of improvement are the means to a continued and successful journey that never ends. The talent resides within people, not tools. Success is about developing and nurturing the right improvement Kata.

9. *The United States and Western organizations have lost improvement ground with their instant gratification approaches and their fanatical focus on decoupling and branding individual tools.* Dozens of twentieth-century pioneers of industrial process and quality improvement created an extensive body of knowledge called *industrial and systems engineering.* The *whole* of industrial engineering was exported to Japan after World War II. By the 1980s it was being imported back

to Western organizations in the form of individual translated tools and applications. Western organizations have spent decades building single-point improvement programs from the tools themselves. Organizations have spent too much time, effort, and money on intellectual exercises and debating the relative value of various methodologies and tools. There are hundreds of articles about the superiority of value stream mapping, why kanban is, and is not compatible with ERP, why you should begin with 5S, Lean is easier than Six Sigma, Lean versus TOC, Kaizen versus DMIAC, or the right sequence of tools to use to begin a Lean journey. Others argue that Six Sigma should be avoided because Toyota does not use Six Sigma. Does anyone really believe that Tagucchi developed his experimental design methodologies just so he could send them to Motorola for inclusion in Six Sigma? Make no mistake about it: Toyota has adapted data-driven analytical problem solving for decades without the fancy labels. It just does it! Many practitioners run around pulling a tool out of the toolbox and then looking for a problem to solve. Some refer to this approach as "fools with tools." No single-point tool is all exclusionary or all inclusive. Organizations must return to the integrated body of knowledge way of thinking about improvement.

10. *The architecture and process of how organizations improve have not changed in decades and are now obsolete.* Western organizations have followed an approach that is best described as the big bang, top down, executive mandated, talk-the-talk, token agreement versus true commitment, train the masses, launch across the entire organization, require strict compliance, get the belt or certificate, move on to the next program. This huge process often replaces the original objective of improvement. *Going through the motions* of this model often creates resource conflicts and overloads, with dozens of lengthy projects always in process but with questionable benefits. Lean, Six Sigma, and other improvement initiatives that are structured in this manner eventually become hierarchies of overhead, detractors to improvement, and questionable value contribution efforts. This explains part of why management loses interest and commitment in light of other conflicting business needs and abandons such efforts or moves on to the next vogue program. This approach is definitely not a systematic management system.

History underscores common threads of failure with improvement. Western organizations have been on a path of improvement that is fascinated with colored belts, sensei certificates, rebranded fad programs, tools, and more tools. These approaches have produced temporary success but have failed to create the much needed, autonomous and continuous, culturally grounded systematic way of thinking about improvement. Before our very eyes are the fundamental and timeless design criteria that create the foundation for a better systematic process of improvement. Organizations that are missing committed and unwavering leadership and constancy of purpose will continually take a ride down the maturity and death side of the improvement cycles. Herein lies a major objective of this book: How can we help organizations reverse this trend and implement a permanent, adaptive systematic process of improvement? How can organizations create the right improvement Kata that keeps this process running at full speed—equal to or superior to the Toyota Production System? How can organizations address new and higher-order business improvement requirements of the more complex global, knowledge- and technology-based processes? How can organizations evolve from a production system to a for-real, business system approach to strategic improvement? The answers to all these questions are provided in great depth throughout the book.

Shingo Prizes and Best Plants Awards

What about the Shingo Institute prizes and Industry Week's Best Plants Awards? Where are these organizations today? A few years back, people were asking the same questions of Baldrige winners. Some have even criticized the value of these awards. Personally, I admire the people and organizations that win these awards. These are all very noble accomplishments for a particular moment in time based on an assessment of using specific methodologies and tools, but they do not guarantee long-term success. Remember that the impressive winners represent a very small piece of the total manufacturing population. The majority of Lean initiatives in organizations are not even remote contenders for these prestigious awards. Many previous winners have all but abandoned their Lean initiatives with multiple changes in leadership, business conditions, and priorities. A few winners continue to triumph far beyond the original awards (Ahrens, Flextronics,

Lincoln Electric, Avery Dennison, General Cable, GE, Harley Davidson, Motorola, IBM, Deere, Lockheed Martin, Raytheon, Dana, Boeing, Johnson Controls, Visteon, Emerson Electric, Caterpillar, Honeywell, and dozens of other great organizations). All these organizations continue to face the same or greater operating obstacles as organizations do everywhere else, yet they continue to lead and win at improvement.

The XPS Trend

Another trendy movement today is something called XPS which stands for X (your company name) production system. The intent of XPS is to institute a corporatewide system that aims to create an operational system of improvement. Many multinational companies like the Bosch Production System, Boeing Production System, Audi Production System, Lego Production System, John Deere Quality and Production System, Alcoa Business System, REC Production System, Electrolux Manufacturing System, Danaher Business System, and others are successful XPS examples. The majority of XPS systems in other organizations are simply copy-and-paste efforts and superficial imitations of the Toyota Production System or the XPS of other successful organizations. Some organizations have chosen the brand names "X business system (XBS)" or "X management system (XMS)." A closer look at many of these initiatives reveals that their XPS, XBS, and XMS are simply Lean renaming exercises and that the companies are going through the same motions with the same recipe of tools and template-based approaches. Most are narrowly focused on Lean *manufacturing*. These organizations have simply renamed their same *process* of improvement and are expecting different results. New acronyms might create a sense of improvement and renewal, but they are often fallacious solutions to much more complex leadership, cultural, and operating problems. Organizations that have created a true, successful XPS, XBS, or XMS openly admit to the continued challenges of keeping momentum and results high and maintaining their status on the Lean leaderboard.

The Short-Term Performance Dilemma

As we mention earlier in this chapter, Western organizations have reached a historical tipping point with Lean and continuous improvement in general.

The present global economic situation and in particular the rising debt and political uncertainty of the U.S. economy has caused many organizations to pull back on their formal improvement initiatives. A recent executive comment drives this point home:

> Our industry has set aside Lean due to being forced to look at more short term problems. I think we will be in this mode for the next two years or so. Then we will rebuild our Lean program and value-focused methods once the immediate impact of the current situation subsides. I believe then that some of the gains made in the previous three years can be recovered.

Wrong! Everyone knows that statements like these make no sense. But too many organizations are spending more time getting out of recurring jams or immediate trouble than solving problems via a structured and disciplined, universally accepted approach (the cultural standard of excellence) yet they call it "improvement." Other executives make empty claims that people are using the huge investment in Lean, Six Sigma, and continuous improvement skills in autopilot mode. Their people are the first to admit that they are missing the leadership commitment, time, and resources to do the right things right the first time. And they are totally frustrated by the firefighting trap they find themselves in. Winging it based on opinions and perceptions sometimes works and meets management's immediate timetable, but it destroys commitment, loyalty, and team spirit when people feel that they are being undermined in trying to do their best job. People will never feel a sense of pride and accomplishment when they are forced to take symptomatic actions that (they know) do not fix problems. Most of the time these problems keep returning as larger problems. One executive offers his thoughts:

> We don't need Lean or Six Sigma because we already know our problems, and we are good at fixing these problems every time they occur. We have real jobs to worry about here before we think about Lean and besides—Lean is not in my goals and objectives.

It is both unfortunate and sad when leaders are allowed to interpret executive directions in this manner because these actions have far-reaching consequences for people in organizations. There are so many executives running their organizations as if they were 90-day wonders. Short-term profit-and-loss (P&L) and cash flow performance temporarily hide the hidden waste in organizations when improvement is moved down on the priority list. Great organizations understand that success involves much more than hitting the numbers. When organizations sit on cash and refuse to advance Lean and disciplined improvement in general in their organizations, this is the modern-day equivalent of a "robber barons" strategy. Many organizations have decided to postpone investments in future infrastructure in favor of performance bonuses in this uncertain economy.

Procrastination, postponement, complacency, and abandonment are losing strategies for improvement. History demonstrates that the piper always comes a-calling with significant consequences such as lost customers, excess and obsolete inventory, warehouses full of defective product, warranties, returns and allowances, hidden financial variances, unplanned discounts, cannibalized equipment bone yards, nontransacted material review board (MRB) and return to vendor (RTV) stockpiles, invoicing errors, and uncollectable accounts—all of which remain hidden until they *hit* the bottom line. Unfortunately, accounting rules allow management to conveniently perform "accounting *heijunka*" (i.e., level out the numbers) and pretty up the financial statements, while putting the burden on the next leadership regime to explain away these wastes with write-offs and restructuring costs. These costs are very real but invisible—and it's all avoidable waste and incremental profits. The piper never seems to be paid by those who allowed these wastes to accumulate in the first place.

Adaptive Systematic Improvement: The Winning Future Strategy

Continuing while adapting and changing the process of improvement is the winning strategy of improvement. This all points to the serious need to change the *process* of improvement in order to meet new requirements and operating criteria of our competitive world. The answer is not abandoning or postponing improvement; it comes down to *rethinking the process* of how organizations achieve the desired results. Organizations can rediscover Lean and continuous improvement as critical enablers of success across all time frames: immediate, short term, long term (which is about 12–18 months these days). It all comes down to replacing an out-dated model of improvement and architecting a new and adaptive model of improvement by *improving how we improve*. For Western organizations, this next evolution of improvement is an adaptive systematic process that recognizes the soul and spirit of improvement throughout the entire enterprise and views continuous improvement first and foremost as a cultural standard of excellence.

Organizations and their people typically have different perspectives of and motivations for improvement and how it should be rolled out. In the absence of a cohesive systematic process, formal improvement initiatives can (and have) run astray very quickly and in many different directions. Organizations will never get continuous improvement right by a copy-and-paste strategy or by slapping a new label on what they have been doing all along. The challenge is about evolving a higher-order philosophy of improvement and cultural standard of excellence (Kata)—the soul of the greatest organizations in the world. The soul of improvement emphasizes the immaterial essence, animating principle, and moral purpose of the total organization's existence and not the quick wealth of a few individuals.

Executives have a moral obligation to build great organizations and encourage and develop superior talent. They also have the moral obligation to swing the leadership pendulum back to a state where the whole organization benefits both short and long term. The Puritan values and characteristics of Western culture have evolved over three centuries. Their origins are from the industrial revolutions in Europe and the United States. These basic human values and beliefs are timeless; these values turned a handful of small American colonies into the greatest economic and political power on earth. Many countries around the globe have been influenced by these fundamental cultural values. Puritan roots are synonymous with energy, social mobility, competitiveness, and capacity for innovation. In recent times, many of these basic Puritan values are being replaced by charlatan values that focus more on instant gratification, short-term financial success, personal prosperity, and other get-rich-quick mindsets. Generally there are no shortcuts to success; Charlatan success is success that benefits a subgroup at the expense of the whole. The *next greatest generation* is already busy developing direct digital and additive manufacturing technologies (3D printing); reshoring manufacturing jobs back to the United States based on fully loaded costs versus labor rates; integrating improvement, and emerging technologies within the high-impact professional, knowledge-based transactional processes and using technology to transform traditional manufacturing and storefront businesses into large software logistics organizations that happen to have physical and human assets attached to them (e.g., FedEx, Apple, Amazon, Google, Williams-Sonoma, Dell, Walmart, Staples, Best Buy, Deluxe, etc.).

It is time to break the old mold of improvement and innovate a superior, *for-real* Lean Business System. The need for strategic and operating improvement never goes away, and there are *millions upon millions* of new improvement opportunities in this economy—particularly in customer service and order fulfillment, global supply chain management, new product development, software development, product management, R&D and innovation, sales and marketing, outsourcing and supplier management, technology-enabled improvement, global operations, distribution and logistics, facilities management, and all other professional knowledge-based enterprise processes.

Bibliography

Burton, Terence T. 2012. *Out of the Present Crisis: Rediscovering Improvement in the New Economy.* CRC Productivity Press, New York.

The Center for Excellence in Operations, Inc. (CEO). 2013. *Tell-Tale Signs of a Failing Improvement Initiative.* Blog on www.ceobreakthrough.com. New Hampshire.

The Center for Excellence in Operations, Inc. (CEO). 2015. *A History of Lean and Continuous Improvement.* White paper on www.ceobreakthrough.com. New Hampshire.

Deming, W. Edwards. 1982. *Out of the Crisis.* MIT Center for Advanced Engineering Study, Cambridge, Massachusetts.

Ford, H., and Bodek, N. (Foreword). 2002. *Today and Tomorrow, Commemorative Edition of Ford's 1926 Classic.* Taylor & Francis, Boca Raton, Florida.

Goldratt, E. 1986. *The Goal: A Process of Ongoing Improvement.* North River Press, Great Barrington, Massachusetts.

Hammer, M. and Champy 1995. *Reengineering the Corporation.* Harper Collins, New York.

Imai, M. 1986. *Kaizen—The Key to Japan's Competitive Success.* McGraw-Hill, New York.

Imai, M. 1997. *Gemba Kaizen—A Commonsense Approach to a Continuous Improvement Strategy.* McGraw-Hill, New York.

Juran, J. 1951. *Quality Control Handbook.* McGraw-Hill, New York.

Liker, J., and Franz, J. 2011. *The Toyota Way to Continuous Improvement.* McGraw-Hill, New York.

Rother, M. 2010. *Toyota KATA.* McGraw-Hill, New York.

Taylor, F. W. 1911. *The Principles of Scientific Management by Frederick Winslow Taylor.* A monograph. Harper & Brothers, New York.

Womack, J., and Jones, D., Roos, D., and Carpenter, S. 1990. *The Machine That Changed the World.* Free Press, a division of Simon & Schuster, New York.

Zandin, K., and Maynard, H. 2001. *Maynard's Industrial Engineering Handbook.* 5th ed. McGraw-Hill, New York.

CHAPTER 2

The Lean Business System Reference Model

This chapter introduces our Lean Business System Reference Model™. This reference model provides the business and operating architecture of a superior adaptive systematic process of improvement.

Confusion 101: Lean Production, Business, or Management System

It is important to address this issue right up front. Organizations have called their broader systematic improvement initiatives by many names such as the XYZ Company production system, the XYZ business system, the XYZ Lean system, or the XYZ management system. It is the content and substance, not the name, that makes these initiatives successful systematic processes of improvement. A humdrum rebrand of a traditional Lean manufacturing program that mimics the successes of the Toyota Production System, and the successes of other companies, will not bring sustained improvement.

Caution: If an organization chooses to call its systematic process of improvement the XYZ Lean management system, it needs to redefine *Lean* as a broader body of improvement knowledge focused on the enterprise, not the newest flavor of Lean *manufacturing*. Many organizations have joined this growing trend of renaming Lean *manufacturing* (as it has always existed) to the Company X business system. This does not make it a business system—an adaptive systematic process of enterprisewide improvement. We have already discussed the severe limitations of business improvement with a narrowly focused tool-set approach or simply attaching a new label to an old malfunctioning or peaked-out improvement program. Many speakers talk about their company's Lean business system and jump right into discussions about Lean *manufacturing* and *tools*. Most authors conceptually introduce a Lean business system and also jump right into discussions about production storyboards and action plans, A3s, kanban, 5S, leveling production, and floor gemba walks, all of which relate to *manufacturing* and *tools*. Peel back the onion and it is more mimicking of the visible Toyota Production System (TPS) details.

In this chapter we introduce our generic architecture of an adaptive systematic improvement process called our Lean Business System Reference Model. This reference model goes far beyond Womack's five principles of Lean or Toyota's 14 points or Toyota Kata's manufacturing focus or a limited list of TPS improvement tools. Organizations that keep their scope on the traditional principles of Lean *manufacturing* only will miss the point. None of this is intended to be a put-down; the world has changed and so too have the requirements and approaches to achieving a higher order of improvement. In practice, a preferred name for our architecture is the XYZ Corporation management system or XYZ Corporation business system because people and organizations are tainted by previous Westernized improvement programs and their associated terminology and tool sets. Nothing against Toyota, but I recommend that organizations avoid the name XYZ Corporation production system. It becomes much easier to describe adaptive systematic improvement as a generic enterprise-focused name with a clean slate, rather than redefining Lean or production or operations excellence into something other than what people know it to be from past experiences. People in some organizations think that they already have this management system or business system in place. A closer look reveals that it is in name only, while the substance of a limited, mediocre, go-through-the-motions *Lean manufacturing* program has remained the same. We are talking about an authentically new generation of expanded, higher-order Lean. Most importantly, we are talking about a totally integrated, enterprisewide *business system* or *management system*. A major objective of the Lean Business System Reference Model is to guide organizations away from the superficial mimicking and success-limiting scope of Lean manufacturing principles and tools and to think, innovate, expand boundaries, develop the right improvement Kata culture, and become the next global Toyota organization *in their own way*.

Thinking Enterprise Operating System Versus Tools

Throughout the book we use the terms *Lean, Lean Six Sigma, continuous improvement, strategic improvement,* and *business improvement* interchangeably when discussing the broader topic of adaptive systematic improvement because it no longer makes sense to treat the specific methodologies and tools of improvement as stand-alone programs. We also encourage the reader to avoid the great debates about tools. Pigeonholing improvement methodologies is success-limiting thinking, not Lean thinking. We understand that there are different definitions, terminology, and tools at the micro level, but there are just as many overlaps. Besides, this is how Western organizations and experts chose to package these individual manufacturing-focused improvement programs. The term *Lean Six Sigma* was a positive attempt to integrate the methodologies and tools toward a unified body of knowledge. The term *operations excellence* was a further positive attempt to "detool" improvement with a nontool label. Fact is, it is all improvement. For example, does Lean not promote standardization thereby reducing process variation? Does Six Sigma not eliminate one or more of the eight wastes when process variation is reduced or eliminated? Does enterprise resource planning (ERP) and theory of constraints (TOC) not enable Lean and Six Sigma? Does *hoshin kanri* thinking not apply to all forms of improvement? Does Six Sigma not enable Lean through data analytics and simulation? Is value stream mapping (VSM) a Kaizen, Lean, or Six Sigma tool? Are there not Kaizen activities that stem from all types of Lean, Six Sigma, IT, supply chain, or new product development projects and improvement activities? Is it right to avoid Six Sigma because Lean is easier? Which is better: Lean, mobility, business analytics, or 5S? What is the most popular tool to use when implementing Lean? Which tools accelerate innovation or technology integration? What's next after Lean and Six Sigma? If I had a dollar for every time I have been asked the last question and many other naive questions about improvement, I could go on an exotic vacation!

These comments are symptomatic of naive improvement organizations and their wavering leadership and fanatical focus on tools and terminology, while missing the point of the integrated system, spirit, and deep cultural foundation of improvement. Many practitioners continue to view Lean as a magical set of improvement tools, principles, and buzzwords to solve every problem. On top of this, there is no shortage of misinformation, silly debates, misunderstanding, misapplication, and totally incorrect advice about the use of the various improvement tools themselves. This is easier than addressing *why* the problem is there and *how* to prevent or eliminate it. This approach to Lean ("improvement toolitis") is a psychological phenomenon about how organizations have attempted to implement Lean and continuous improvement in general. I have heard people in organizations ask questions like, "What are we doing today—Kaizen, Lean, or Six Sigma?" or, "Is it time to do 5S yet?" Organizations need to break out of this improvement toolitis trap because it confuses the hell out of their organizations. Even Frederick Taylor and other pioneers would think that we lost our way by separating his principles of scientific management into individual tools-based programs and disconnected tool sets. The purpose of improvement is most important, and the *means* of improvement (i.e., methodologies and tools) are inseparable.

Toyota Kata Goes Global

Now we are learning about Kata—originally the teaching and training methods by which successful combat techniques were preserved and passed on in Japan. Practicing Kata allowed a company of warriors to engage in a struggle using a systematic approach, rather than as individuals in a disorderly manner. The basic goal of Kata is to preserve and transmit proven techniques and to practice self-defense. By practicing in a repetitive manner, the learner develops the ability to execute those techniques and movements in a natural, reflexlike manner. The goal is to internalize the movements and techniques of a Kata so they can be executed and adapted under different circumstances without thought or hesitation. Toyota Kata demonstrates the company's serious, relentless, and never-ending philosophy about continuous improvement. The book, *Toyota Kata* by Mike Rother, is a great reference to advance Lean manufacturing; it reinforces Toyota's philosophy, autonomous thinking, mentoring, and collaboration regarding improvement, and Kata is a great descriptor for this process. Toyota and other Eastern corporations have learned to work this way as a natural national standard out of sheer necessity. Toyota's culture was not naturally omnipresent; it was developed over the past 70 years by Toyota managers who were often ruthless about success. Their employees and their families were starving, respected authority, and viewed group success as being more important than their own self-interests. Western organizations on the other hand are motivated by crisis, immediate reason, and self-interests. Western organizations have more than enough talent and capacity to create a permanent, adaptive, systematic process of improvement. The difference is choice, which is directly related to cultures. Global Kata is our answer for an integrated operating system to the future of improvement. When various other basic industrial engineering fundamentals were exported to Japan after World War II, Kata was incorporated with them. Japanese corporations learned and became the global grand masters of improvement. What is the age-old secret? *Adaptive systematic process driven by people, innovation, and culture.* The philosophy and principles are universally applicable to all organizations interested in discovering their next generation of improvement. Adaptive systematic improvement means a return to the *integrated body of knowledge* and a culturally grounded, adaptive systems thinking approach about improvement.

Let's talk about the title of this book. What is the difference between Toyota Kata and Global Kata? Toyota Kata is based on the Toyota Production System and is focused on Toyota's meticulous behaviors and thinking (Kata) in *production*. In this setting, processes are typically more defined, standardized, and visible (via our senses) by specifications, routings, operator and equipment work instructions, maintenance schedules, production boards, and so on. Some organizations have directly applied TPS concepts to the office with some degree of success, but it is an exception rather than a widespread best practice. The objective of Global Kata is to *design, integrate, adapt, systematize,* and *scale* Lean across the entire enterprise and beyond.

Global Kata is a broader interpretation of Kata based on the *visible* and *invisible* aspects of how organizations define, create, nurture, and reinforce patterns of behavior and attribute codes in their enterprisewide culture. *Visible* includes the principles, methodologies, and best practices; *invisible* includes patterns of behavior and cultural attributes plus unknown and undiscovered opportunities (which are also invisible). There is an unlimited amount of unknown and undiscovered improvement opportunities in the broader and more complex interconnected network of professional knowledge and technology-based transactional processes. These opportunities also are invisible and cannot be harvested with a narrow *production* tools and principles focus. Here is the big differentiator: The visible and invisible complexity of improvement increases with the level of globalization and the human professional and technological content of processes, but so does the incremental value contribution of improvement. The challenge is that organizations cannot uncover and harvest these opportunities with a limited Lean *manufacturing* tool-set mindset, and a single production model for patterns of behavior and cultural attributes. Global Kata nurtures and reinforces the right desired patterns of behavior or Kata across the global enterprise, but it also recognizes and adjusts to local cultural norms and customs. Kata is different in every organization and in every geography. The objectives of improvement may be uniform, but *how* it is achieved and sustained around the world is influenced by idiosyncrasies between cultures.

Lean manufacturing matters, but it is shrinking in terms of its impact on the total cost of doing business globally. Let's be clear: Global Kata is not a put-down of Lean manufacturing, TPS, or Toyota Kata. In fact, it is an endorsement based on the need to correctly scale Lean globally in all organizations, in all industries, in all types of different operating environments, in all operating processes, and in all cultures. This is a very challenging undertaking from organization to organization. How does an organization address these challenges of improvement correctly? It involves *designing* the conceptual architecture, structure, processes, and measurements for a company-specific Lean Business System. It involves *integrating* all improvement methodologies and tools (e.g., Kaizen, Lean, Six Sigma, theory of constraints, and a big plus—technology) into a consolidated, higher-order body of knowledge. It involves *adapting* improvement to very different improvement situations—through the existing body of knowledge, or through creating and expanding the body of knowledge with new approaches. It involves *systematizing* the planning, deployment, execution, sustainability, and internalization components of strategic, continuous improvement. Finally it involves developing talent beyond the tools tradesperson level to innovative and creative problem solving. The degree to which these activities occur (i.e., customization) in our Lean Business System Reference Model is driven by business requirements and cultural development needs. In our architecture, the customer and market requirements are a given. Adaptive systematic improvement is always customer-centric. A true enterprisewide Lean Business System is the next generation of improvement.

Figure 2.1 illustrates the journey to Global Kata. The benefits of a Lean Business System are significant because the system creates direct improvements on processes, interaction improvements between processes, and residual improvements on other processes throughout the entire enterprise network. Also, it is routine for forward-thinking organizations to

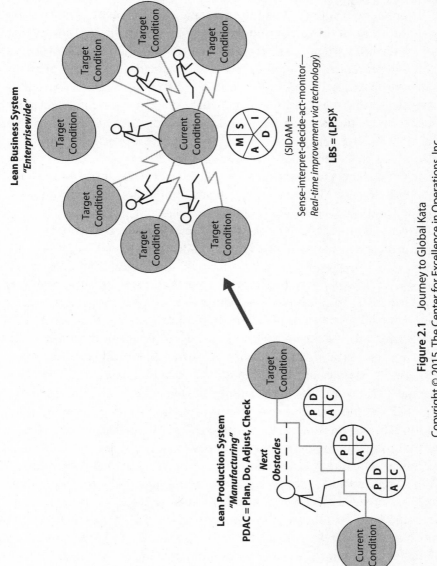

Lean Business System
"Enterprisewide"

Target Condition

(SIDAM =
Sense-interpret-decide-act-monitor—
Real-time improvement via technology)

LBS = (LPS)ˣ

Lean Production System
"Manufacturing"
PDAC = Plan, Do, Adjust, Check

Next
Obstacles

Current Condition

Figure 2.1 Journey to Global Kata
Copyright © 2015, The Center for Excellence in Operations, Inc.

have collaborative improvement initiatives underway beyond the enterprise with customers and suppliers. This creates a single enterprise model of thinking about improvement. The path to success is very challenging and confusing from organization to organization. It involves the precise integration of improvement plus technology. Another variation is that part of the infrastructure of a Lean Business System manages the obstacles (through preventive and predictive analytics) and ideally reduces or eliminates the obstacles. Does it really eliminate obstacles? No, but it minimizes obstacles so that they become small manageable bumps in the road, and it builds the confidence and capability to deal with them without fear. The limit of improvement is the self-imposed limit that executives choose to place on their organizations; otherwise, the sky is the limit! There is no recipe of concepts or a standard tool set to get there. Our Lean Business System Reference Model provides guidance about how to proceed on the journey to this next generation of improvement.

Throughout the book I frequently remind the reader that my message is not a criticism of Toyota or the Toyota Production System (TPS). I admire Toyota and many other great organizations that enjoy Lean benchmark success—the 20 percenters. The real problem is how other organizations have superficially interpreted and deployed the TPS without an appreciation of its deep, holistic, and systematic architecture (i.e., the visible principles and tools *and* the invisible Kata). The largest takeaway for the reader is this: If organizations remain on the same "mimic the manufacturing tools and principles of TPS," they will achieve diminishing results in an economy that demands higher, enterprisewide expectations. Additionally, they will never become a great adaptive systematic improvement organization like Toyota. A different Lean paradigm is needed to achieve new breakthroughs in improvement and superior performance. Let's now shift to Toyota's quality problems in the past few years: Millions of automobiles were recalled for accelerator pedal entrapment by out-of-place floor mats, unintended acceleration, stability control problems, corrosion, faulty air bags, and a few others. No organization is perfect at everything all the time, and *stuff* happens! A further look into the recalls reveals questions about whether these issues were product, dealer, or customer caused. Nevertheless, did anyone notice how quickly Toyota rectified these problems? Do you know how it did it? It was not with the TPS. It was with its TCSWRS (Toyota customer service and warranty repair system) and TDES

(Toyota design and engineering system). Has anyone heard of these? Is anyone aware of the TCSWRS and TDES tools? Of course not. Do you know that in this same time period Toyota's growth in market share, profitability, gross margins, and earnings before interest, taxes, depreciation, and amortization (EBIDTA) performance was superior to all competitors? Incredible! My point is that the behaviors, thinking, spirit, and culture of excellence (Kata) of the TPS exists beyond production and throughout Toyota's entire corporation. However, these values and code of conduct of perfection are invisible. Toyota understands that success requires more than TPS tools and terminology and a limited focus on manufacturing. For Toyota, TPS is really a holistic business system or Total Business System (TBS). Now it's time for other organizations to look beyond the visible and oversimplified tools and signage, and see the whole of Lean and its greater possibilities. This is the essence of Global Kata.

Understanding Adaptive Systematic Improvement

The next stage in the evolution of improvement is being driven by a combination of experiences and lessons learned, as well as the rapid evolution of globalization, redefinition of industry structures, technology, and sheer velocity to play in this game. These complex changes present new opportunities because they are leveling the playing field of improvement where the aggressive winner takes all. All industries and organizations have new and much greater opportunities for improvement that they have not discovered yet. Executives and their organizations must integrate strategic and operating improvement into their business model DNA if they can ever hope to harvest these new opportunities.

For most global organizations, the next stage of evolution of improvement is the challenge of how to design and implement a culturally grounded, continuous, and sustainable *process* of improvement successfully with the right approach, velocity, focus, simplification, efficiency, and ease, while eliminating or working within the dynamic operating models, realistic constraints, and absorption bandwidths of organizations—i.e., how much people and organizations can really do before they become totally overloaded and less efficient at everything. An adaptive systematic process of improvement incorporates many higher-order characteristics. *Adaptive* implies a customized design around specific requirements and evolving needs and opportunities. *Systematic* implies an integrated and precise, sociotechnical system of improvement. Systematic requires the existence of a formal system. *Process* implies that there is a standardized protocol of best practices for *improving how we improve. Improvement* implies a core competency of management approaches (plural) for raising the organization to a higher state of overall performance and competitive success through structured means and deliberate actions. An adaptive systematic process of improvement is the combined strategy of Deming's back-to-basics and other timeless fundamentals, innovation and creativity, the integration of enabling technology, and adaptive improvement across diverse industries and environments. Organizations can bring these complex elements together only through a systematic planning and execution architecture that leverages culture and fosters a natural way of process thinking and improvement—an improved Kata or cultural standard of excellence in how people autonomously think and work, which is the soul of the organization that embodies its meaning, vision, purpose, and inner identity of greatness.

The Historical Foundation Requirements

Before we hastily take off into the future, let us not forget to integrate the history and the lessons learned into our systematic process of improvement. These are the timeless fundamental requirements of a systematic process of improvement provided in Chapter 1. An adaptive systematic process of improvement must integrate these timeless fundamentals from the past that are still very relevant for the future. Western organizations must acknowledge these lessons and make sure that they do not repeat the same mistakes in the future. Otherwise their adaptive systematic process will be nothing more than another new label for another fad program.

New Global Competitive Requirements

There are many new global challenges and cultural factors that are driving the need to invent a superior process for how Western organizations improve. Executives and their organizations need the capability to expand the competitive space and quickly and in real time to understand gaps between current and desired performance. Consistent with this is to innovate and execute superior strategies and industry practices to become the *best*. Organizations must invent a superior integrated process of planning and implementing change while growing talent and evolving culture. This process must be a fit with both business needs and cultural values: simplified and easily managed, laser-targeted on the largest challenges, rapid deployment, rapid results, and visible improvement that enable both short- and longer-term performance, yet continuous and able to develop talent and evolve culture (e.g., smaller, continuous, high-impact increments rather than waves of large 6–12 month projects, with some exceptions of course). They also need to integrate technology and improvement through the use of more integrated business architectures, business analytics, mobility, and real-time digital performance dashboards, to name a few.

The following points summarize our future requirements discussion into eight specific areas. These are broad business requirements for an adaptive, systematic management process. We explode these basic requirements into our full Lean Business System Reference Model later in this chapter. The general requirements are included below.

Adaptive Systematic Improvement: General and Future Requirements

1. *Adaptive, systematic leadership.* The process of leadership and governance that continuously scans for new opportunities and deliberately evolves the cultural standard of excellence through the right improvement-enabling behaviors, choices, and actions.

2. *A living strategy and alignment process.* A formal best practice of continuously scanning new business requirements, recognizing needs to change, and prioritizing and aligning improvement activities with the business plan and operating plan.

3. *A formal systematic infrastructure of improvement.* This is the basic physical, organizational, cultural, social, technical, and feedback structure that enables improvement to function as a precise, sociotechnical operating system.

4. *Continuous cultural and talent development.* A means of continuously educating and developing the employee talents and skills to evolve the systematic management system to higher levels of achievement performance.

5. *Integration of all improvement methodologies.* The unification of all improvement methodologies and tools into a holistic body of knowledge and sociotechnical system of improvement.

6. *Efficient planning, deployment, and execution process.* Reinventing the process of improvement that is both *aligned to* and *evolves* with Western culture and values (e.g., laser-targeted, simplified, multiple shorter horizons; rapid deployment and results; high-impact, continuous, manageable, positive experiences; enabling monthly, quarterly, and annual performance; people and cultural advancement).

7. *Business performance-based success.* A crystal clear picture of how improvement is directly contributing to stakeholder value using "hard metrics" (e.g., growth, market share, brand loyalty, cost reduction, quality and reliability, velocity, EBITDA, accumulated rate of improvement, and superior customer experience).

8. *Improvement of the invisible underpinnings.* More focus on behavioral alignment, talent expansion, coaching and mentoring, and cultural evolution. The *soft stuff* is the *tough stuff* because it is not observable through one's natural senses, but it is a "must do" for *autonomous* adaptive systematic improvement.

The requirements provided are critical to a successful systematic process of improvement. This chapter provides the detailed architectural design of the Lean Business System Reference Model and its critical success factors. This is the architecture for what ends up as (*your company name*) business system, business improvement system, management system, or another relevant name of choice. It is the total operating system of an integrated, adaptive systematic process of improvement. The architecture incorporates both the timeless fundamentals of improvement that history has taught us and the challenging future requirements that drive the need for improvement higher than ever before in the history of improvement.

Introduction to the Lean Business System Reference Model

As a prelude, let us look at the decades-old Western definition of industrial engineering:

Industrial engineering is concerned with the design, improvement and installation of integrated systems of people, materials, information, equipment and energy. It draws upon specialized knowledge and skill in the mathematical, physical, and social sciences together with the principles and methods of engineering analysis and design, to specify, predict, and evaluate the results to be obtained from such systems.

Institute of Industrial Engineers (IIE)

The definition talks about a very important principle of improvement in terms of a *system*, not an independent collection of tools. When the basic discipline of industrial engineering was exported to Japan for its reconstruction efforts, managers there understood and adapted this principle as a religion. *Integrated system* is the heart of the Toyota Production System. Taiichi Ohno, an industrial engineer by trade, kept this integrated system together as an improvement operating system. The Japanese implemented quality and process improvements as an integrated system, a systematic process of improvement. They evolved the discipline of continuous improvement into a deep philosophy and culturally grounded way of thinking and working. They mastered adaptive systematic improvement because that is how the U.S. reconstruction support was presented to them, not knowing that they would evolve to a global reference point for improvement.

There is a major difference between a well-architected, organization-centric adaptive systematic process of improvement and a typical Lean program. Lean and other continuous improvement programs of the past have been more focused on tools to make improvements in manufacturing operations and equipment. These initiatives have come and gone as discrete, short-lived programs, while Toyota enjoys a unified continuous process of improvement and the spirit and culture to keep it alive. Continuing on the same path of improvement in light of all the structural and technology changes is the main reason why organizations are achieving *less with more* in their Lean initiatives. As the work content of organizations advances more toward professional, technology, and transactional processes, organizations must progress from a tools-based silo approach focused on manufacturing to a systematic process of improvement across the enterprise and extended enterprise. It is becoming increasingly difficult to generate substantial proportions of business improvement with a production-based Lean improvement initiative. Additionally it is becoming more complex to adapt and scale Lean correctly throughout the entire enterprise. Executives and their organizations need more practical guidance to evolve to this next generation of improvement. The basic Toyota philosophy is applicable, but the "production system" concepts and tool set are not enough to harvest the larger opportunities in complex global supply chain management, new product development, outsourcing rationalization, product portfolio management, inventory pipeline performance, R&D and innovation, customer relationship management, integration of enabling technologies (e.g., real-time digital performance dashboards, business analytics, mobility, cloud Lean applications, visualization, system modeling, etc.) and contractor/supplier management issues. There is a major need to expand Lean correctly across the enterprise and extended enterprise, and across diverse industry sectors with very different goals and operating conditions. To accomplish this major objective, the level of talent, knowledge, and body of (Lean and continuous improvement) knowledge must be both integrated and expanded.

Figure 2.2 provides a concept overview of the Lean Business System Reference Model. What is the purpose of a reference model and why is it needed? Our reference model is an architectural framework of integrated concepts, processes, and best practices that is used as a guide to communicate, educate, and create a shared understanding of a holistic, enterprisewide Lean Business System. The Lean Business System Reference Model helps organizations to *design, integrate, adapt,* and *systematize* improvement in a variety of different industry environments, business requirements, situational conditions, cultures, and industry segments. The philosophy of improvement is universal, but the correct path to adaptive systematic improvement is very different in different industries, operating environments, and cultures. Like all reference models, it evolves every day as we acquire new knowledge through our own experiences and the successes of others.

The remainder of this book reveals the architecture, principles, and best practices for creating *your own* signature Lean Business System. By the way, this is not a replacement for the Toyota House or TPS. Think of it as a major addition to the Toyota House and the TPS concepts, which are very important parts of a holistic, enterprisewide Lean Business System.

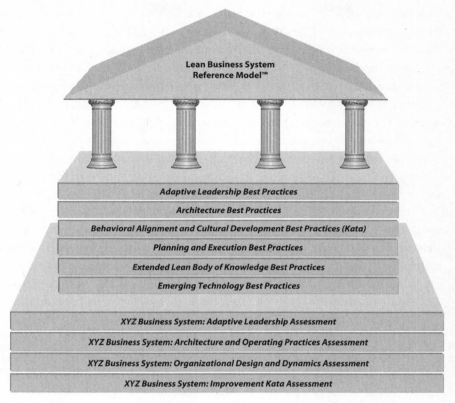

**Lean Business System
Reference Model™**

Adaptive Leadership Best Practices

Architecture Best Practices

Behavioral Alignment and Cultural Development Best Practices (Kata)

Planning and Execution Best Practices

Extended Lean Body of Knowledge Best Practices

Emerging Technology Best Practices

XYZ Business System: Adaptive Leadership Assessment

XYZ Business System: Architecture and Operating Practices Assessment

XYZ Business System: Organizational Design and Dynamics Assessment

XYZ Business System: Improvement Kata Assessment

Figure 2.2 Concept Diagram: Lean Business System Reference Model
Copyright © 2015, The Center for Excellence in Operations, Inc.

What is different about this next stage in the evolution of improvement? Adaptive systematic improvement is a higher-order human, sociotechnical system of improvement for the enterprise. The sociotechnical aspect is a dynamic system (a Lean Business System), a hybrid of art and science that recognizes the interaction between people, technology, and behaviors in terms of the structure and process of how organizations improve (and *improve how they improve*). The architecture of adaptive systematic improvement includes critical operating processes powered by a soul (i.e., Adaptive Leadership in Chapter 3) that keeps it in a continuous living state. Within the architecture is an integrated body of knowledge of traditional and emerging improvement methodologies. Adaptive systematic improvement is a combined strategy of Deming back-to-basics and other timeless fundamentals, innovation and creativity, the integration of enabling technology, and adaptive improvement across diverse industries and environments. It brings together both the historical fundamentals and the future competitive requirements into a powerhouse improvement capability for organizations. The goal of adaptive systematic improvement is to optimize the requirements of strategy, finance, technology, quality of life in organizations, and the broader social and competitive well-being of society. A systematic process is always in balance and not tilted toward one of the above requirements at the expense of other requirements. These combined characteristics create a superior operating system of improvement.

At first glance this might appear as an idealistic view of improvement, but this is becoming the international standard of excellence. It is alive and working well in several global organizations. However, for the majority of Western organizations this is a new management and operating process. It might exist in name, but it does not exist in daily practice as a natural cultural core competency—and it does not exist in terms of a formal improvement ROI and business value contribution. Adaptive systematic improvement is a very different and advanced operating system of improvement. It requires a huge leadership mindset change from the deterministic sequence of tasks, recipes, and tools-based approaches of the past to adapting a systems thinking approach to improvement. The leadership challenge for most organizations is to evolve, adapt, implement, and internalize adaptive systematic improvement as the cultural standard and expected code of conduct in daily thinking, behaviors, choices, actions, and interactions. The larger challenge is to create a culture that learns how to *improve how it improves* while doing all of this naturally and continuously.

Purpose of the Lean Business System Reference Model

The Lean Business System Reference Model provides a shared framework for designing, developing, and implementing best practices relative to adaptive systematic improvement. Why is a reference model approach valuable? A true, organization-centric Lean Business System is very complex and difficult to implement correctly but is much easier to sustain once the critical success factors are well-thought-out and incorporated into the total architecture. Much has been written about the Toyota Production System over the past decades. Much effort has been invested by organizations in attempting to achieve the same levels of Lean success. Several organizations have figured out the success behind the Toyota Way and have achieved the same impressive levels of success. Yet, globally organizations as a whole have a 20 percent batting average with Lean and continuous improvement in general. Today there is a significant amount of confusion and misinformation floating around about Lean and continuous improvement in general. Many organizations are convinced that a tools-based approach following the TPS recipe is the road to success. Others continue to believe that Lean and technology architectures are incompatible, which is a huge misconception and reason for failure. Coincidently the improvement tools by themselves represent about 20 percent of the factors of success. Leadership, a strong grounded culture of excellence, the moral soul and spirit of improvement, and the ability to adapt improvement systematically to a variety of evolving scenarios and requirements represent the 80 percent factors of success. Organizations tend to focus on the 20 percent and get some pieces of the total architecture right. However, when a Lean Business System is partially implemented, it functions at a low level of performance and is not sustainable for long. The word *continuous* always falls out of continuous improvement.

To help organizations through this journey to the next generation of Lean, we developed a reference model for adaptive systematic improvement. This reference model provides the total architecture and subprocesses for creating a *for-real, forever* Lean Business System. We have chosen to call our adaptive systematic process of improvement the Lean Business System Reference Model. It serves as the organization's relentless, neverending operating system of improvement. Figure 2.3 shows the overall architecture of this operating system.

A true Lean Business System is a finely tuned network of integrated and interdependent subprocesses working together. The Lean Business System Reference Model helps organizations to adapt the architecture, subprocesses, and underlying best practices to their own operating environments. The intent of our reference model is a design guide for Lean Business System success. Initially, the degree to which our architecture and its subprocesses are customized is a function of a specific organization's business requirements and cultural development needs.

There is some level of order to architect a systematic process of improvement and its subprocesses to an up-and-running state. However, the order is eventually replaced by a precise operating system that responds to time-based requirements. It is a highly intelligent and interactive management process, not a discrete and disconnected batch program model of improvement. Adaptive systematic improvement is more proactive, more predictive, and prevention-based. Every activity in every subprocess is requirements-driven in as near real time as possible. Adaptive systematic improvement is deliberate, efficient, and effective—and plans for and achieves breakthrough results. It is called adaptive systematic improvement because it is a formal, integrated system of how the most critical success factors of improvement work together to produce breakthroughs in performance. The integration of evolving technologies is moving plan-do-check-act (PDCA) into a more real-time sense-interpret-decide-act-monitor (SIDAM) model of improvement.

The reference model does not display evolving and enabling technology as a separate subprocess. However, technology is a key requirement and the underlying differentiator for adaptive systematic improvement, interconnectivity, and higher-order success in an enterprisewide Lean Business System.

Benefits of the Lean Business System Reference Model

The Lean Business System Reference Model is a very useful framework because it presents a true Lean Business System as an integrated system of leadership; strategy; and critical processes of improvement, people, and performance into a unified structure. The benefits of the reference model include:

▲ A shared awareness and blueprint of the specific elements in the total architecture of a true, internalized Lean Business System.

▲ An understanding of how the critical subprocesses interconnect to create an adaptive systematic process of improvement.

▲ A reference point for rapid assessment of current Lean approaches and performance to a higher standard of Lean as an enterprisewide operating system.

▲ A clarified understanding of new needs, design criteria, and architecture requirements to develop and adapt a Lean Business System in any global organization.

▲ Information on how to align strategy, operating plans, and improvement to achieve best-in-class performance and superior business results.

The Lean Business System Reference Model can help any organization around the globe to develop an exceptional core competency of improvement and a higher cultural standard of excellence throughout the total value chain (i.e., customers, stakeholders, the enterprise, supply chain partners).

The Lean Business System Reference Model Architecture

Following is a brief overview of the mission-critical subprocesses in our reference model architecture.

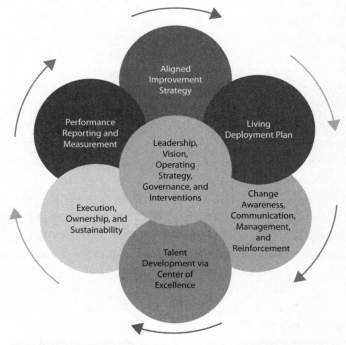

Figure 2.3 Architecture: Lean Business System Reference Model
Copyright © 2014, The Center for Excellence in Operations, Inc.

Leadership, Vision, Operating Strategy, Governance, and Interventions

The "soul-building" elements of our operating system are leadership, vision, operating strategy, governance, and interventions. Adaptive systematic improvement requires leadership, discipline, structure, daily management, cultural acceptance, and clear evidence that things are improving for all stakeholders in order to generate *continuous* success. Leadership creates the vision, strategy, sense of urgency, recognition of the need, and culturally grounded rules of engagement for a successful Lean Business System. Leadership defines very specifically the overall purpose of the organization's systematic process of improvement; the organization and reporting relationships; the dynamics of how improvement will be defined, deployed, and supported to business units and sectors; and how to manage and resolve conflicting priorities and barriers to change. It keeps our operating system in a healthy and living state through a continuous cycle of reckoning, renewal, enlightenment, and higher levels of organizational achievement— including cultural evolution. Finally, it keeps a balance between short-term financial performance and the overall well-being of organizations.

How is this soul-building achieved? Through Adaptive Leadership, a systematic form of leadership that continuously drives adaptive systematic improvement. (Note: We discuss Adaptive Leadership in detail in Chapter 3.) The soul-building function in adaptive systematic improvement establishes true constancy of purpose. Successful organizations have constancy of purpose as their operating foundation. For everyone else, this element replaces the temporary interest, wavering commitment, or token agreements that have been present in the stream of previous fad improvement programs. The best way to begin this adaptive systematic improvement journey is with an accountable executive steering group, a small highly skilled central support group for common and special development needs, and deployment leaders decentralized to business units. The initial objective of the executive steering group is to establish the strong momentum of adaptive systematic improvement by achieving significant breakthroughs within the first 90 days. At the same time, members of this group are innovating and architecting a longer-term, requirements-driven, and culturally grounded systematic process. Organizations that think and casually lead improvement initiatives in terms of years achieve questionable results or fail outright. This is a big change from the big-bang fad improvement programs with their huge dedicated Lean and Six Sigma departments and the bureaucracy of resources and questionable value that have been commonplace for the past decades.

Aligned Improvement Strategy

The subprocess of aligned improvement strategy serves as the perpetual hopper of strategic issues or detractors from superior performance and the organization's respective requirements for improvement. The most important operating characteristic of this subprocess is how the customer, market, and overall competitive environment is scanned, and how the right improvement opportunities and requirements are identified. Aligned improvement strategy is just that; it is always up to date and on point, and it constantly prioritizes and distills broader strategic improvement themes with more specific improvement objectives.

One of the more familiar approaches to accomplish this is *hoshin kanri* or simply policy deployment. Originally used in Japan in the 1950s, it serves as an annual management system where all employees participate in identifying key business issues, defining a vision and goals of improvement, establishing quantifiable goals, defining supporting tactics to facilitate success in each initiative, and defining performance metrics. The result is a large set of standardized hoshin tables that show each improvement goal and its supporting strategies for success. These tables are typically reviewed and updated on a monthly basis. Hoshin kanri works brilliantly in Japan's patient and meticulous attention-to-details industrial culture.

Like other improvement tools, many Western organizations have installed hoshin kanri into their Lean or continuous improvement initiative. Most organizations spend more time being puzzled with how to fill out the templates and matrices than actually understanding the spirit of the methodology. Many organizations have their matrix sets and symbolic A3 reviews to encourage people to be brief and to the point. By the way, why use an A3 international paper size (297mm by 420mm) that is not even used as a standard paper size in the United States? Wouldn't the sensible thing be to use U.S. B size paper (11 inches by 17 inches)? It folds nicely into our standard A size format. How about redesigning the content to fit our spirit of a U.S. systematic process of improvement? Copying and imitating a methodology based on a fixed set of templates and an international paper size to constrain decision making seems almost obsessive.

Furthermore the sheer time it takes to keep all of the matrices and templates updated can become a detractor (or take the place of) improvement in Western cultures. Fact is, it is difficult for most Western organizations to actually use hoshin kanri naturally as a *living* strategy of adaptive systematic improvement. The methodology of hoshin kanri is sound for sure. In a systematic process Western organizations should be asking themselves what the best implementation of hoshin kanri is for their specific business requirements and organizational culture. The answer is to adapt the methodology to Western culture with more focused and nearer-in goals, and simplified tables and templates. We have developed a "MacroCharter™" and "MicroCharter™" methodology which we share with you in Chapter 4. The MacroCharter and MicroCharter methodology translates the essence of hoshin kanri into a simple, easy-to-maintain improvement planning and deployment process. While it is not as administratively elaborate as hoshin kanri, it keeps the right improvement objectives and details in front of the organization, and it incorporates a continuous closed-loop process of monitoring and measuring progress.

Living Deployment Plan

This subprocess of the living deployment plan provides a level of detail below the aligned improvement strategy. In essence, it is the subprocess of how broad opportunities and needs are broken down into smaller but very specific and assignable-ready improvement activities. The living deployment plan is a *laser-targeted plan* in which the attention is always on the vital few issues that yield breakthroughs in improvement rather than the trivial many issues that end up as improvement for improvement's sake. This subprocess ensures the detailed planning and definition, prioritization, alignment, and control of released improvement activities and their respective teams and limited resources. This subprocess also regulates the amount of improvement activity in the right areas, thus providing sufficient capacity to execute quickly and successfully. There are essentially four parts to this subprocess of adaptive systematic improvement:

1. Translate broader strategic improvement themes into smaller manageable improvement activities using our MicroCharter methodology. The primary focus is more near-in prescriptive, but the reality is a mix of quick and longer-term efforts. The objective is to break the larger

improvement themes into many smaller, simpler, time-phased, and rapidly executable improvement activities.

2. For each planned improvement need, define the specific problem statement, objectives and scope, baseline performance (metric and level), improvement goals and objectives, expected deliverables and timing, entitled benefits of success, executive and/or process sponsor, resource(s) or team leader and team (if necessary), and a go-forward plan, including a Gantt chart (a type of bar chart that graphically describes a project schedule). Note that this step and step 3 below are performed concurrently to acquire enough information for decision making, but to avoid non-value-added definition efforts for activities that land further down the priority list.

3. Evaluate and force rank the relative value contribution of planned improvement activities in the MicroCharter relative to key attributes (revenue growth, cost reduction, cash flow, quality improvement, customer need, time, resources, cost, risk versus rewards, capital requirements, complexity, dependencies, etc.). This is a process of separating the vital few from the trivial many, where the most achievable, highest-impact opportunities move to the top of the list. This seems like a lot of up-front work, but it provides much clarity and reduces the required cycle time to complete improvement activities by 50–75 percent or higher.

4. Organize and release improvement activities, and monitor weekly progress. The MicroCharter serves as a *living* planning and deployment methodology because it is directly linked to the MacroCharter. The MacroCharter and MicroCharter are always updated and synchronized to align with broader business issues and requirements. There are no *waves* of lengthy projects in a systematic process; improvement activities are managed by priority and capacity, and each begins and may reach completion at a different time.

This element of our operating system introduces a major change to improvement planning and deployment from the historical batch, wave, train the masses, full widespread rollouts of improvement programs in organizations. Organizations were anxious to improve and hoped that throwing enough improvement tools at the ceiling would cause something to stick. Associates were also eager to respond with demonstrations of what they were asked to do. In retrospect, executives overloaded their entire organizations with too much mandated incremental improvement. The *process* of improvement replaced the original objectives of improvement, and the program eventually dwindled away or stepped aside for the next silver bullet program. It is nobody's fault. This was the standard accepted protocol and *process* for introducing improvement in Western organizations. This subprocess of systematic improvement recognizes the organization's realistic capacity to improve and responds to this reality with smaller and well-scoped improvement activities and a regulating feature to manage the realistic capacity for executing with great results. Adaptive systematic improvement requires that organizations reinvent the *process* of how they improve, wrapped around their specific business issues and culture. By now, the reader should recognize that a systematic process of improvement requires a major overhaul in the traditional Western approaches to improvement.

Change Awareness, Communication, Reinforcement, and Management

The subprocess for changing awareness, communication, reinforcement, and management is the most overlooked and oversimplified factor in large-scale improvement initiatives. In many cases it is a poorly conceived mechanical procedure to disseminate information, often creating more confusion than clarity of purpose and missing the mark of its intended objectives and spirit. In a systematic process, these factors—change awareness, communication, reinforcement, and management—are the fuel, lubricants, maintenance, and customer service that keeps the soul of improvement alive and at attention at all times. This subprocess most directly influences the defining, creating, nurturing, and reinforcing of the right improvement Kata. The rate of Kata's development is directly proportional to executive behaviors, choices, and actions—and how well executives communicate, engage their people, and act as the greatest role models.

The purpose of this subprocess is to create awareness, commitment, trust, inspiration, engagement, and other positive behavioral and cultural attributes of excellence. These factors help to deal with the invisible human drama of change that we cannot see in the data and metrics. Organizations are complex entities in which leadership actions can unintentionally transmit the wrong signal about improvement or other priorities.

This subprocess of our operating system builds the human and emotional foundation for improvement and change. There are two simple thoughts to remember about communication:

▲ The strategy that the CEO and executive team choose to communicate the message about improvement and change (e.g., what, when, why, where, how) significantly influences the initial recognition of the need, receptivity, and acceptance on the part of the organization.

▲ The process, content, candor, method/media choices, and frequency of communication significantly influence ongoing awareness, proactive participation, reinforcement, and internalization of change. This determines the "continuousness" of the effort.

Why is the most important question to answer. People need to understand and internalize the urgency and recognition of the need to change and the consequences and risks of staying the same. They need to know what to expect if the organization does not change—particularly at the individual level.

People need constant renewal and recognition about their stake in improvement. The practices and media to support effective change awareness, communication, reinforcement, and management must be deliberately designed and adjusted based on organizational issues and needs. We provide additional guidance on change awareness, communication, reinforcement, and management in Chapter 6. One design criterion that is important in this area is how to design and deploy these factors to different parts of the organization. A pretentious gemba walk, a company newsletter article, an e-mail blast, or an occasional video is not enough to achieve success.

Infrastructure and Talent Development via Center of Excellence

Every systematic process of improvement requires a standardized education and continuing professional development function. This is not the typical *attend the course, check the box, get the certificate* operation. This is the organization's "improvement boot camp," where the right success-enabling thinking, skill sets, and behaviors are created, delivered to the organization, and continuously reinforced. This subprocess helps to develop a uniform body of knowledge and operating guidelines for everything from the specific improvement methodologies, tools, and applications to more advanced analytics, teaming and group dynamics fundamentals, change of leadership and management, performance management, basic finance and cost analysis, technology and integration, business process fundamentals, nonlinear improvement methodologies for accelerating innovation, and other skill sets necessary to support an evolving systematic process of improvement.

Remember, it is important to visualize the interaction of all of the subprocesses in our operating system. For example, the initial education and professional development needed to support a systematic process of improvement are best determined by the specific improvement activities and their supporting tactical requirements in the MacroCharter and MicroCharter. Prior improvement programs have included a "train the masses on everything" approach, whether it was relevant or not. Our operating system is always in tune with development needs and delivers more targeted education continuously on a just-in-time basis. This creates an achievement-based (versus attendance-based) education where associates learn, apply, and experience success in a quicker cycle. The operating system ensures that this cycle is *continuous,* so improvement is *continuous.*

The concept of a center of excellence is to be the education and talent development entity of our Lean Business System. The purpose of the center of excellence is to provide leadership development, design and deliver technical and soft skills education, create new methodologies for new situations, provide education and talent development regarding cultural evangelization, build a best practices benchmarking knowledge system, and conduct external research on specific topics of need. A center of excellence develops both talented corporate citizens and talented improvement associates. This is the subprocess of our operating model that plans, executes, and monitors this monumental effort of standardization and uniformity in the various improvement methodologies across all business units of the corporation. Often, organizations set up satellite centers of excellence in larger business units to work with the division executive and lead deployment executive.

A critical success factor in a center of excellence is customization: providing professional development that is tailored to, aligned with, and success-enabling to the organization's strategic issues, operating plan, and cultural and organizational development needs. We have talked previously about the need to return to an integrated body of knowledge for our adaptive systematic improvement operating system. There are many different types of improvement opportunities in organizations. Some are simple, while others are complex. A center of excellence education typically includes (but is not limited to) a much wider variety of these topics:

▲ Leadership and management development (e.g., company policies and procedures, best practices of leaders and managers, planning, controls, metrics, mentoring and coaching, and handling difficult situations and disciplinary policies).

▲ Teaming and soft skills education (e.g., teaming fundamentals, group dynamics, communication, barrier resolution, change management, virtual teaming).

▲ Lean enterprise (with more focus on business process improvement and transactional process improvement).

▲ Six Sigma (basics, intermediate, advanced) and other process analytics to support all improvement activities with fact-based and data-driven approaches.

▲ Technology-enabled improvement—e.g., enterprise resource planning (ERP), Internet, business analytics, data visualization, mobility and cloud technology, and business process fundamentals.

▲ Nonlinear improvement methodologies (e.g., mind and dialogue mapping, prioritization grids, affinity diagrams, free-form value mapping, worth factor analysis, abstraction analysis, risk and decision tree analysis, simulation, and modeling).

We provide more guidance about how to establish a center of excellence with the right improvement methodologies and talent development-enabling content in Chapter 7. For those with a fascination for *tools,* they are presented in this chapter as an integrated body of knowledge. Initially, a seasoned improvement expert can review the details of the MacroCharter and MicroCharter and define a basic body of knowledge required to enable a systematic process from a talent and execution standpoint. These components of our operating system are dynamic and needs-based; one can never sit down and define the full scope of talent needs and educational offerings because they are ever-evolving with internal progress and external influences. Organizations require constant injections of new skills in this operating system. They are always needs-driven and evolve as new and uncovered situations arise or as business improvement requirements evolve over time. In Chapter 1 we mention that the largest opportunities are the ones that are not known yet; the talent and specific improvement methodologies may need to be developed to deal with these unknown opportunities.

Execution and Talent Development Infrastructure

The objective of the subprocess execution and talent development is to replace "broad improvement for improvement sake" efforts with precisely regulated, high-impact activities that are completed efficiently and that produce rapid results. Infrastructure includes the set of standard rules about how projects are launched, tracked, completed, measured, and archived: in essence "execution." Several organizations have set up a searchable improvement intranet to avoid duplicating previous work of other teams or to leverage their documentation, analysis, and lessons learned. Another objective of this subprocess is to replace the "train the masses in everything, get the belts" mindset with a very specific and deliberate professional talent development plan based on the true requirements of the company (e.g., develop and expand the "go-to" champion talent pool). This subprocess also ensures that continuous improvement is a "pull" into business units based on defined needs rather than the traditional centralized "push" (i.e., throw everything at the ceiling and hope something sticks) out to the entire organization.

An important component of this subprocess is Scalable Improvement™. This is a more adaptive "middle out" model of improvement. Our Scalable Improvement model *adapts the process of improvement* to the organization, its culture, and mission-critical success factors. It's all about continuously defining the organization's 80-20 sweet spot of opportunities and then navigating through the barriers to success while developing internal talent and "internalized" participation and momentum. This approach builds a true, permanent, cultural standard of excellence in how people think and work. Scalable Improvement is a laser-targeted, rapid deployment, and rapid results model that eliminates all the non-value-added waste that exists in traditional approaches to improvement—the waste that kills improvement initiatives and makes it nearly impossible to keep the word "continuous" in continuous improvement. *Scalable* implies a living cycle of developing improvement talent in small increments—giving people just what they need at the right times in order for them to achieve success, and then repeating the cycle at a higher order of learning. The model is also designed to position organizations quickly in a positive self-funding mode with their strategic improvement initiatives.

We also use a process of daily check-ins with critical resources to stay on top of progress and intervene as necessary. This intervention is mentoring and technical support, not undermining the engagement and empowerment of individuals and teams. It is helping individuals and teams to become committed to improvement naturally (spiritually by Toyota standards) by experiencing multiple successes efficiently and the personal growth inherent in making a difference in the organization.

Performance Reporting and Measurement

This subprocess of performance reporting and measurement is straightforward, but can be a severe weakness in most internal improvement initiatives. In some cases, the management pressure to produce results while skipping all the other important ingredients for success can spur a host of funny money savings games. To start off, a number of factors drive behaviors in organizations: beliefs, perceptions, values, emotions, politics, safety and security, observations, messaging, motivation, underemployment, and a number of other factors. The purpose of performance reporting and management is to align behaviors with the organization's mission, vision, and purpose. This is a balanced set of metrics that maintains somewhat of a controlled process in our operating system. Reality introduces changes daily, and success is a function of how these changes are sifted through and acted upon. There will always be noise in our operating system and in all other complex systems.

There are several caveats about measurement system analysis worth mentioning:

▲ Organizations cannot manage what they cannot measure.

▲ What gets measured gets attention, even if it is pointless to measure and manage it.

▲ Organizations must make sure that they are measuring and communicating the right things.

▲ Measurements change behaviors and establish priorities in the right or wrong directions.

▲ Measurements create the right enabling behaviors, which lead to the right enabling actions for achieving the right enabling results—and the inverse is also true.

▲ Be careful what you measure because you just might get it.

▲ In the absence of measurement, everything is fine.

The need for performance reporting and measurement is evident in a systematic process of improvement. The most important role is that it provides instant closed-loop feedback to the business and to all the other subprocesses of our operating system so it becomes a true Lean Business System. Contrast this attribute to improvement programs of the past and present. I have observed where it required a special finance project to go out and determine the costs and benefits of Lean programs. Most organizations do not know the ROI on their improvement efforts but can mention a few significant accomplishments. Previous Lean, Six Sigma, and other continuous improvement initiatives might have started out publicizing successes, but most of these fad programs became "fly by night" programs. See the difference in a systematic process? Performance reporting and measurement continuously interact with other subprocesses of our operating system. In effect, this subprocess is validating that the content of the MacroCharter and MicroCharter is happening and moving the business positively toward its strategic and operating intent. This subprocess is involved early on when proposed benefits are being planned and estimated. It is involved during in-process improvement activities to assist teams in standard financial assumptions and calculations (to avoid incorrect financial assumptions, double counting, and *funny money* savings). Finally it serves as the verification of results achieved. Our operating system allows executives and their organizations to sense, interpret, decide, act, and monitor (SIDAM) the value contribution of their XYZ business system on the spot and adjust the subprocesses to realign desired outcomes to customer, business, and talent needs.

This subprocess incorporates several levels of improvement (which are not listed in order of priority):

▲ Individual/team performance, where improvement is an important criterion in performance reviews.

▲ Activity and project performance, a postmortem of all improvement activities with lessons learned formally integrated into future efforts.

▲ Organizational and cultural adaptation, an attribute-based evaluation to assess the degree of acceptance and internalization in the way people think and work every day.

▲ Effectiveness of the overall Lean Business System on strategic performance, including consolidated value contribution by strategic objective, functional area, budgeted improvement achievement, and overall rate of improvement.

▲ Business and operating performance, a formal pegging process of improvement activities to individual accounts in top-line customer and/or market growth, profit and loss (P&L), cash flow, and measures within other financial ratios (asset turns, operating leverage, cash-to-cash conversion, EBITDA, etc.).

Without going into more details, it is assumed that recognition and rewards go hand in hand with performance management. At any given time, this subprocess provides information about projects completed, projects in process, planned and prioritized projects, accumulated benefits and rate of improvement, adaptability by organizational function, and direct linkage of activities to financial impact in the operating plan. Several organizations incorporate a planned level of improvement into their budgeting process. As we mention above, performance measurement and reporting *close the loop* in the overall systematic process of improvement, enabling organizations to continuously *improve how they improve.*

Adaptive Systematic Improvement by Design

Our Lean Business System Reference Model provides a thorough and extensive guide for success. The reference model also incorporates four formal and extensive assessments to determine gaps and probable causes between current and best practice XYZ Lean Business System performance:

1. *The Adaptive Leadership Assessment.* An evaluation of how well leadership adapts to changing conditions and builds an improvement-enabling, Kata-compatible culture through their own daily behaviors, choices, and actions.

2. *The Architecture and Operating Practices Assessment.* An evaluation of the performance of architecture subprocesses in the reference model, and how well these elements work synchronously to create an adaptive systematic process of improvement.

3. *The Organizational Design and Dynamics Assessment.* An evaluation of the present organizational structure and operating norms, and the ability to naturally integrate distributed authority, stakeholder engagement, empowerment, and Kata development into the culture.

4. *The Improvement Kata Assessment.* An evaluation of the relative existence and strength of the right, improvement-enabling aligned behaviors and cultural attributes of a true and continuously evolving Kata-based culture.

These assessments help to design, measure, and analyze how well an organization's XYZ Business System is working relative to strategic, operational, financial, technology, and cultural development needs. Keep in mind that as a reference model, these formal assessments are a continuous work-in-progress based on new learning and future requirements.

Recognize that the reference model is a guide, not a tool or practice to be mimicked. Adaptive systematic improvement is a complex management system, and it requires architecting by the right skilled design professionals. However, it is not another improvement bureaucracy that requires years of effort before an ROI is achieved. A well-designed, organization-centric Lean Business System is an endless journey to quantum levels of excellence that organizations have not yet discovered. There are also plenty of known immediate opportunities for improvement where organizations can achieve breakthroughs in improvement within the first 90 days or sooner.

A true Lean Business System and its subprocesses must be designed around a specific organization's business requirements and cultural development needs. Adaptive systematic improvement is a deliberate design with a highly integrated operating system and high expectations for results. Most organizations lack a formal and deliberately designed and operating Lean Business System as we have outlined. When developing this operating system, appreciate the detailed design architecture of *adaptive, systematic, process,* and *improvement* mentioned throughout the chapter. The most critical subprocess is at the center of our total architecture: leadership, vision, operating strategy, governance, and interventions. Building this operating system requires a systematic leadership model as well—one that continually builds the soul, vitality, and robustness that enable the Lean Business System to operate as a living whole. These leaders typically understand how to maintain a delicate balance between operational and financial performance and building an organization that acts as a big team, a big family. Figure 2.4 provides a general overview of adaptive systematic improvement.

Note that the goals include many goals that are different from the normal list of leadership roles and responsibilities. Let's save the details of this leadership style for now. We refer to this systematic leadership model as Adaptive Leadership which we cover in great detail in the next chapter. The means of success is our Lean Business System. The outcomes are much bigger and bolder than the results from previous improvement programs.

The purpose of the Lean Business System Reference Model is to stimulate thinking and dialogue and provide guidance toward a true, holistic and organization-centric Lean Business System. The scope of the reference model includes the enterprise and extended enterprise, particularly collaborative improvements within the network of global customers and suppliers. It is a reference model, and it is perfectly acceptable to agree, disagree, modify, or add content to create a better fit within your own organization. It takes a very special kind of leadership to see a systematic process of improvement through design to daily work. It's easy to launch a few improvement programs and achieve some positive results. It's a different animal to transform culture to a higher spirit of improvement that resembles a religious or sophisticated military movement. This is the challenge of growing your organization to be a Toyota—or superior to Toyota. Several Western organizations like GE, Honeywell, Emerson Electric, Deere, and others have made the grade. This is the future of improvement—a living systematic, technology-enabled, culturally grounded operating system of

Systematic Leadership Goals

- Business Strategy and Operating Plans
- Streamline Concept to Cash
- Reckoning, Renewal, Enlightenment
- Constancy of Purpose
- Adaptive, Systematic, Evolving
- Chronic Disruption Is the Norm
- Cultural Embracement
- Interdependent Key Processes
- Collaborative Team Environment
- "Continuous" Improvement
- Learning to Observe
- Mentoring and Coaching Kata
- Talent Development
- Boundaryless Fluid Organizations
- Collapsed Nimble Hierarchy
- Family-Oriented Work Environment
- Barrier Resolution
- One Big Team, All on Board
- Risk and Entrepreneurial Spirit
- "Look Under All Rugs" Mindset
- How Much Better Can We Get
- Achieve Financial performance and Other Critical-to-Customer Metrics

The Means
Lean Business System Reference Model™

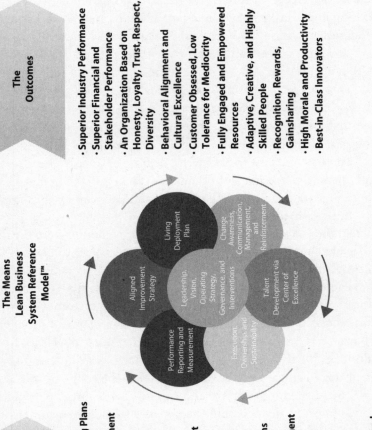

The Outcomes

- Superior Industry Performance
- Superior Financial and Stakeholder Performance
- An Organization Based on Honesty, Loyalty, Trust, Respect, Diversity
- Behavioral Alignment and Cultural Excellence
- Customer Obsessed, Low Tolerance for Mediocrity
- Fully Engaged and Empowered Resources
- Adaptive, Creative, and Highly Skilled People
- Recognition, Rewards, Gainsharing
- High Morale and Productivity
- Best-in-Class Innovators

Figure 2.4   Adaptive Systematic Improvement Process
Copyright © 2015, The Center for Excellence in Operations, Inc.

improvement. A natural, higher-order, and well-functioning Lean Business System will produce more benefits for an organization (hands down!) than any other approach to improvement to date. Because it is *adaptive* and *living*, it continuously evolves to enable new and often unknown opportunities for improvement.

Bibliography

Burton, T., and Boeder, S. 2003. *The Lean Extended Enterprise: Moving Beyond the Four Walls to Value Stream Excellence.* J. Ross Publishing, Plantation, Florida.

Burton, T. T. 2012. *Out of the Present Crisis: Rediscovering Improvement in the New Economy.* Productivity Press, Boca Raton, Florida.

Jackson, T. L. 2006. *Hoshin Kanri for the Lean Enterprise.* Productivity Press, Boca Raton, Florida.

Liker, J. 2004. *The Toyota Way.* McGraw-Hill, New York.

Rother, M. 2011. *Toyota Kata: Managing People for Adaptiveness, Improvement, and Superior Results.* McGraw-Hill, New York.

SAP, The Center for Excellence in Operations, Inc. (CEO). 2006. "Special Report: Creating a Lean Extended Enterprise Through Adaptive Supply Chain Networks." Collaborative white paper published by CEO.

CHAPTER 3

Reinventing Lean Leadership

Not surprisingly, leadership is the soul builder of a Lean Business System. Leadership tends to be a topic that everyone understands at an intellectual level, but has difficulty practicing effective leadership on a daily basis. Furthermore, the composition of executives' leadership style is largely a function of what they achieved in the past that enabled them to rise to their positions. Many executives have reached the executive suite because of subject matter knowledge rather than leadership expertise. This chapter is not about bashing leadership for a failed fad improvement program, because everyone is only human. Besides, this excuse is not the real root cause; it is symptomatic of deeper conflicting and misaligned issues in the organization. It's a cop-out to suggest that *everything is leadership's fault* and that *the buck stops there* because this destructive thinking prevents organizations from turning that axiom buck into millions of real bucks!

Today many organizations are constrained by a leadership style that is outdated. To be candid, it's apparent that Western leadership is based on a combination of military organizational theory, principles of scientific management, and short-term financial performance. When leadership limits itself to hitting the numbers each month, it creates a false sense of success. Great organizations hit the numbers, but they also build high-performance organizations with a high-performance culture composed of high-performance people, talent, and skills. This style of leadership enables organizations to keep hitting the numbers because all associates are hunting down and eliminating the wastes that increase the risk of not hitting the numbers. Culture is deliberate—it is difficult to transform and easy to reverse direction of basic core values. Leadership has been talking a good game about engagement and empowerment for decades, but the majority of organizations have yet to leverage the knowledge and skills of their associates. This chapter is about evolving traditional leadership in order to achieve continuous renewal and associate engagement top down, bottom up, middle out, and laterally. Leadership for adaptive systematic improvement must originate from as many sources as possible in the organization. This is engagement and empowerment—for real and is living every day.

The Governance of Greatness

Being a leader is not an easy job in today's fierce global economy. Executives are constantly challenged and surprised at all the issues they must face, always operating at extended bandwidth mode. Many executives got to where they are because they were great at getting things done in their particular area of subject matter expertise. Executives can no longer make the same amount and type of decisions they have made in the past because the content is too complex and cannot be resolved by immediate actions taken by a single individual. Leadership must engage the entire organization in decision making and improvement. We are not insinuating that the shipping clerk develop the company's marketing plan. But we are insisting that organizational engagement is influenced significantly by leadership: executive behaviors, choices, actions, how they scan for opportunities, how they mentor and grow their organizations, how they communicate, how they balance the needs of multiple stakeholders, how they run interference, how they achieve goals through the positive engagement of others, and how they achieve the success of the whole enterprise. One of the best references on organizational engagement is contained within *Disney Great Leader Strategies*. This reference demonstrates that leadership starts top down to set the objectives and direction. Then leadership evolves to a very powerful hybrid of highly skilled, engaged, and empowered associates that *live and breathe* horizontal, vertical, lateral, bottom-up, top-down, and middle-out leadership. Great leadership comes from all directions when it develops and engages talent. When you ask for help from one of the Disney associates, you always get your questions answered on the spot. You never get a "Please hold" or, "I'm not sure," or, "Let me speak to my manager." Disney understands how to manage customer touch points and deliver the superior customer experience.

This chapter stresses the importance of this type of leadership in a systematic process of improvement, and provides a systematic model of leadership (Adaptive Leadership) to create new breakthroughs in operating performance. Why is leadership so important? Because organizations naturally adapt to the personality of a CEO and his or her executive team through their behaviors, choices, and actions. Leadership shapes culture, harmony, productivity, and in general how their associates think and work. Engagement and empowerment are crucial to this process because they develop associates who are customer-friendly, ambitious, motivated, enthusiastic, happy, intelligent, polite, respectful, conscientious, honest, curious, high energy, collaborative, and focused—and many more positive adjectives. There are no *Cliff Notes* for this stuff; it is a learned and developed competency. In a Lean Business System, organizations are challenged to develop Disney-like talent that has no fear of discussing or fixing problems on the spot. Such organizations have employees with the skills and talent to identify new opportunities, and they have a culture that engages people where they work, encouraging associates to proactively respond to problems and new opportunities. In short, adaptive systematic improvement evolves to become a 360-degree process.

When Gemba Walks Are Not Enough

Back in the 1970s a concept called *management by wandering around* was popular. It returned in the 1990s as *going to the gemba*. In Western organizations many of these efforts have turned into informal visits to talk to employees and get a better understanding of what is going on at a daily microlevel. For some people it literally became wandering around, kibitzing with employees about everything but improvement and going through the motions for their superiors. By the way, this is but another example of blindly copying a standard Lean or TPS practice and missing the technical discipline, culture, and spirit that makes it work. We mentioned previously with technology and changing process structures that we are all connected to the gemba 24/7. In a well-functioning adaptive systematic management process, leadership must evolve and integrate this concept so that it becomes more of a continuous and formal scanning of the external competitive world as well as a scanning of the internal culture and a response to this competitive world. It is a very formal, structured, disciplined, and fact-based leadership process of always looking for new opportunities and always looking at how to build a more robust, culture-enabled organization.

It is a process of *everyone* using structure and discipline, hunting for the next opportunity.

There is no room for complacency, procrastination, postponement, or confusing priorities in a systematic process of improvement. These actions are organization killers in this economy. Why? Because they breed *Maladaptive Leadership* and a cultural mode that inhibits the ability of executives and their organizations to adjust to particular changing situations. Maladaptive Leadership shuts down formal and structured improvement. It promotes avoidance, denial, reactionary efforts, working harder instead of smarter, emergency hot list meetings, and other similar behaviors that might create activity and reduce the immediate anxiety of a problem. However, the result is dysfunctional and non-value-added, and it does not alleviate the actual problem in the long term. In fact, this cultural condition typically increases the size of the main problem, creates other new interrelated problems, and demotivates an already confused and overloaded organization. A common outcome in these environments is the *separation disorder of improvement* where improvement is perceived (and allowed) to be *in addition to* rather than an *integral part of* daily work. Maladaptive Leadership drives culture backwards and cultivates the negative traits of helplessly overloaded resources, political motivations, dishonesty, loss of interest, protectionism, lack of risk, concealment of problems, lack of trust, loss of caring and loyalty, disinterest in the next silver bullet program, and associates who are just putting in their time to name a few. Organizations can never expect to become best in class with this kind of culture—no matter how many improvement programs, tools, and Lean or TPS jargon they throw into the mix.

There is an explanation of why some organizations are successful year after year while other seemingly extraordinary companies eventually fall by the wayside. It comes down to a cohesive executive team that understands how to systematically conceive, lead, and continually rediscover innovation, growth, improvement, and change management throughout their business life cycles. It is becoming increasingly more difficult to sustain competitiveness and superior performance, especially with the same course of action and talent pool. For organizations that get temporarily lucky, their success does not go unnoticed for too long in this economy. Success attracts competitors and imitators, so eventually maturity sets in and success becomes a commodity.

Superior competitiveness and operating performance can only be achieved with a deep-rooted adaptive systematic improvement culture—one that continually raises the bar for the organization and keeps the bar out of reach for competitors. This is the common underpinning in superior performing organizations: improvement as the cultural standard of excellence and expected code of conduct. Adaptive Leadership is the element that keeps the momentum of innovation, growth, improvement, and change management at superior levels of industry performance. Leaders are always at center stage in their organizations, sending formal and informal messages about what matters most. Constancy of purpose and constant two-way communication are very important to this process. Simply, Adaptive Leadership provides the moral compass and navigation system of adaptive systematic improvement.

Adaptive Leadership

Adaptive Leadership is the soul and spirit behind a systematic process of improvement. Adaptive Leadership serves as the permanent senior architects, operators, and sustainers of a systematic process of improvement. In the Lean Business System Reference Model™, leadership provides the harmony of this operating system through the integration of its interconnected subprocesses, and the lower-level interactive elements within each subprocess at any given moment in time. A closer look at this architecture clearly indicates that the scope includes total enterprise success, not just a good Lean *manufacturing* program. At the core of Adaptive Leadership are the executive values, vision, purpose, operating style, behaviors, and cultural attributes that create the right improvement Kata. These are the make-or-break factors on culture and adaptive systematic improvement. Let's make sure that this is well understood: Leadership does not create this soul and spirit of an organization by launching the latest improvement program. Leadership is not following some standard linear recipe of instructions or mandating the use of improvement tools and copied practices, or encouraging a shibboleth of improvement jargon and sending everyone off on ritual gemba walks. Leadership's primary role is to create an organizational environment for success (i.e., vision, purpose, strategy, core behaviors, and cultural expectations). Leaders also nurture themselves and their organizations through the creative human development practices of *learning to learn, learning to observe, learning to coach,* and *learning to develop culture.* These unified factors in turn nurture organizational experiences and create an evolving cultural standard of excellence—the right, higher-order improvement Kata as the foundation of a Lean Business System.

The soul and spirit of a systematic process of improvement are living and essential phenomena. Figure 3.1 provides a graphic overview of Adaptive Leadership. It is the leadership mechanisms behind this style of leadership that are important to understand.

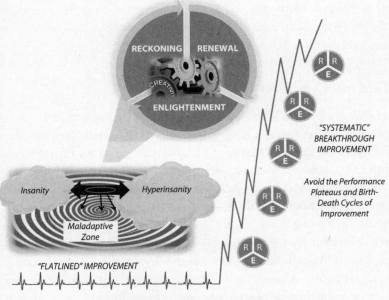

Figure 3.1   Adaptive Leadership
Copyright © 2015, The Center for Excellence in Operations, Inc.

In the center and right side of the figure is the Adaptive Leadership mode. The figure illustrates leadership cycles through stages where their organizations hit natural performance plateaus. Enlightened leaders recognize these performance plateaus immediately and either modify the current course or rediscover a totally new course through a continuous cycle of *reckoning, renewal,* and *enlightenment.* In effect, their leadership behaviors, choices, and actions prevent performance plateaus and other disruptions to improvement. Reckoning is the immediate recognition of the need to change course, and renewal is the vision and execution of change to a higher level of excellence and performance. Enlightenment is the positive outcome of this successful, continuous cycle of reckoning and renewal. This continuous cycle transforms improvement from another wish or short-lived program into a long -term cultural standard of excellence. Enlightened leaders know when to make minor adjustments and when bolder changes in direction are necessary. They are decisive and armed with the facts. They make the right tough decisions swiftly. They involve themselves from strategy to execution to make sure that there is continuity of purpose and that strategy and plans are executed swiftly and are on point. They use a balanced scored approach to performance management and expect the same cascading standard through their organizations. They maintain the *continuous* in continuous improvement.

Adaptive Leadership relies on executives who understand the importance of a combined strategy of Deming's back to basics and other timeless fundamentals; innovation and creativity; the integration of enabling technology, and adaptive improvement across diverse industries and environments. Adaptive Leadership creates an environment of near real-time "fast forward improvement" called SIDAM (sense, interpret, decide, act, monitor). It also leads to business model innovation through improvement. The more executives think "beyond the box," the better they and their organizations become at discovery and innovation.

Adaptive Leadership is the future of leadership: a style of leadership excellence that is timeless because it continuously develops leadership talent and organizational competencies in both current and future-focused time horizons. This style of leadership replaces the traditional life cycles of discrete leadership stages with one of continuous cycles of leadership and discovery. Adaptive Leadership continuously strives to achieve a more holistic form of greatness that goes way beyond the self. The best-in-class Lean and continuous improvement organizations get it and fully understand that short-sighted, reactionary leadership is not sustainable in the new economy. Leaders who allow themselves and their organizations to twirl and toss in the modes of insanity and hyperinsanity are not innovating their business models and creating the business conditions and cultures that will lead to continuous future successes. Executives and their organizations need to figure out very quickly how to spend all their time in the reckoning, renewal, and enlightenment areas of our model. This is the essence of a Lean Business System, as well as everything else an organization does to become a great organization with great people.

Avoiding the Insanity and Hyperinsanity Traps

The lower left region of Figure 3.1 is a leadership trap for many organizations. The figure illustrates two distinct cycles of leadership:

▲ *Insanity.* "*Doing more of the same and expecting different results,*" which is usually followed by a more acute cycle of hyperinsanity.

▲ *Hyperinsanity.* "*Doing more of the same with greater urgency and velocity, and expecting different results.*"

These styles of leadership are very common in organizations today because there is so much to accomplish in so little time, and people are stretched beyond their bandwidths. Additional work keeps arriving on people's plates, but nothing is being removed from their plates. Leadership is not: "Do the best that you can," "Try harder," and "Just figure it out." Figure 3.1 shows an area that we call the *maladaptive zone.* The insanity and hyperinsanity cycle occurs when leaders choose to "rabbit" themselves and their organizations around from one crisis to the next. Everyone knows that this approach is incorrect intellectually, yet many leaders give in to *immediate reason*: the act of attempting to correct a situation at hand with unreasonable actions based on opinions, perceptions, or direct orders from others who are missing the facts. The objective is *instant gratification.* This certainly does not achieve Deming's point about continuity of purpose, and often these efforts create bad improvement Kata and a demoralized organization. When leadership becomes an activity of managing one crisis after another and puts too much focus on short-term revenue and profits, executives quickly lose sight of the bigger picture. They lead by and perpetuate a "whack-a-mole" style of leadership in their organizations, and this style of leadership is more common than most executives and managers would like to admit. Executives cannot continue to do the same things and expect to achieve different results. Too many organizations are stuck in this vicious cycle of insanity and hyperinsanity and risk falling behind in this challenging economy. Constancy of purpose is dealing with uncertainty in a more adaptive equilibrium state. Adaptive Leadership is about shutting down these large reactive pendulum swings in leadership behaviors, choices, and actions that appear to correct symptomatic issues in one direction while creating more and larger problems in the opposite direction.

The Process of Reckoning, Renewal, and Enlightenment

The process of reckoning, renewal, and enlightenment is the center point of Adaptive Leadership. To refresh the reader's memory:

▲ *Reckoning* is the immediate recognition of the need to change course. Reckoning is not a negative activity; it is a reflection of successes, mistakes and misdeeds, and emerging issues facing the organization. Without reckoning, organizations cannot plan for change and improvement. Reckoning formally defines the gaps between current performance and desired performance over various time horizons. Managers are forced to deal with change after it hits. We have already discussed the results: insanity and hyperinsanity.

▲ *Renewal* is the vision and execution of change to a higher level of excellence and performance. Renewal is the process of developing the right improvement strategy and tactics to keep the systematic process of improvement alive, further develop the organization's talent, and achieve superior industry performance.

▲ *Enlightenment* is the positive outcome of this successful, continuous cycle of reckoning and renewal. Enlightenment covers the full cycle from idea to execution and standardization of an improved process. One cannot feel enlightenment from the idea alone. Enlightenment is experienced by the full success of improvement.

The big question in all of this is, "How do I and my executive team, managers, and entire organization adapt this approach to leadership?" Figure 3.2 provides an overview of this process.

Adaptive Leadership is based upon the principle of inclusion. Executives cannot go through all the details of reckoning, renewal, and enlightenment on their own. Adaptive Leadership also includes creating a safe, collaborative workplace ecosystem that nurtures trust, mutual understanding, continuous coaching and development, and total freedom of expression.

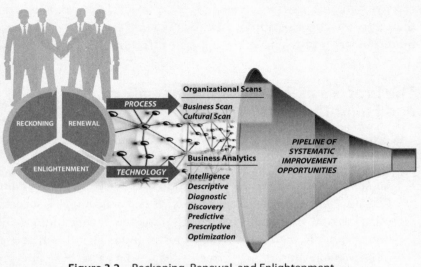

Figure 3.2   Reckoning, Renewal, and Enlightenment
Copyright © 2015, The Center for Excellence in Operations, Inc.

Inclusion builds a culture that invites total participation, engagement, multiple perspectives, and contribution to holistic success. The very first step is *invisible* and not shown but it is the toughest step. It's often painful for executives to come to the realization that what they have been doing isn't working anymore. Many might feel the emotions of this realization as a personal reflection on their leadership competence. The entire organization shares this pain. The pain increases the longer executives and their organizations remain in the same situation. This first step involves rethinking the journey. Recognition of the need to change is a healthy leadership discovery; it is how good leaders grow to become great leaders.

A Combination of Process and Technology

Adaptive Leadership is state-of-the-art leadership that requires a combination of process and technology, namely:

▲ Organizational scans that include both an internal and external check-in on the organization's health and well-being of the business as a whole. Organizational scans are continuing disciplined processes and include two categories: the business scan and the cultural scan.

The *business scan* is a structured operations due-diligence activity, while the *cultural scan* is a status and needs update on the human capital side of the business. These continued scans are the basis for identifying new business and cultural requirements and for feeding our Lean Business System Reference Model with laser-targeted, high-impact improvement opportunities.

▲   A formal analytics support system that integrates the scanning processes above with technology; namely, business analytics. Technology enables the continuous iterative exploration and investigation of prior business performance and helps executives to gain insight into future business requirements and competitive issues. Business analytics provide the data-driven and fact-based view of the business and its challenges. There are several types of business analytics methods that answer questions like what is the current state, what happened, how many, how often, where the problems exist, and what actions are needed. Business analytics can answer questions like, "Why is this happening?" "What if these trends continue?" "What will happen next?" and, "What is the best that can happen?"

The Business Scan

The business scan is a formal methodology used for conducting a diagnostic and assessment of the organization's strengths and weaknesses relative to competitors and emerging market opportunities. The purpose of this scan is to identify gaps between current operating performance and where the organization needs to be in order to remain a superior player in its industry.

The business scan is a four-step process:

1. Review the business strategy and operating plan: This is a review of goals rather than current operating performance. Its purpose is to identify specific gaps between current and desired performance. The result of this step is the identification of high-level improvement themes, which are later detailed in specific, assignment-ready, improvement activities in step 4.

2. Benchmark the organization's current and potential performance against relevant best practices and demonstrated best-in-class

performance: The purpose of this step is to identify how the organization is performing relative to inside industry and outside industry best-in-class organizations. Adaptive systematic improvement encourages organizations to learn from the experiences of others but *adapt* (not copy and paste) best practices to specific business requirements and culture.

3. Develop the adaptive systematic improvement strategy and implementation needs: This involves developing the Aligned Improvement Strategy, using the MacroCharter planning template.

4. Define improvement goals, benefits, and risks/consequences of not changing: This is the more tactical aspects of deployment planning, where the improvement themes are further detailed into specific, assignment-ready improvement activities, using the MicroCharter planning template.

The diagnostic reveals both current inefficiencies and future business requirements. It also provides the working road map for a successful systematic process of improvement because it provides the up-front, deep-core drilling into the organization's key strategic, business, and operations issues.

The Cultural Scan

The cultural scan is a check-in on the organization's readiness and willingness to change. It is designed to surface any people issues, frustrations, opinions and perceptions, communication issues, political issues, or other human resource issues that may become detractors to improvement. The cultural scan is checking the vital signs of Kata—the behavioral and cultural development needs. Many organizations conduct periodic internal scans through formal surveys, structured evaluations, focus groups, town hall meetings, functional area meetings, or some combination thereof. The aim is to continually identify how the organization can support its associates and help them in any way to operate in a safer, productive, and positive environment. The *internal scan* determines the organizational and cultural alignment with the organization's intended strategic goals and improvement plans.

Some of the results from a cultural scan that are very necessary to adaptive systematic improvement include but are not limited to the following areas:

▲ Communication and reinforcement of mission/vision/purpose.

▲ Understanding the corporate values communicated compared with those actually practiced.

▲ Organizational structure and reporting relationships, and how these might impact associates' abilities to get things done.

▲ Code of conduct assessment—real or symbolic.

▲ Personal growth and career and talent development plans.

▲ Adjustments to leadership and management behaviors, choices, and actions.

▲ Management practices, degree of command versus empowerment.

▲ Individual, group, and department issues and barriers to success.

▲ Communication issues.

▲ Overall climate and attitudes in the organizations.

▲ Effectiveness or inefficiencies in policies and procedures.

▲ Progress with systems and key business processes.

▲ Performance measurement systems.

▲ Workplace environment and conditions; safety issues.

An assessment of the executive leadership team and key organizational positions, talent backstops, the organization's abilities to implement new strategic improvement initiatives, and additional talent and skill development needs are also part of the cultural scan.

The Role of Business Analytics

The new requirements of organizations are evolving at a much faster rate than can be identified and responded to—especially in a manual world.

Business analytics allows for the efficient exploration and investigation of current conditions, performance gaps, and strategic and operating needs. Developing an analytics support capability for a Lean Business System is not a big deal or a year-long IT project. For simplicity and clarification, business analytics can be grouped into the following types of information:

▲ *Intelligence analytics* is information that provides a continuous snapshot of what is going on in a business. Real-time, digital performance dashboards and data visualization technologies that display metrics and other graphical information are examples of intelligence analytics. The objective is to get everyone on the same page in terms of current conditions and issues.

▲ *Descriptive analytics* is like descriptive statistics. Information is analyzed by predetermined methods and displayed in various tabular or graphical summaries (e.g., averages of customer fill rates by product, Pareto analysis of revenue and profit contribution by product, customer, territory, and so on. The objective is to break down obscure data into smaller attributed clusters through statistical profiling, segmentation, and other statistical means.

▲ *Diagnostic analytics* is a deeper dive into information with more advanced statistical engineering techniques to better understand cause-and-effect relationships in performance data. Diagnostic analytics strives to identify and explain the relative influence of root causes on a particular business outcome. For example, what are the primary drivers of delivery performance or pipeline inventory performance or product quality or late time to market? These are known problems.

▲ *Discovery analytics* involves advanced inferential statistical tools like hypothesis testing, analysis of variance (ANOVA), and design of experiments (DOE). We start off with a pure "we don't know what we don't know" condition. There exists perceptions, opinions, and speculation about corrective actions but we are normally dealing with issues that we have never been able to improve. These are unknown problems. Through the use of discovery analytics, the factors that most influence process performance can be isolated. It's a discovery, because we discover problems and root causes with data and facts. If we solve this 20 percent of the root causes, we will eliminate 80 percent of the problem.

▲ *Predictive analytics* usually involves simulations and modeling of future scenarios based on a predetermined set of assumptions. These assumptions can be modified to create a sensitivity analysis of what-if capability to analyze future scenarios or predict the outcomes of remaining in the same state. These are often complex and carefully structured statistical simulations in which the likelihood of certain outcomes are predicted based on various factors or input assumptions.

▲ *Prescriptive analytics* is the summary of one or more other different types of business analytics. Once a situation is well defined and understood with data and facts, prescriptive analytics is useful in consolidating findings and conclusions, and in evaluating the feasibility and likelihood of success of various options or recommended courses of action (prior to taking physical actions). Prescriptive analytics is also useful in weighing the pros, cons, costs, barriers, and risks of various options.

▲ *Optimization analytics* is a higher order of predictive analytics that seeks to optimize process performance around conflicting constraints. The goal of optimization analytics is to either maximize or minimize a business given limited inputs (e.g., resources, capacity, capital, and other constraints). In these complex systems, these limited constraints are at conflict with each other for given situations. For example, how do we optimize the global supply chain? One answer is unlimited inventory, which is not feasible. Another answer might be to build more and larger production facilities or to spread our spend out to a hundred new suppliers or design reliable and defect-free products. I was involved with an optimization analytics study a few years ago in which the organization wanted to determine which metrics optimized profitability and EBITDA. Optimization analytics may produce a recommendation that minimizes operating costs or maximizes profitability, but keep in mind that one cannot possibly build all the factors in organizations (especially the unpredictable human factors) into these analytical exercises.

The most applicable to the organizational scans are the intelligence, descriptive, diagnostic, and discovery analytics. Predictive, prescriptive, and optimization analytics are used more in a larger specific and complex improvement project.

A word of caution is in order when designing this business analytics support process. This applies to all technology solutions like mobility, cloud computing, data warehousing, virtualization. Technology is a powerful enabler for conducting these scans efficiently, but technology can also quickly overwhelm people with information—more information than they can possibly understand, distill, and use in a true value-added way. A major consideration of technology-enabled improvement that must not be overlooked is that the real intelligence lies in the improvement practitioner and the user community in the form of human intelligence. There is no improvement intelligence software or mobile application that plans and executes adaptive systematic improvement automatically.

The process of improvement still relies on human intelligence to organize and structure the right business queries, define and scan the right baseline data, define and segment the right root cause information, analyze data with the right methodologies and tools, draw the right, data-driven conclusions, take the right fact-based actions, and close the loop with the right performance metrics.

This is often the big disconnect with business analytics activities in organizations today. If one is missing this core competency of structured and disciplined improvement, then technology is reduced to providing more information quicker—the old data rich/analysis poor syndrome. Organizations must be very wary of looking at the wrong data just because it is available, and then drawing the wrong conclusions and developing a wrong improvement strategy.

Governance and Interventions: Organizing for Adaptive, Systematic Improvement

A Lean Business System is much more than an architecture; it holds a formal executive role in the organization. There is no single right way to design an organization in order to maintain a systematic process of improvement. It is always a function of the organizational business requirements and business unit structures that are currently in place, and the structure is very different in larger multinational corporations from the structure in smaller and midsized organizations.

The purpose of this section is to provide a guide for leading and organizing a systematic process of improvement. Unlike the early Six Sigma deployments most organizations do not have hundreds of people hanging around whom they can dedicate as full-time, centralized black belts. The thought for dedicated resources is there, but it is impractical and not sustainable for most organizations. We have used a different model that is shown in Figure 3.3. A Lean Business System is lead by a vice president of the XYZ Corporation business system. This role has worked well reporting directly to the CEO, or a senior operating vice president (global operations, global quality). This individual is the chair and lead facilitator of the executive core team. This is definitely a role that organizations want to keep visible in the executive suite so as to send the right message of its importance to the organization.

Next we suggest that an executive core team be established and tasked with the overall continuous success of the systematic process. The organization chart in Figure 3.3 is an abbreviated representation: This group is composed of a cross-functional subgroup of the executive team, business unit executives, and other influential executives. The core functions of sales and marketing, finance, operations, and engineering are represented on the team. Sometimes the CEO chooses to be an active member of the core team. The executive core team plays a key governing role in adaptive systematic improvement by:

▲ Synchronizing and aligning the Lean Business System to the business plan and operating plan.

▲ Updating the CEO and executive team on progress and issues.

▲ Providing overall leadership and governance.

▲ Conducting, analyzing, and drawing requirements from the business scans and cultural scans.

▲ Continuously maintaining the MacroCharter and MicroCharter, the living hopper of improvement activities in process, queued up, and new requirements.

▲ Encouraging and mentoring executive and process owner engagement and objectivity.

▲ Acting as the barrier resolution, resource balancer, and interference factor to keep adaptive systematic improvement on track, efficient, and continuously successful.

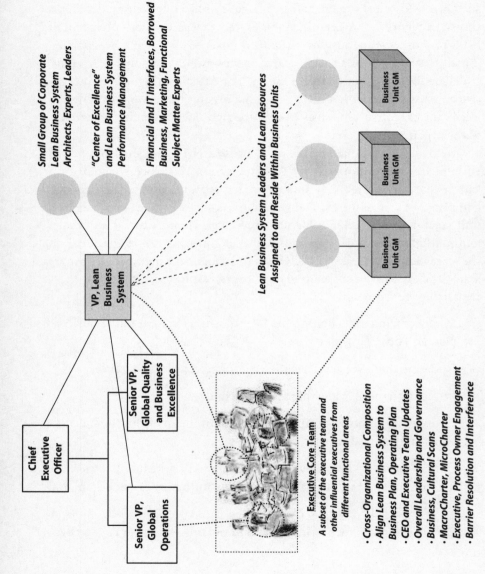

Chief Executive Officer

Senior VP, Global Operations

Senior VP, Global Quality and Business Excellence

VP, Lean Business System

Small Group of Corporate Lean Business System Architects, Experts, Leaders

"Center of Excellence" and Lean Business System Performance Management

Financial and IT Interfaces, Borrowed Business, Marketing, Functional Subject Matter Experts

Lean Business System Leaders and Lean Resources Assigned to and Reside Within Business Units

Business Unit GM

Business Unit GM

Business Unit GM

Executive Core Team
A subset of the executive team and other influential executives from different functional areas

- *Cross-Organizational Composition*
- *Align Lean Business System to Business Plan, Operating Plan*
- *CEO and Executive Team Updates*
- *Overall Leadership and Governance*
- *Business, Cultural Scans*
- *MacroCharter, MicroCharter*
- *Executive, Process Owner Engagement*
- *Barrier Resolution and Interference*

Figure 3.3   Organizing for Systematic Improvement
Copyright © 2015, The Center for Excellence in Operations, Inc. (CEO)

The executive core team usually meets every week for a quick flash report of improvement initiatives and other activities in process. Its mission is to seek out the greatest improvement opportunities, engage the organization to set and hit goals quickly and efficiently, and to keep mining for the next big improvement opportunities—and most importantly, to keep adaptive systematic improvement on point. There are occasions when the executive core team has an emergency meeting for an important improvement activity, or it might dedicate a two- to four-hour working session if it is conducting a spin on the business scan and cultural scan, discuss how to accelerate improvement activities in process, or when the need arises to reprioritize and realign the contents of the MacroCharter and MicroCharter. At the conclusion of these executive core team meetings, members have action items to support the overall adaptive systematic improvement role.

In smaller and midsized, self-contained organizations (e.g., two to three sites) this organizational description provides an adequate start. However, in larger, independent multinationals, the vice president, Lean Business System, and an executive core team provides more of a policy deployment and shared services role. Larger independent business units need their own Lean Business System site leader and their own executive core team. In the Lean Business System Reference Model, the specific corporate and business unit roles and responsibilities are requirements-driven and must be architected to address particular business and cultural development needs.

One of the most important elements of a successful executive core team is to consciously disallow participant perceptions, opinions, and political issues from shaping the work of the group. Business analytics provides an objective analytics support system that is both targeted and focused on identifying the right data-driven and fact-based improvement requirements for the organization. It is the executive core team's role to define the best and highest-impact opportunities for improvement and then to prioritize and align these activities to the business plan and annual operating plan. Members of the team should be in tune with the organization's needs as operating executives, and they must tee up the right, fact-based improvement activities to enable high monthly performance, quarterly performance, and annual performance. This is a very important, precision-oriented role for achieving success.

Our Lean Business System Reference Model avoids the large armies of dedicated centralized black belts and other Lean resources prevalent in the past decade. The vice president of the XYZ business system needs a small centralized group of highly skilled improvement leaders and practitioners that report directly to him or her, and who focus on planning, development, providing a uniform center of excellence for talent development, maintaining overall performance of adaptive systematic improvement, recruiting special support needs such as financial analysis and validation or IT support, and assisting with special business unit improvement needs. The vice president of the XYZ business system works with each business unit general manager to plan staffing needs based on the MacroCharter and MicroCharter plans. In large organizations with large business units, it makes sense to plan on a business unit executive core team and senior improvement executive/architect and a few skilled practitioners to work *with* business units. This role is to develop the internal competency of adaptive systematic improvement throughout the business unit. This smaller group adapts systematic improvement and the MicroCharter even further to the specific requirements and uniqueness of a business unit. Members of this group serve as adaptive systematic improvement leaders and mentors, not doers for the business units. In smaller organizations the responsibility may reside with the business unit GM and executive team (who also serve as the executive core team) with a designated business unit lead improvement resource. This individual serves more in a project management role, organizing and prioritizing improvement needs with the executive team, providing technical mentoring and mentoring managers, teams, and individuals through the successful completion of their improvement activities. In all cases, the central XYZ business system organization works with and mentors business unit resources to develop talent through the center of excellence, and to organize and mentor business unit improvement resources through their successful activities. Another role of the business unit improvement leaders is to help business units balance the requirements of daily distractions with continuous improvement.

Overall, we have found this to be a simple and very efficient organizational approach to planning, deploying, executing, and sustaining a Lean Business System. Please keep in mind that this is one of several different options to organize adaptive systematic improvement as the organization's business or operating system. The proper organization and infrastructure design for adaptive systematic improvement is critical to sustainable success. The actual design is driven by business requirements; present organizational structure, size, and scope; and specific adaptive systematic improvement needs. In very small, single-site organizations, for example, the best option might be to create a site executive core team and appoint a senior improvement leader. This individual is responsible for the XYZ business system and works with the executive core team and functional champions on detailed deployment planning and execution.

In every scenario there is also the option to engage *proven* outside experts or to proceed with an organic approach. *Proven* means true Lean Business System architect resource(s) that bring originality, credibility, creativity, customization, industry recognition, and a track record of successes. These professionals are much more skilled than the typical, narrowly focused "TPS preachers" of *manufacturing and tools*. The majority of the best Lean Business System organizations have engaged *proven* outside expertise to help organize and expedite the front end of their journey. This is not a statistical anomaly. While Lean Business System consulting expenses increase short-term discretionary spending, it is a great investment with a significant ROI (*return on investment*) when the right credible resources are engaged as executive mentors, architects, and advisors. A true Lean Business System is a legitimate core competency that organizations develop and nurture over time. It is much more than another casual replication of the TPS principles and tools. Adaptive systematic improvement is logical and looks simple, but it is *not* easy. The risks of failure are high when systematic improvement is not well organized and architected at the front end. The only option is to get it right!

The Best Practice Leadership Behaviors

Adaptive Leadership recognizes that behaviors influence executive choices and actions. This is Leadership 101 in theory. However, in order to evolve to an adaptive style of leadership, it helps to better understand and quantify these specific behaviors. Adaptive Leadership is supported by a conscious set of executive behaviors that can be *adapted* by leadership and instilled in the organization. Organizational awareness is the prerequisite for adaptivity. These behaviors are the essence of what enables adaptive systematic improvement and what creates great cultural organizations, where one continuously evolves into the other. Adaptive Leadership recognizes that organizations cannot *improve how they improve* or change culture by mandating the use of a set of tools or copied practices. Behavioral awareness, alignment, and reinforcement are the underpinning for creating a cultural foundation of excellence and greatness. This cultural foundation adjusts and adapts to changing business and operating conditions, always to a higher level of excellence and superior performance.

Recognizing that we are not dealing with an exact science here, we have developed a best practice leadership behaviors model, a soft control evaluation technique that is simple to use and helpful in building individual and group awareness about certain improvement-detracting behaviors. The model includes the dimensional *Kata* attributes of both great leadership and cultural excellence. Best practice leadership behaviors can be grouped into five major categories:

1. Vision

2. Knowledge

3. Passion

4. Discipline

5. Conscience

Within each of these categories is a set of behavioral attributes that contribute positively to adaptive systematic improvement and, in fact, personal leadership success. This is a quick and simple, attribute-based scan of leadership behaviors and is not limited to the executive suite. The CEO and his or her executive team may choose to complete the scan as a group or on each other's styles. The scan can be used to evaluate middle managers from a 360-degree approach including their manager, direct reports, and internal customers or other individuals who interface with a particular individual. The process is consensus-based, using a scale of 1 to 10 (1 = poor, 5 = average, 10 = outstanding). We do not view the individual scores as a pass/fail competitive test, but we use them to uncover the lower score trends in an individual, a team, a functional area, another organizational segment, or a specific leadership category or its related group of attributes. Often it serves more as an awareness and self-help exercise to improve a particular leadership style or to better understand and resolve organizational conflicts. It is most useful in individual and smaller group applications; it is obvious that a full leadership behavior scan is possible on the entire organization, but it is not actionable. Another useful capability is to look at the relative difference in attribute levels over time, or before and after an educational or career development event. Table 3.1, Figure 3.4, and

Table 3.1 Best Practice Leadership Behaviors Scan Data

Vision	Scores	Knowledge	Scores	Passion	Scores	Discipline	Scores	Conscience	Scores
Courage	6	Logical Thinking	7	Motivating	7	Commitment	9	Trust	8
Conviction	7	Answering Why	7	Challenging	7	Objectivity	7	Authenticity	8
Charisma	5	Answering What	7	People-Oriented	4	Patience	2	Candor	8
Creativity	6	Answering How	7	Team Building	4	Communications	8	Character	7
Curiousity	4	Answering Where	7	Inclusive	4	Competence	9	Ethics	6
Strategic Thinking	4	Answering When	7	Unmeddling	3	Common Sense	9	Respectfulness	7
Guiding Beacon	6	Know-How	9	Engaging	7	Consistency	6	Transparency	5
Goals-Oriented	8	Needs-Driven	8	Empowering	6	Constancy	7	Dignity	7
		Consequence Enforcer	4	Development	5	Balance	7	Admissiveness	3
		Resource Balancer	4			Realism	9	Accessibility	4
		Skill Builder	5			Focus	8	Integrity	7
						Attentiveness	7	Recognition and Rewards	3
								Inspiration	7
Totals	**46**		**72**		**47**		**88**		**80**
Possible Score	**80**		**110**		**90**		**120**		**130**
Category Score	**5.75**		**6.55**		**5.22**		**7.33**		**6.15**

Figure 3.5 provide a sample from the Adaptive Leadership Assessment in the reference model.

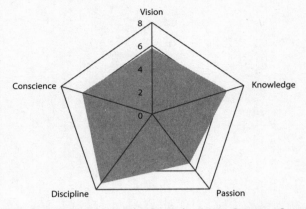

Figure 3.4 Best Practice Leadership Behaviors—Category Summary
Copyright © 2015, The Center for Excellence in Operations, Inc.

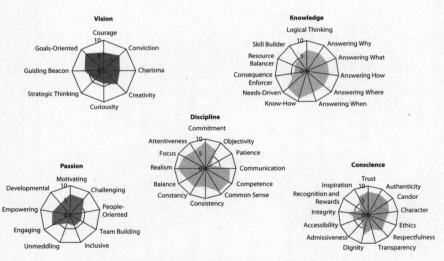

Figure 3.5 Best Practice Leadership Behaviors—Attribute Level Scan
Copyright © 2015, The Center for Excellence in Operations, Inc.

These behavior categories and their detailed attributes used in the model are contained in Table 3.2.

Table 3.2 Best Practice Behaviors

Vision	Vision is the ability to see beyond current challenges and define a new direction for improvement. Vision is only attainable for individuals willing to pick their heads out of the reeds, take a time-out, stop the *insanity*, and dream a bit about how the business can and will improve.	• *Courage:* The ability to confront fear, pain points, risk/danger, uncertainty, or internal and external intimidation. • *Conviction:* The art of convincing oneself and others about reality, risks, and the consequences of not improving. • *Charisma:* The magnetism, communications skills, and personal being to persuade and convince others about improvement. • *Creativity:* The ability to "imagineer," to think beyond the box, and think and act divergently. • *Curiosity:* The desire and inquisitive interest to learn from others. • *Strategic thinking:* Thinking beyond the next quarter and thinking big. • *Guiding beacon:* Behaviors followed by actions that attract others. • *Goals-oriented:* Setting the bar of expectations high but achievable; also raising the bar of expectations above current performance to encourage continuous improvement.
Knowledge	Knowledge is the ability to act based on true facts and data. Knowledge is self-education and self-awareness that enable one to understand how the vision may be possible. This includes taking the time and having the patience to understand what really matters in an adaptive systematic management process.	• *Logical thinking:* The ability to reduce a complex and unsolvable puzzle of improvement into a rational and orderly set of proposed plans and activities. • *Answering why:* The patience to develop the business case so that one can lead with facts and truth and data to construct a solid story of change. • *Answering what:* The ability to synthesize facts and decide on the correct strategic corrective actions. • *Answering how:* The ability to understand and prioritize the true requirements of a challenge and recognize internal shortfalls. • *Answering where:* The ability to prioritize where the organization needs to focus improvement efforts. • *Answering when:* The timing and sense of urgency required to move the business forward. • *Know-how:* Taking the time to build intelligence combined with objectivity so that one avoids reactionary problem solving, underestimating efforts, or hip-shooting leadership. • *Needs-driven:* The ability to understand implementation requirements and admit to barriers to success and gaps in internal expertise.

(Continues)

Table 3.2 Best Practice Behaviors (*Continued*)

		• *Consequence enforcer:* The ability to take a tough stand on fact-based controversy or confrontation or noncompliance to improvement goals and objectives.
		• *Resource balancer:* The ability to help the organization balance priorities versus the perceived piling of additional assignments on current workloads.
		• *Skill builder:* The ability to recognize skill and experience gaps and inject these competencies into the organization.
Passion	*Passion* is the compelling emotion that drives leaders to success. Passion is the "fire in the belly" that gets leaders and organizations through any and all obstacles to success. When leaders possess and transfer passion to the rest of the organization, it is powerful stuff.	• *Motivating:* The ability to activate and energize goal-oriented behaviors in the organization.
		• *Challenging:* The ability to positively call out individuals to explain, justify, or rationalize plans and activities.
		• *People-oriented:* The ability to encourage employees to use all of their talents and skills and to be productive in an organization where learning is a priority.
		• *Team building:* The ability to mentor people to work in cohesive, cross-functional teams, regardless of their home organization.
		• *Inclusive:* The ability to recognize and tap people's experiences and expertise from a variety of backgrounds.
		• *Unmeddling:* Recognizing that leadership is not meddling in or second-guessing others' roles and responsibilities. Leadership is developing others to conduct themselves with excellence in their roles and responsibilities so that meddling is not required.
		• *Engaging:* Developing positive, enthusiastic, and effective connection with people regarding their work in a way that motivates an employee to invest in getting the job done, not just "well" but "with excellence" because the work content energizes the individual.
		• *Empowering:* The ability to give away power and authority to the organization because the organization has developed the sense of responsibility to accept power and authority and act in a correct manner.
		• *Developmental:* The ability to encourage and mentor systematic growth in individual job content skills, broader business skills, communication skills, interpersonal skills, or supervisory/leadership skills.

| Discipline | *Discipline* is the ability to adhere to rules of conduct and expectations for the organization in a manner that establishes logical business conduct and order. The other side of discipline is "walking the talk." Discipline lays down the moral compass and serves to guide organizational behaviors to pursue the right decisions and achieve the right results. | • *Commitment:* The ability to make a personal pledge or emotional contract to a particular course of action without being disrupted by other arising issues.
• *Objectivity:* The ability to express or deal with facts or conditions as perceived or measured without any bias and distortion by personal feelings, prejudices, interpretations, political implications, or personal implications.
• *Patience:* The ability to endure and stay focused in the most difficult situations.
• *Communication:* The ability to foster interchange of the right thoughts and actions by translating information into understandable messages.
• *Competence:* The ability to engage in and complete various actions, to demonstrate true commitment, and to ensure that one is not asking the organization to do something that it will not do itself.
• *Common sense:* The ability to exhibit sound, logical, and practical judgment.
• *Consistency:* The ability to display cohesive, noncontradictory behaviors.
• *Constancy:* A behavior that relates to the quality of unwavering direction and steadiness or faithfulness in action, affections, and purpose.
• *Structure:* The ability to create, follow, and reinforce accepted standards of conduct such as DMAIC (define-measure-analyze-improve-control) and root-cause problem solving.
• *Balance:* The ability to strive for a fact-based state of equilibrium or parity characterized by understanding and stabilizing the organization's driving and restraining forces.
• *Realism:* The ability to deal with people, objects, actions, or business conditions sensibly and levelheadedly as they reveal themselves in actuality.
• *Focus:* The ability to concentrate on a particular challenge, combined to create clarity that allows others also to concentrate on a particular challenge.
• *Attentiveness:* The ability to listen to all sides of an issue with objectivity and without interrupting and providing an answer. Another aspect is the ability to mentor and ask the right questions and develop subordinate decision making. |

(Continues)

Table 3.2 Best Practice Behaviors *(Continued)*

| Conscience | *Conscience* is the leadership ability to distinguish whether the organization's actions, or individual actions, are right or wrong. Some refer to this as the inner voice of the subconscious mind. This inner voice is shaped by values or emotional rules established in one's personal, social, cultural, educational, and business life. Conscience is the inner voice that justifies and rationalizes what is right and what is wrong. | • *Trust:* The reliance on another individual's integrity, abilities, commitment, enabling behaviors, performance, and mutual surety. Trust is the nucleus of leadership.
• *Authenticity:* The truthfulness of origins, attributions, commitments, sincerity, devotion, and intentions.
• *Candor:* The quality of being frank, open, and sincere in speech or expression.
• *Character:* The moral and ethical traits and qualities of a leader as observed by the organization.
• *Ethics:* A leader's observed moral principles and values.
• *Respectfulness:* The ability to exhibit positive esteem and in turn receive the respect of others.
• *Transparency:* The ability to act in a "what you see is what you get" manner and work *with* the organization.
• *Dignity:* The ability to grant the right of respect and ethical treatment to others.
• *Admissive:* The voluntary admission of truth, even if it is a mistake; also the acceptance of others' mistakes and the mentoring of corrective actions as part of the normal learning and development cycle.
• *Accessibility:* The ability to be reachable and in the presence of the organization; also the ability of others to work with leaders without fear.
• *Integrity:* The honesty and consistency of actions, values, methods, measures, principles, expectations, and outcomes as demonstrated by both communications and actions.
• *Recognition and rewards:* The ability to celebrate and recognize organizational successes and reward high-performing individuals and teams, but follow the "Great job" comments with "How good do you think we can get? What are the team's next actions?"
• *Inspiration:* A divine influence, action, or power of leaders to motivate intellect or emotions or to influence great behaviors followed by great actions and great satisfactions. |

How Leaders Adapt and Win

Most executives are extremely challenged by all the issues and information coming at them on a daily basis. This can create a lack of self-awareness of their own strengths and limitations, and can blur the strengths and limitations of their organization. These issues and challenges are complex and come in cyclic streams: many small manageable cycles for adaptive leaders and larger problematic cycles for maladaptive leaders who choose more of the same—postponement, procrastination, or complacency. It is easy for organizations to lose their way, and it is even easier for organizations to remain in denial about losing their way. Again, not a criticism: This is the reality of the warp-speed global economy where we all work.

As mentioned earlier, Adaptive Leadership is a rare commodity. Executives do not come to work one day as an Adaptive Leader and decide that their organization will become effective in an adaptive way immediately. Organizations develop the competency of Adaptive Leadership over time by responding to and resolving the challenges immediately and with the right resources and talent. It requires a major paradigm shift; a personal realization that *you don't know what you don't know;* a recognition of serious organizational voids; a painful cycle of reckoning, renewal, and enlightenment. The ideal situation is to transform every internal executive, leader, manager, and process owner, but it is neither realistic nor timely. This leadership mindset adjustment is not always effective with internal resources that are profoundly accustomed to their various "as-is" and firefighting routines. The most successful organizations embrace talent acquisition—injections of new external talent to make the necessary organizational competency improvements.

Interventions Are Healthy

Intervention plays a large role in Adaptive Leadership. This is not a negative activity but a very healthy organizational development process. Most organizations proactively reinforce cultural expectations and the accepted code of conduct. However, there are a number of reasons why executives, managers, and associates temporarily abandon these values. Many of these reasons are directly attributable to leadership behaviors, choices, and actions. Over time, these diversions become accepted because nothing is done about them. One of my favorite examples is embedded in this executive comment: "We do Lean Monday through Thursday, and Friday is rework and repair day."

Leadership must play a strong intervention role in order to keep adaptive systematic improvement on track; we are not insinuating a "Gestapo" role here. We are talking about systematic interventions in which leaders view these diversions in terms of the whole system rather than reprimanding individuals for doing what they thought they were supposed to do. Leadership's role in adaptive systematic improvement is to set up and maintain a positive environment for success, to create the right improvement Kata. Leaders and managers must learn to act as counselor, mentor, personal coach, technical advisor, coordinator, educator, and barrier and deadlock buster. They must learn to ask the right questions and get their people to think rather than giving answers or direct orders. They must practice the conscious habit of continuous *power hits* to their organizations. Power hits are the quick, informal, conscious 15-second messages that demonstrate commitment, interest, and expectations.

A final thought about interventions. Most executives like to approach this topic in a positive light. Creating a talented, empowered, and happy workforce is the goal and the right thing to do. In the real world, interventions are not always a bed of roses. Occasionally I have worked in organizations where there are a few real improvement troublemakers. Often these people can be turned around with the right attention and guidance. However, when organizations allow one of these characters to undermine all the great work of groups of dedicated people, it is very destructive on any improvement activity. Furthermore, it sends a very negative message that improvement does not matter; improvement is not on the radar screen. Intervention is also about having the leadership fortitude to remove the detractors and obstacles from adaptive systematic improvement.

Courage Is Asking the Tough Questions

Nobody said that Adaptive Leadership (or leadership in general) was easy. A Lean Business System forces executives to step out of a role of moderating the happenings in their organizations, to proactively pushing the limits of what their organizations can achieve. It is a mindset change away from *how well are we doing* to *how great can we become?* Here are a few tough questions that executives should ask themselves about their organizations:

▲ When was the last time you stood back and rated your performance and that of your management team? Is there a shared notion of what, why, where, when, how, and who need to change?

▲ Are you and your team best suited to running your organization in its current stage of operating challenges and growth? Where are the voids in strategy and execution of the desired changes?

▲ Who are the leaders and champions of innovation, improvement, business transformation, and change management? Who are the maintainers and sustainers of the status quo? What and who are the barriers to change?

▲ How are you doing on your organic Lean, Six Sigma, and other strategic and/or continuous improvement initiatives? What is the ROI and validated value contribution to the business? When do you expect to reach the industry benchmark annual savings run rate of 3–10 percent+ of revenues?

▲ What specific strategic transactional initiatives are in place to flush out the hidden waste in knowledge processes such as new product development, supply chain management, R&D and innovation, excess/ obsolete inventory, returns and allowances, warranty and repairs, cash to cash, product portfolio management, marketing and promotions, advertising, sales and channel management, sustaining engineering, quality management, IT, sourcing and procurement, and so on? What has changed, and how has it impacted operating performance?

▲ Do you have a chance of becoming a best-in-class industry performer within the next 12–18 months with the current leadership, strategy, and organization?

Enterprisewide Adaptive Leadership

Organizations develop an Adaptive Leadership competency when they are able to respond to and resolve challenges in real time, with their existing (and acquired) resources and talent capabilities. This anemic economy has swung the needle toward organic improvement with traditional Lean methods in the interest of cost containment, but it is not working out for many organizations. Additionally, organizations have a natural tendency to settle into a comfortable operating mode and delay true, proactive, and adaptive systematic improvement. Adaptive Leadership thinking breaks this traditional cycle and renews the opportunities for improvement in a very precise and systematic way.

At the manager, first-line supervisor, or team leader levels, the form of Adaptive Leadership becomes more of a proactive execution role. Associates need a structured routine and pattern of thinking about process improvement. Toyota uses an approach called the *five questions* which is deeply embedded in how their people think and work. Organizations need to create this competency with executives, managers, and associates. Since 2004 we have used a simplified define-measure-analyze-improve-control (DMAIC) pocket template from our basic improvement skills (BIS) education for associates and individual contributors. It serves the same purpose as Toyota's five questions while providing a consistent way of thinking about adaptive systematic improvement throughout the organization. We have kept the DMAIC structure in our Lean Business System Reference Model because it provides an effective, common universal language of improvement. We have also adapted other open methodologies for non-linear improvement situations.

The following list shows the systematized set of DMAIC questions from our BIS Pocket Guide that managers, supervisors, and team leaders should be instilling in their people as a daily way of thinking:

Basic Improvement Skills Guide

Define:

▲ What is the challenge or detractor?

▲ What is the improvement goal and objective?

▲ What are the general benefits?

▲ What is the next step?

Measure:

▲ What is the baseline performance?

▲ Is the problem confirmed with data?

▲ What are the financial benefits?

Analyze:

▲ What are the root causes of the problem?

▲ What are the options for improvement?

▲ When can improvement be implemented?

Improve:

▲ What is the best improvement option?

▲ What are the barriers, dependencies, and contingencies?

▲ How will you measure and confirm success?

Control:

▲ Did the actions solve the problem?

▲ How will you sustain improvement?

▲ Are there any other actions needed?

▲ What have you learned from this activity?

Today there exists more waste in many organizations than when they first embarked on their Lean journey years previously. It is nobody's fault: The sheer velocity, complexity, and competitive nature of change is moving at a faster rate than the organization's *maintainer and sustainer* leaders can deal with. Waste is an organic phenomenon in organizations that grows without deliberate attention and proactive countermeasures. Regardless of the economic dominos, Adaptive Leadership and best-in-class performance still remain an executive choice.

In this economy, human capital is the most valuable asset in organizations. It all comes down to having the right talent in the right places at the right time. Given that many "A" players move on and that there will be mismatches in leadership styles versus business cycle needs, the process of talent planning, development, retention, rationalization, and acquisition is critical. Chaos and constant change, increased complexity, and "improving how we improve" are givens in this new economy. This notion of *improving how we improve* can be accomplished only with the right improvement Kata. Adaptive leaders create adaptive organizations that are capable of morphing themselves into different structural and customer- and market-focused value stream organizations on demand. Best performing organizations are led by adaptive leaders that recognize and act immediately upon the need to change, including bringing in new talent from outside the organization.

Bibliography

Burton, T. 1995. *The Future Focused Organization.* Prentice Hall, Upper Saddle River, New Jersey.

Cockerell, L. 2006. *Disney Great Leader Strategies.* Disney Institute, Orlando, Florida.

Collins, J. 2011. *Great by Choice.* Harper-Collins, New York.

Iacocca, L. 2008. *Where Have All the Leaders Gone.* Scribner, New York.

Liker, J., and Convis, G. 2012. *The Toyota Way to Lean Leadership.* McGraw-Hill, New York.

MacKey, J., and Sisodia, R. 2013. *Conscious Capitalism: Liberating the Heroic Spirit of Business.* Harvard Business School Press, Boston, Massachusetts.

CHAPTER 4

Living Laser-Targeted Planning

This chapter provides guidance on how to create and maintain a *living laser-targeted planning* process. This is not a replacement for the corporation's strategic planning process; it is a direct replacement for hoshin planning as it is known today. These two subprocesses (aligned improvement strategy and the living deployment plan) of the Lean Business System Reference Model™ provide an expansion of the capabilities of planning and policy deployment. Before we get into this chapter, let's clarify a few things as they are presented in this chapter:

▲ A *strategic plan* is the longer-range plan outlining customer and market conditions, opportunities, and the organization's high-level business strategy, goals, objectives, major directives, high-level outlines of how to achieve the strategy, and decisions about how resources and capital will be allocated to achieve the strategy.

▲ *Hoshin kanri* (also known as *policy deployment*) is a strategic planning framework popularized in Japan and used by many Western organizations. It is a systematic planning process that uses an integrated set of "step-down" tables for strategy to tactics for execution and metrics. Hoshin tables are typically reviewed on a quarterly basis. Hoshin kanri is effective as long as the process of filling in templates and matrices does not take the place of planning itself.

▲ An *operating plan* is the organization's annual tactical plan that specifies goals, objectives, revenue and financial expectations, milestones, and desired performance metrics to achieve the strategic plan. The plan includes the aggregate corporation and its functional segments (e.g., customer sales and marketing, R&D, new product development, manufacturing and supply chain, finance, capital spend, etc.) and provides the basis for annual operating budgets. The operating plan provides the basis for monthly reviews that drive the organization toward its annual and strategic goals.

▲ *Living laser-targeted planning* provides the overall infrastructure and master plan for identifying critical business improvement needs, how key improvement issues are being addressed, what has changed for the positive, and where adjustments to the overall systematic process of improvement must be made to keep everything synchronized and generating the right results in the right places and at the right time to achieve or exceed the larger strategic and operating plans. It includes two subprocesses of our Lean Business System Reference Model: aligned improvement strategy and living deployment plan. Simply, living laser-targeted improvement is the engine that drives adaptive systematic improvement.

Living laser-targeted planning is not a replacement for strategic planning, hoshin planning, or the operating plan above. It is a more near real-time plan of business improvements needed to achieve the strategic and operating plans. Living laser-targeted planning provides a more granular and actionable level of detail below the strategic plan. Strategic planning and operational planning are *calendar-driven*. Living laser-targeted planning includes two subprocesses in its architecture:

▲ Aligned improvement strategy

▲ Living deployment plan

Both of these subprocesses are unique in that they are *demand- and event-driven,* thus creating more of a near real-time plan for adaptive systematic improvement. We chose not to cover these subprocesses in separate chapters because of their interrelationships and interconnectivity. One cannot function without the other. Therefore, both subprocesses are covered in this chapter.

Living laser-targeted planning (Figure 4.1) precisely aligns specific improvement themes, priorities, timing, and value contribution to present and evolving business requirements. Then these subprocesses further define specific improvement activities and their associated alignment, priorities, and control mechanisms at a much lower level of detail. It also provides a continuous and up-to-date reference of critical business

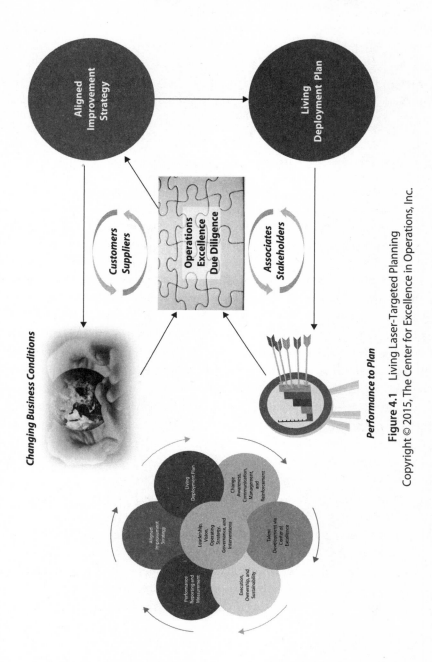

Figure 4.1 Living Laser-Targeted Planning
Copyright © 2015, The Center for Excellence in Operations, Inc.

107

improvement requirements and an evaluation of how the organization's strategic and operating plans are working out vis-à-vis major improvement in general. It does so through a double closed-loop feedback feature, and visualize that each loop may be working at variable rates. Living laser-targeted planning is essentially the subprocess that creates and maintains the *living* improvement strategy and implementation plans in our Lean Business System Reference Model.

A Lean Business System Requires Systematic Planning

Is all of this sophisticated planning necessary for Lean? Just go out there and do it. Hurry up and finish your Lean projects. This is the very executive mindset that has taken major improvement initiatives off track. First, living laser-targeted planning is not sophisticated once the baseline process is developed and put into natural practice. Second, attitudes about Lean and continuous improvement in general come from an oversimplification and underestimation of what it takes to achieve success. This is the first major obstacle of creating a systematic process of improvement, and this way of thinking needs to go—now! I have always prided myself on practicing the leadership values of honesty, integrity, courage, dignity and respect for other people, active listening, empathy, inspiration, entrepreneurship, fact-based and a logical, event- and data-driven subprocess. Executives can often get irritated at news that they do not want to hear, but they respect candor and the ability that takes them forward to new levels of superior performance. So here are the facts about why planning is necessary. The historical focus of Lean has been on *manufacturing* and *tools.* Most of the books and existing body of knowledge are focused on *manufacturing* and *tools.* Education has been focused on *tools.* Lean has been practiced as a generic recipe of *tools* for improving *manufacturing,* much of which has been photocopied from and between other organizations. There is this accepted notion that winging it with the *tools* create improvement opportunities, but it is the exact opposite. Improvement needs drive selection and deployment of the right combination of skills and tools to the highest-impact opportunities. Maybe the *Lean speak* of practitioners is correct, but their actions resemble a *Kata sonata*: a single-point approach to Lean with a very limited toolset. Lean manufacturing has evolved to a confusing set of tools and Toyota Production System terminology that practitioners can't even agree upon. Ask 50 experts the definition of *Lean*, and you will receive 50 different answers. Many who agree are blindly memorizing and regurgitating TPS *principles and tools* as the cure-all and end all. Lean is a bit like ice cream and children when each child thinks that his or her favorite flavor is better. There have been many varieties of *du jour* improvement. Where does this leave the people in the rest of the organization who are the direct recipients of a long parade of fad improvement programs and jargon in the hope that something will stick?

Having said all this, it is not a criticism of Lean manufacturing but a call to action to expand Lean to an enterprisewide systematic process. Lean *manufacturing* is still very important to preserve and grow the domestic manufacturing that remains in the United States. Lean *manufacturing* is an integral part of a Lean Business System. When one looks at the entire spectrum of opportunities across the enterprise and extended enterprise, these opportunities are more complex and require a much broader set of principles and approaches. It also requires planning to figure out this puzzle. Understand that whatever Lean and continuous improvement have included in the past it is insufficient to deal with the future. Systematic planning develops entire organizations to *improve how they improve*.

Mimicking Is Not Planning

Like it or not, Western culture is not compatible with Eastern-style Lean and continuous improvement initiatives. This is not a bad thing; we are who we are. Overlaying the Lean practices of other global companies is quick, but fundamentally flawed and short lived. Organizations lose interest when Lean becomes more of a cultural detractor than an enabler of success within *their* cultural belief system. This is exactly what happens when an organization attempts to "press fit" the Toyota Production System verbatim on their own culture. Learning and benefiting from external experiences is encouraged, but copying the Lean practices of other organizations makes an organization a questionable follower by definition. There is no soul in this quick knock-off improvement strategy. History demonstrates over and over that we are capable of creating superior performance with our own Western cultural beliefs and values. Yet Lean and general continuous improvement initiatives have resembled a generic copy-and-paste exercise for the past three decades. Toyota's success lies in evolving basic Western industrial and systems engineering fundamentals with *its* culture, values, and business requirements. Lean's failure has been in people attempting to evolve continuous improvement with tools, while forcing the culture and values of Toyota and other external organizations on their own environments. The irony in all of this is that much of the Toyota Production System is grounded in basic fundamentals of "Made in America" productivity improvement. Western organizations were the original leaders and architects of the Lean evolution for over 100 years!

The Complex Morphing of Enterprise Structures

The competitive leverage of *process* has transcended away from physical content and moved toward human, knowledge, and technology content. Think about it: When 70 percent of an organization's manufacturing content is outsourced to other parts of the globe, then Lean *manufacturing* in the smallest remaining plant in Canton, Ohio, is just not enough. What used to be the factory floor is now the enterprise and extended enterprise infrastructure. What is left of the factory floor is in flux daily with the introduction of new products, customer and market needs, demand and supply schedules, global supplier issues, international requirements, and other constant changes that demolish the manual, steady-state Lean manufacturing approaches. Transactional process improvement presents a whole new set of complexities and challenges that extend far beyond traditional Lean *manufacturing* thinking and practice. With these complexities come enormous benefits worth hundreds of millions of dollars in new incremental value contribution for many organizations.

The Gemba Is Now in Your Hands

The emergence of technologies and integrated business architectures is also changing the landscape of business. It's hard to believe how we existed a quarter of a century ago without the Internet, cell phones and mobile technology, e-mail, PCs, iPads, data warehousing, business analytics, real-time digital performance dashboards, visualization, and other technologies that are readily available today. Technology is the enabler that is taking traditional Lean and continuous improvement programs to new levels of possibilities, but it is not a replacement for systematic planning.

Lean *manufacturing* with its kanban cards, color-coded bins, magnetic scheduling boards, and manually maintained storyboards are just not responsive enough. Furthermore, their relevance is significantly reduced in an enterprisewide adaptive systematic improvement process.

The root causes of many problems that Lean manufacturing addresses are created in the transactional processes and are preventable. As processes become more transactional and knowledge- and technology-dependent, the process of how we improve these integrated networks of processes also must adapt and evolve. The gemba is now in everyone's hands 24/7! The process of how Lean is being implemented and maintained is stuck in a *same people + same process + same thinking + same approaches + same information = same results* dilemma. Traditional Lean *manufacturing* is becoming a trivial pursuit of improvement in the larger scale of global competitiveness.

Outsourcing Problems Has Not Worked

Western organizations improved manufacturing by a bandwagon strategy of fad improvement programs, including outsourcing manufacturing to other low-cost countries. In retrospect, many of those outsourcing decisions were based on a flimsy foundation, driven by a cursory spreadsheet analysis that focused on labor and other visible profit-and-loss (P&L) elements of costs. These costs are often irrelevant in the total scheme of outsourcing. Some organizations, moreover, blindly followed the outsourcing paths taken by other companies. Several executives even mandated that "X levels of outsourcing be achieved by Y date" without any analysis at all. Along the way, companies became confused about the difference between price and total landed cost, and they failed to consider *all* the cost factors associated with outsourcing. Those overlooked factors—the hidden costs and risks of outsourcing—were not considered or even recognized in the outsourcing strategies of most organizations. However, they are very real costs that can represent anywhere from 14 percent to as much as 2×–3×+ of total production cost. Organizations can't fix their problems by outsourcing them. Changing cost structures have recently brought these decisions under scrutiny and created a strong interest in reshoring manufacturing back to the United States. Manufacturing jobs in the United States will not be restored to previous levels because advances in technology have automated and/or eliminated many positions. Technology also continues to create new professional jobs. But many off-shored manufacturing jobs are unlikely to ever return. Reshoring America's manufacturing base is great, but it must be supplemented with many other innovative strategic business improvements to maintain our superior global competitiveness.

Collapsed Planning Horizons

Globalization, technology, and industry structure changes have collapsed the planning horizons of strategic planning, operational planning, new product planning, financial planning, and planning in general. Strategic planning is a *calendar-driven* function. It is a structured annual exercise that defines the mission, vision, and purpose of the organization and establishes realistic, consistent goals and objectives in a defined time frame and within the organization's capacity for implementation. The strategic plan is not always communicated effectively, leaving the organization with a confused sense of direction. The time horizon has typically looked out five years with annual updates. Does anyone know today what will be happening in five years? These days, two to three years out is a stretch. The strategic plan is intended to be *strategic*, keeping the organization focused on the future and preventing competitive convergence. Organizations are now moving toward a more segmented strategic planning approach with shorter horizons and quarterly updates.

The Obsolete "Process" of Improvement

The *architecture* of how Lean and other continuous improvement initiatives have been introduced to Western organizations has remained the same for decades: top-down, executive-mandated, rally the troops, train the masses, launch across the organization, edict strict compliance, go through the motions, promote showboating, hope for success, move on to the next fad improvement program. Improvement for improvement's sake, Field of Dreams improvement. A series of limited, single-point birth-death programs focused around tools (the means) rather than a philosophy and moral purpose of improvement as the permanent cultural standard of excellence (the ends). Recently there has been a trend toward merely renaming Lean and continuous improvement efforts "the XYZ business system" with the same old process architecture. This process architecture is obsolete. It is the equivalent of overhead and waste in our new economy demanding laser-targeted improvement, rapid deployment, and rapid and sustainable results. Repackaging improvement under a new brand is out. Substance and results are what matters most to success, not a name and its associated buzzwords and templates. Organizations must adapt and design a new process architecture that is culturally grounded and continuously aligned to the business strategy on operating requirements.

Systematic Planning Pulls Improvement into the Present

As executives we should not become angry or defensive or deny the above facts or feel a sense of failure. Lean has produced (and continues to produce) significant value contribution for many organizations. But the industrial structure of the world has changed, and it's time to make some major adjustments to regain America's competitive edge. Despite the widespread awareness and presence of Lean and continuous improvement, the United States has been losing its competitive edge in the global marketplace for the past two decades. Lean and general continuous improvement are a career-long adaptive learning and development experience. Executives and organizations that accept this fact are taking the first step into a new Lean renaissance.

To better understand the value of living laser-targeted improvement, let's reflect on how organizations have planned their previous improvement programs—including most recently Lean and Six Sigma. Executives were anxious to get going with the exuberant program launches, mass training, widespread improvement projects, and mandated acceptance. They underestimated and oversimplified the importance of an age-old problem called "planning." All these programs achieved early success because of an abundance of low-hanging fruit in organizations. A familiar occurrence with Six Sigma, for example, was to schedule black belt education and then tell all participants to make sure that they bring a project to the first class. Some of these projects were more Lean- and Kaizen-oriented than Six Sigma; participants knew how to make improvements in the first few days but were dragged through five to six months of heavy statistical problem solving in order to receive their black belt certification. We have mentioned earlier in this book that most Lean manufacturing programs were focused on tools-based education. All in all, these programs were not systematic and sustainable because they lacked the formal infrastructure (including planning) to continuously synchronize improvement efforts with business relevance, linkage, and alignment. Many organizations jumped into Lean and other improvement programs while turning a blind eye toward planning and hoping for success. A familiar response to this was, "We have an improvement plan. It just is not written down and as formalized as you would like it to be." These organizations did not have a plan; they were winging it with their Lean efforts and hoping that these efforts generated some P&L benefits. This is "Field of Dreams" improvement where organizations assume that if they launch and spread out enough teams and improvement assignments, the results will come. They lacked substance, achieved disappointing results, and eventually faded away. In a more complex world with higher risks of failure, adaptive systematic improvement can never become a reality with a continuation of an improvisational (improv), tools-based approach. Their living laser-targeted improvement avoids these experiences by continuously keeping organizations and their improvement activities on point.

Think about the impact on execution and achievement of the strategic plan, operating plan, new product plan, financial plan, or capital plan. Today executives are more focused on near-in results than tools demonstrations when it comes to improvement initiatives. They are interested in knowing the incremental value contribution of the improvement, when a change will be fully implemented, and when the company will realize the benefits. Many organizations are now factoring planned improvements into their operating budgets. If an organization is trying to achieve millions of dollars through adaptive systematic improvement over the next 12–18 months, it must look at how it is doing more often than on a quarterly basis. In fact, the millions of dollars may require a hundred or more very targeted improvement activities coming together successfully. Measuring progress requires continuous monitoring of progress against business requirements and plans. A monthly review of the operating plan or the hoshin plan doesn't cut it because the paths to improvement have gone *cold case*; and lack of planning definitely does not cut it in a more near real-time environment. This is not a hoshin kanri problem; it is a user problem. The reference model endorses hoshin kanri as an effective policy deployment and management best practice. Many organizations have discovered how to use hoshin kanri effectively and should continue to use and improve upon this best practice. The reference model does not endorse *going through the motions* of hoshin kanri, when it becomes a misunderstood and narrowly accepted ritual of filling out and hanging up matrices for the sake of using a tool. Not to be critical, but many more organizations are not using hoshin planning as an internalized and widely accepted best practice. Later in this chapter we introduce a simplified, daily management process that further aids in the execution of the hoshin plan.

Scalable Improvement Methodology

Through dozens of successful strategic improvement engagements, we have applied the Pareto thinking to the design of our high-performance Scalable Improvement Methodology, namely:

▲ 20 percent of the improvement opportunities yield 80 percent of the benefits.

▲ 20 percent of the improvement methodologies and tools are used to achieve 80 percent of the benefits.

▲ 20 percent of the organization becomes the outstanding champion of improvement, and attempting to make this 100 percent instantly is a game of diminishing returns.

▲ 20 percent of the supply base creates 80 percent of the sourcing and procurement issues.

This has become a best practice in the Lean Business System Reference Model. The traditional top down, executive mandated, train the masses model of improvement is a shotgun approach to improvement, hoping that something sticks. Historically we all know how much overhead, cost, time, and resources it takes to keep these improvement programs alive before they eventually fizzle away. Dozens of fad programs have passed through this model of improvement with their respective birth-death cycles during the past decades, and then organizations slide back into their inefficient norms. (See Figure 4.2.)

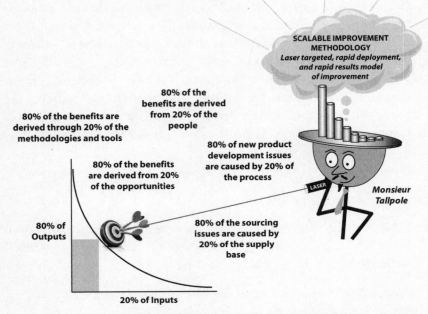

Figure 4.2 Scalable Improvement Methodology

Scalable improvement is a more adaptive "middle out" model of improvement. The Scalable Improvement Methodology *adapts the process of improvement* to the organization, its culture, and mission-critical success factors. It's all about defining the organization's 80/20 sweet spot of opportunities and then navigating through the barriers to success while developing internal talent and "internalized" participation and momentum. This is a good time to introduce *Monsieur Tallpole* (a descendent of Wilfredo Pareto), the figure in our illustration whom the reader will meet throughout the rest of the book. The Scalable Improvement Methodology is a laser-targeted, rapid deployment, and rapid results model that eliminates all of the non-value-added waste in traditional approaches to improvement—the waste that kills improvement initiatives and makes it nearly impossible to keep the word "continuous" in continuous improvement. At the same time this approach focuses deeply on building the right behavioral patterns and permanent cultural standard of excellence in how people think and work. This is very different from the scattered, "improvement for improvement's sake" approach of traditional deployments. The Scalable Improvement Methodology is a "low-risk, surgical, high ROI, bull's-eye" approach to improvement. The strategy behind the Scalable Improvement Model is to ensure that our clients' improvement initiatives are solid investments in the right mission-critical areas with a significant ROI and not a sunk cost or another fad, check-the-box program.

When implementing a scalable improvement approach, a word of caution is encouraged concerning the use of Pareto analysis. In our reference model, the Pareto analysis is extensive and multileveled. In other words, do not be fooled by a single pass at a problem with Pareto analysis. For example, the most frequently occurring reasons for downtime may be the easiest to fix, while the reasons at the bottom of the pile require the most time and cost to repair. The most frequently occurring billing errors may not be the most costly or severe errors. It is a good practice to combine Pareto analysis with five-why thinking and other analytics and to view problems from different angles during the calibration process. For example, in the case of billing errors, often in the normal distribution there are overbilling situations which customers respond to immediately and there are underbilling situations which remain unknown because a customer may not respond at all. The point here is high-velocity improvement, but with an understanding of the true problem prior to corrective actions.

Scalable implies a living cycle of developing improved talent in small increments—giving people just what they need at the right times to achieve success and then repeating the cycle at a higher order of learning. In the reference model the Scalable Improvement Methodology also incorporates *ten accelerators* or best practices that are designed to reduce the *time-to-improvement* (TTI) cycle. It is a different approach from a workout or other fast-action effort of the past because it is highly disciplined, fact-based, and data-driven. In the past many quick improvement "tiger" teams operated in a mode of *sufficient cause* problem solving based on group perceptions, opinions, and limited evidence. Some of these efforts diminished the impact of problems but did not eliminate them, and in some cases they introduced additional problems in other areas. Scalable improvement is laser-targeted, but with all the structured means and deliberate actions within it to achieve real *root-cause* problem solving effectively and efficiently. In the reference model, it is one of many best practices aimed at helping organizations *improve how they improve*. The model is also designed to position organizations quickly in a self-funding mode with their strategic improvement initiatives.

CEO views Lean, Six Sigma, Lean Six Sigma, and other certifications as a longer-term professional development endeavor rather than a prerequisite to improvement. In the past 10–15 years, too much improvement began and ended with a "belt." Our scalable model promotes rapid injections of new knowledge followed by engagement in a never-ending cycle of professional development and growth. By the time individuals become certified, they are highly technically qualified and experienced as a result of their participating in several improvement initiatives, and they are also much more likely to lead and champion continuous improvement as a living cultural and organizational standard well into the future. This process of achievement-based talent development is celebrated with formal recognition and rewards, but not necessarily with a "belt."

Let's face it. The traditional approaches to improvement are irrelevant in this challenging economy. What do organizations do when their processes are not working? They improve their processes. Scalable improvement is an enhancement of the overall process of how improvement is implemented that is fitted to the quick response realities that executives find themselves in today. Scalable improvement is an implementation model that enables organizations to *improve how they improve*—plain and simple.

Creating the Aligned Improvement Strategy

Throughout this book our intent is to provide as much "how to do" guidance as possible about the Lean Business System Reference Model and its critical subprocesses. Living laser-targeted improvement is developed and maintained from the organizational scan (i.e., the business scan and cultural scan).

What is the purpose of an aligned improvement strategy in a systematic process of improvement? Like any strategy, it is a reference point for what the organization needs and wants to achieve, but it is specific and aligned to the improvements that are required in order to achieve the strategic and operational plans. The aligned improvement strategy is a higher-level vision and plan for improvement that incorporates the following objectives:

▲ *Establish an unquestionable recognition of the need to improve.* This is accomplished by describing the current status of the organization, sharing customer and competitor information, and pointing out the gaps between current and desired performance. This objective includes the packaging and communication of critical business challenges and the consequences of not moving forward with change.

▲ *Create a bold and compelling image of the future.* The aligned improvement strategy activates the organization's conscience and creates a renewed sense of purpose, direction, urgency, and reason. Reason is accomplished by being prepared to respond to the organization's questions and concerns with real data and facts from the organizational scans. A fact-based image of where the organization needs to be in order to remain competitive appeals to people's emotions positively and builds cohesion, trust, and critical mass.

▲ *Build executive cohesion and commitment.* The aligned improvement strategy builds a shared sense of direction, priorities, and specific details about the why, what, where, how, and when questions. Answering these questions results in the superglue of holding the executive team together in unity of purpose and with a consistent message of improvement. Although it is often underestimated, there is forward movement to improve when executives can agree on and communicate a universal story of improvement to their organizations.

▲ *Build stakeholder engagement and commitment.* A fact-based and data-driven vision is effective in setting uniform direction, expectations, and thinking with executives and managers about adaptive systematic improvement. At this stage of the game, no organization or expert has all the answers to their challenges, but it is never too soon to engage the *talent machine.* Success with adaptive systematic improvement requires real and unwavering executive and stakeholder engagement and commitment.

▲ *Act as the strategic reference point.* The aligned improvement strategy is the organization's reference point of systematic improvement and how it will enable achievement of the strategic plan and operating plan. It creates constancy of purpose and constancy of progress.

The aligned improvement strategy is the top tier of what we refer to as living laser-targeted planning. This aligns improvement with business requirements, sets in motion the living deployment plan, which in turn drives daily improvement activities. The aligned improvement strategy outlines the what, where, why, when, who, and how of a broad set of improvement themes. Often we describe improvement themes as the challenges that keep executives awake at night (the *insomnia* challenges). Examples might include the urgent need to simplify the global supply chain, reduce time-to-market of new products and services, rationalize global manufacturing and outsourcing, reinvent order fulfillment, improve field quality and reliability, and so on. Two points to note here:

1. The aligned improvement strategy is not the business strategy, but a strategy of challenges to be addressed through adaptive systematic improvement.

2. The *insomnia* challenges are broad and require the right multiple improvement activities over time to achieve breakthroughs in performance. If an organization attempts to treat these as projects, it is the equivalent of boiling the ocean where there may be high levels of symptomatic activity, but nothing changes.

A final note: The aligned improvement strategy includes the improvement mind map for the organization. Some organizations refer to this as a strategy map or value creation diagram (Figure 4.3). Mind mapping typically removes the fear of the unknown and replaces it with logical,

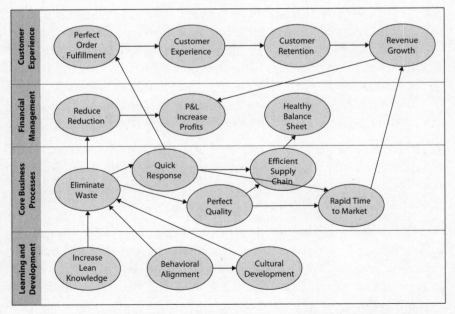

Figure 4.3 Lean Business System Reference Model™: Simplified Strategy Map
Copyright © 2015, The Center for Excellence in Operations, Inc.

graphical thought. This element of the aligned improvement strategy provides clearer insight into designing a balanced scorecard performance system. The more people connect to and believe in this strategy, the less likely they become about the fear of change, and the more autonomous they become about improvement.

The Operations Excellence Due Diligence

The prerequisite for planning in adaptive systematic improvement is the organizational scans. For a refresher, this includes both a business scan and a cultural scan. Both are diagnostic efforts to check the vital signs and needs in each respective area. We have developed a methodology called an *Operations Excellence Due Diligence*™, a structured and efficient means of identifying and updating an organization's business, operating, and competitive challenges.

The Operations Excellence Due Diligence is very different from the typical operations due diligence practices used by private equity and venture capital firms. These operational diagnostics are often focused on manufacturing versus enterprise operations, and the assessments do not go deep enough to validate the actual success of Lean, or to uncover the larger hidden transactional process opportunities for improvement. Finally, these diagnostics are usually academic and superficial, accounting- and spreadsheet-oriented, with data collected from standard templates and questionnaires. The Operations Excellence Due Diligence is designed to complement our Lean Business System Reference Model by continually probing with the right questions to uncover new improvement opportunities.

The purpose of the Operations Excellence Due Diligence is twofold:

1. Identify, prioritize, and deploy the right corrective improvement efforts to create maximum operational value and competitive strengths quickly—ideally in the next 45–90 days, and on a rolling basis. Transactional process improvement presents the largest opportunities these days, and these improvements may require a longer horizon to integrate and implement process improvements and enable technology.

2. Develop an aligned, organization wide improvement strategy and vision, deployment plan, and practical implementation approach. This effort represents the unlimited unknown opportunities for improvement that must be continuously mined, prioritized, and scoped relative to alignment with the company's business plan.

The other aspect here is process creativity and innovation, beyond the incremental As-Is improvements. These activities are the larger, cross-functional improvement projects that create best-in-class practices and millions of dollars in breakthrough operating performance. Below is a cursory outline of our Operations Excellence Due Diligence.

Review the business strategy and operating plan:

▲ What are the organization's goals and expectations?

▲ What are the strategies for capturing and growing market share?

▲ What are the plans for new products and services?

▲ How does the current portfolio of activities align with the business plan?

▲ How is the organization performing relative to the plan?

▲ Where are the voids and risks of lower performance?

▲ Have we conducted a structured operations assessment to better understand current performance?

▲ How are the current processes and practices working?

▲ What key processes are working well, are working okay, and are severely "broken"?

▲ What is the current performance in all areas of the business?

▲ Is current performance characterized with data and facts?

▲ What are the key sales and marketing issues?

▲ What are the key manufacturing operations issues?

▲ What are the key supply chain issues?

▲ What are the key supplier management issues?

▲ What are the key engineering/facilities issues?

▲ What are the new product development process issues?

▲ What are the key service delivery issues?

▲ What are the key financial operations issues?

▲ What are the key customer service issues?

▲ What are the key aftermarket service, repair, spares, upgrade issues?

▲ What are the current legal or regulatory operations issues?

▲ What improvements have been made internally and by what means?

▲ What have been the experiences of prior improvement initiatives?

▲ Where are the significant operating "pain points" or detractors to success?

Benchmark the organization's current and potential performance against relevant best practices and demonstrated best-in-class performance:

▲ What are the dynamics of the cost structure and major cost drivers?

▲ Is the organization aware of industry benchmarks and competitor performance in key strategic areas?

▲ How do the organization's performance and key business processes stand up to industry best practices? What are the specific gaps and strategic improvement opportunities?

▲ What are the accepted industry practices, and how could the organization differentiate its industry performance from that of competitors? (Benchmarking is a single data point and is sometimes either outdated or irrelevant to the mission.)

▲ What are the best-in-class practices in "outside" industry organizations that are admired by their customers?

▲ Have we defined the gaps between current and potential performance?

▲ How is the organization performing vis-à-vis the strongest "within" industry competitors and "external" companies in the areas of product and services availability, profitability, cost, delivery, flexibility, responsiveness, innovation, new products, financial ratios, inventory performance, quality and reliability, productivity, customer intimacy, leadership, stakeholder development, or other key performance areas?

▲ What are the five to six improvement themes that create insomnia for the organization?

Develop the aligned improvement strategy:

▲ What are the focal points, priorities, and plans for improvement?

▲ What deployment scope and magnitude are best for the organization?

▲ What level of deployment will achieve results and rates of improvement compatible with the business plan?

▲ What is the right implementation infrastructure for success?

▲ What is the top-level plan for moving forward?

▲ How will the organization align its customer with improvement activities?

▲ How do we establish the clear need for improvement?

▲ How will the organization provide a shared vision of change?

Develop the living deployment plan:

▲ What are the strategic opportunities by key process area?

▲ What are the big quick strike (next 45–90 days) opportunities by key process area?

▲ What are the larger specific scoped and prioritized improvement initiatives, baseline performance, entitlement goals, and savings/value creation targets?

▲ Have we defined reasonable but stretch performance objectives?

▲ What are the specific, assignable-ready, improvement activities?

▲ What can the organization expect to achieve and by when?

▲ How do we successfully launch, execute, and monitor the performance and overall success of this initiative?

▲ How does leadership best engage other powerful people in the organization who are not part of the executive team?

▲ Who are the organization's champions of and spectators, resistors, and showstoppers to improvement?

▲ What additional internal education and talent development is needed to execute and sustain a true systematic process of improvement?

Define and address the cultural issues of adaptive systematic improvement:

▲ Have we summarized the people and cultural issues learned during the Operations Excellence Due Diligence™ diagnostic?

▲ What are the leadership, political, cultural, administrative, or other barriers to success?

▲ What needs to happen around the executive conference table to set the strategic improvement initiative on a successful course?

▲ Do we understand what is on our employees' minds relative to change?

▲ Have stakeholder needs been factored into the living improvement strategy and living deployment plan?

▲ Are associate and cultural values aligned for success?

▲ What is the plan for dealing with resistance to change?

▲ How will the organization improve and take care of day-to-day activities?

▲ Does the organization have all the right skill sets internally?

▲ How will the organization communicate with all stakeholders and reinforce the need to improve?

▲ What communication media are best for various segments of the organization?

Many aspects of the culture scan are covered in Operations Excellence Due Diligence. However, these are evaluated at a level relative to the *plan* for improvement. Many Lean attempts have failed because they have not focused enough on the people and culture side of change management. There are some who have professed, "Use the tools; change the process—and you will change culture." This simply is not true. Organizations must focus on the full sociotechnical aspects of improvement. It is important to understand and fold current cultural conditions into our aligned improvement strategy and living deployment plan subprocesses. Executives must put the effort into thinking through the type of culture that they want to create, and the type of culture that enables both company and personal success. There are a number of formal survey methods beyond the Operations Excellence Due Diligence that assess individual personalities and organizational culture.

The Operations Excellence Due Diligence should be revisited at least three to four times per year and should be updated in real time when new intelligence or requirements are identified. It is permitted to add additional questions provided that you are not altering the diagnostic's intent. Otherwise you lose the capability to measure progress over time. The results of this activity provide updates to the organization's "living" improvement strategy, the MacroCharter and MicroCharter templates, and adaptive systematic improvement in general. Technology makes it possible for organizations to conduct these organizational scans quickly and efficiently. Keep in mind that after the first time through, each iteration will be more of a "what's new" update rather than a 100 percent redo.

Elements of an Aligned Improvement Strategy

Business diagnostic activities drive the chief executive officer (CEO) and the executive team to do their homework about strategic improvement. During this process, there should be several excellent discussions about new challenges, priorities, and barriers—all of which build shared learning and commitment among executives and their organizations.

The aligned improvement strategy includes the following elements:

▲ A recognition of the need for change (why)

▲ A believable but aggressive image of change (what and how)

▲ Bold and broad improvement goals (where and when)

▲ Narrower objectives—the five to six *insomnia challenges* (what and how—more detail); accountability (who)

▲ Deployment timeline and expectations (what, when, where)

▲ The adaptive systematic improvement monitoring system (deployment progress)

The aligned improvement strategy becomes very powerful and compelling when, and only when, executives can communicate the above points to their organizations with a uniform story based on knowledge and facts. Keep in mind that the aligned improvement strategy and living deployment plan are developed and maintained through listening to the voices and data of external and internal sources (e.g., customers and internal associates). When the aligned improvement strategy is shared with the organization, it begins to create urgency, understanding, knowledge, and commitment to the five to six improvement themes and adaptive systematic improvement in general. It also demonstrates that leadership is listening to the organization and is committed to taking the right corrective actions in a collaborative way.

The MacroCharter

Living laser-targeted improvement is the master plan of adaptive systematic improvement. It includes two subprocesses: an aligned improvement strategy and a living deployment plan. The first subprocess provides formal infrastructure for the purpose of identifying major improvement themes that must meet or exceed the strategic and operating plans. The second subprocess explodes these higher-level improvement themes into smaller, well-defined, and assignable-ready improvement activities. We have mentioned the MacroCharter and MicroCharter previously. These are simplified templates used to manage these two subprocesses. The aligned improvement strategy uses the MacroCharter template, while the living deployment plan uses the MicroCharter template set.

The MacroCharter template (Table 4.1) is used to summarize high-level information from the Operations Excellence Due Diligence. It also adds a little *meat to the bones* of the aligned improvement strategy. The MacroCharter includes the improvement themes or insomnia challenges, the organization's five to six mission-critical improvement requirements. Each improvement theme includes a statement of a problem and symptomatic evidence, clue information and metrics, probable root causes, rough-cut cost of quality/waste, proposed objectives, improvement goals, benefits, and deliverables. Keep in mind that this is a high-level, single-page template that is used to keep everyone tuned in to the organization's most critical improvement needs. It does not include all the details of specific improvement activities (this is the function of the MicroCharter in the living deployment plan subprocess). The intent is to keep a simple,

Table 4.1 MacroCharter Consumer Business Unit, 11/29/15
Copyright © 2015, The Center for Excellence in Operations, Inc.

Area	Situation Summary	Observations and Clue Data	Improvement Theme	Goals and Objectives	Target Benefits
Inventory Performance	Poor performance. Customers are canceling orders and going to competitors. Shipping wrong products, quantities. Ridiculous lead times and lack of reliability from suppliers.	Inventory turns 3.4 Excess/Obsolete exposure is $38M (50/50) Shipping and in-transit freight damage ($3M) Premium freight $18M	Improve Inventory Performance to breakthrough levels.	Increase turns to 4.5–5.0 in the next year, and 6.5–7 turns in next 24 months. Reduce excess inventory by $15M in 6–12 months. Reduce premium freight to a reasonable level. Reduce freight damage	Incremental Revenue from Customer Service $50M. Cost Reduction $14M. Cash Flow $5M
Supply Chain Management	Never have the right mix of items in the right locations. Missing revenue goals due to product shortages, planning of supply and demand. Supply chain is too complicated for customers. Too many complexities and touch points. Order entry slow clerical process. Supplier quality and delivery performance is unacceptable.	Forecast accuracy 22%. Customer fill rate 61%, 4800 SKUs, 90% of revenue from 168 SKUs. Backorders rising. Customer and Sales complaints. Too much manual planning and kluge worksheets, people not using SAP. Supplier on-time delivery 50%. Not responsive. Quality and rework issues. Too many warehouses?	The "perfect order" Off-the-shelf fulfillment Increase Internet orders. Customer options (e.g., pick up same day at local store). Link customer topology to sourcing locations. Weed out poor performing suppliers. Revisit make vs. outsource opportunities	100% fill rate performance. Reduce order-to-invoice and cash-to-cash cycles by 40%+. Need to relook at SKUs vs. margin contribution	Cost Reduction $9M

New Product Development	New products are always late to market, over budget, and require significant sustaining engineering after release. Too much development resources spending time firefighting supplier problems. Several poor launches with field quality and warranty/exchange problems. Constant disruptions and changes in specs, priorities, canceling projects, etc.	All new products fail to hit original revenue goals. Development cycle times 18–24 months unacceptable. Misinterpretation of customer requirements and expectations. Design verification spins/project = 2.1 at average cost of $67K. Poor track record of supplier selection. High turnover, long hours, never enough time. COPQ $14M	All development projects completed on time and on budget. More scrutiny and justification for development projects. Better utilization of technical resources	Reduce time-to-market by 50%+. Reduce need for development resources post-release. Develop supplier evaluation and selection guide and involve Purchasing	Incremental Revenue from New Products $100M. Cost reduction $14M
Product Management	All things to all customers approach. Proliferation of SKUs. Selling too many products to small customers at negative margins	Over 2,300 SKUs have no or minimum sales activity (<$50/yr) and 28% have negative margins	Product rationalization and pruning use of distributors for low end products	Reduce the number of SKUs by 30%+. Improve profitability from selling planned vs. available products	Incremental margins $3.7M. Warehouse space/resource reduction

consistent, and relevant message in front of the organization. If an organization has multiple business units (e.g., consumer, industrial, medical, defense), it is recommended that a MacroCharter be created for each of these specific segments. It is also useful to display this aligned improvement strategy and MacroCharter into graphic displays to enable visualization and promote ownership.

Table 4.1 is but a section of the MacroCharter. It displays more than three out of the usual five to six improvement themes in its content. These improvement themes are then exploded into many smaller, manageable, and quickly executable improvement activities in the MicroCharter template for the living deployment plan subprocess. The MacroCharter and its full content provide an actionable *why-why-why-why-why* level of detail below the hoshin plan. Both of these instruments are living templates that are updated as priorities change or new problematic situations arise.

The Living Deployment Plan

The living improvement plan is a well-defined and laser-targeted improvement road map designed to achieve the strategic and operational plans. The living improvement plan explodes the higher-level improvement themes into smaller, well-defined, and assignable-ready improvement activities. The purpose of the living deployment plan is to focus the organization's attention and efforts on the vital few issues that lead to breakthroughs in improvement. This subprocess improves execution because it breaks the larger themes into several smaller chunks. Ideally, these chunks are one- to four-week efforts—"small bits with large hits." The smaller Kaizen activities fall out and can be implemented within hours to a week, and there may be efforts (i.e., technology integration) that exceed four weeks. Since this subprocess is *living*, it facilitates continuous improvement. This subprocess ensures the detailed planning and definition, prioritization, alignment, and control of released improvement activities and their respective teams and limited resources.

Elements of the Living Deployment Plan

One of the terms we use in association with the living improvement plan is *assignable-ready* improvement activities. In the past, many improvement programs hastily came up with fuzzy projects and then assembled a team to implement improvement. For some executives, this was their philosophy of improvement: "We have a black belt and a team working on it." We sometimes refer to these approaches as *over-the-wall* improvement where the ownership for results is figuratively thrown over the wall to the teams. Teams waste significant time and effort trying to figure out what they were really supposed to do, often without the commitment and support necessary to complete their assignment successfully. Teams become frustrated and flounder, which leads to team member absenteeism, substitutes, or replacements. In short it is a very inefficient and non-value-added practice. A systematic process of improvement requires very efficient planning, deployment, and execution to achieve rapid results. At the same time it requires effective planning, deployment, and execution on the right highest-impact improvement opportunities. Assignable-ready improvement activities are well defined by the following attributes:

▲ Problem statement

▲ Objectives and scope

▲ Leadership owner

▲ Baseline performance

▲ Improvement goals and objectives

▲ Expected benefits

▲ Timing, milestones, and deliverables

▲ Well-designed team composition

▲ An initial go-forward Gantt chart

Teams are much more efficient at execution and achieving results because they are set on their course knowing exactly what to do and exactly what is expected of them. They also have a leadership owner who can provide mentoring support and run interference for them.

The elements of this assignable-ready best practice are the essence of success with systematic planning. The living deployment plan has other infrastructure elements contained within the MicroCharter planning templates that ensure continuous prioritization, alignment, and control of the overall *process* of improvement.

The MicroCharter

The living deployment plan subprocess uses a step-down methodology in the MicroCharter a set of detailed planning templates that translates the broader improvement themes into actionable improvement activities. The sections of the MicroCharter include:

▲ *Specific improvement activities matrix:* The identification and detailed definition of improvement activities down to the assignable-ready level of detail. There is also a *below the line* section in this matrix for improvement activities that may be feasible but require more characterization. This section also includes *quick-strike* improvements that require no further scoping and can be immediately assigned for implementation.

▲ *Prioritization and alignment matrix:* A relative worth factor analysis of planned improvement activities in which each is scored and force-ranked against a list of predetermined attributes. Improvement activities are *weighed in* relative to their value contribution. The matrix is sorted in descending score order, leaving the most important improvement activities at the top of the template. Sometimes it is necessary to review the individual attribute ratings when an activity perceived to be important does not end up at the top of the list (and vice versa).

▲ *Organization and staffing matrix:* This identifies the sponsorship, resources, the right team leader and team, extended team resources including a financial representative, set meeting times, and the initial go-forward plans for the team. The expectations and ground rules are also part of this matrix.

▲ *Talent development inventory matrix:* An analysis of individual associates' strengths and weaknesses relative to improvement talent and skills. Also considers the need to develop and build bench strength for improvement.

▲ *Resource allocation and control matrix:* An ongoing tracking of released and completed improvement activities, engaged and planned resource assignments, and an overall assessment of resource utilization (e.g., are we developing bench or relying on the same people?).

Tables 4.2 and 4.3 provide a sample of the first two templates in the MicroCharter. The MicroCharter may include a running balance of 30–50

Table 4.2 MicroCharter, Template 1
Copyright © 2015, The Center for Excellence in Operations, Inc.

Improvement Theme	Project Name	Objectives and Scope	Baseline Performance	Goal	Benefits Vision	Quantified Benefits	Expected Deliverables	Barriers and Dependencies
Supply Chain Management	Sales & Operations Planning	Improve the S&OP process; consider a segmented or hybrid process for different groups of SKUs, customers, etc.	Delivery Performance 50%	100% fill rate on time	A quick-response S&OP process that uses different approaches for A, B, & C SKUs	Incremental Revenue $50M	A reengineered company "single plan" S&OP process that closely synchronizes demand and supply in near real time	Will require IT resources; need to increase sales involvement
	SKU Analysis and Rationalization	Reduce the number of SKUs that are planned and sold; eliminate redundant and non essential SKUs	4800 SKUs, 168 SKUs=90% of revenue; negative margins	Reduce SKUs by 30%	A smaller, more profitable product line; resources focused more on the customers and products that matter the most	Incremental P&L impact $3.7M	List of obsolete SKUs; plan for disposition	Sales resistance; they sell many of these SKUs at EOM to make quotas; many planned items out of stock

(Continues)

Table 4.2 MicroCharter, Template 1

Copyright © 2015, The Center for Excellence in Operations, Inc. (Continued)

						Cost Reduction		Conflicts with
	Complexity and Cycle Time Reduction	Analyze the factors that most influence supply chain performance and implement improvements; reduce SC cycle time by 20%+ and reduce complexity and touch points	Lead times too unpredictable 1–120 days Supplier delivery 50% on time	100% availability of A, B, C$_1$ SKUs, 3–5 days C$_2$, C$_3$	Off-the-shelf delivery, higher Internet content, customer fulfillment options	Cost Reduction $3M–$4M; 100% on time A&B	A streamlined supply chain supported by before and after metrics	Conflicts with daily work, short on resources in some areas
New Product Development	Improve New Product Development Process	Streamline the NPD and stage-gate process; eliminate bottlenecks and waste; continuous flow development	Time to market 18–24 months; Over $5M due to DV spins and spec changes; cost and time overruns; quality problems $14M	6–12 month cycle; Reduce change by 50%	A robust and responsive NPD process that enables 1st to market, best product quality, high performing supply base	$100M incremental revenue; COPQ reduction of $10M	New products developed in half the time; eliminate quality and reliability problems; eliminate supplier-related problems	Will need to evaluate suppliers as adjunct to this activity; "taming" of engineering culture

Table 4.3 MicroCharter, Template 2
Copyright © 2015, The Center for Excellence in Operations, Inc.

Project Prioritization Matrix

Project Name	Project Objectives and Scope	Growth Impact	P&L Impact	Cash Flow Impact	Strategic Synergies	Resource Availability	Availability of Data	Risk/Return Factor	Probability of Success	Timliness of Completion	Ease of Implementation	Cost of Implementation*	Total Score
		9	10	9	7	5	6	4	6	5	7	9	
SOP Improvement	Improve Forecast Accuracy (the combo of forecast and MPS that drives MRP)	7	9	9	7	8	8	8	9	7	8	9	629
Customer Rationalization	Develop more targeted sales, customer service, and fulfillment practices that recognize distinctions between customers; Eliminate excess hidden costs to service low-volume, unprofitable market segments; Look for other options to smooth out selling cycle. Might consider new policy for small customers to deal direct with dealers but determine based on data	4	9	7	6	6	5	7	7	7	6	8	510
Product Rationalization and Pruning	Reduce the number of SKUs through data-driven logic and analytical science; also develop a formal ongoing process to evaluate and phase out old SKUs	6	9	9	8	7	7	7	8	7	6	8	569
Premiun Freight Reduction	Define best practice to control and reduce premium freight by 75%; to be at goal by year end	5	10	8	8	9	9	9	9	9	9	9	651

*=Reverse Scoring, High Score=Low Cost, Low Difficulty

specific improvement activities at any given time. Specific improvement ideas can come from many sources in the organization. In fact we do not want these sources to be limited by the Operations Excellence Due Diligence™ and the executive core team. In practice, released improvement activities uncover the need for additional improvements which are placed in the hopper. Associates from around the organization are also welcome to submit their ideas to the executive core team. With a fully engaged and empowered culture, there is never a shortage of ideas.

Completed improvement activities are moved to a different matrix that is used for performance measurement and tracking, and there are new additions over time. Also in our example, all the improvement activities ended up at the top of the priority and alignment matrix. The process worked well because the improvement strategy and deployment plan are in sync. Envision 30–50 specific improvement activities with a wider range of scores (maybe from 200 to 700), and it clarifies the usefulness of this matrix. Controlled execution is critical: If we assign all 30–50 activities and call them priorities, we create an overload situation where nothing is a priority. These instruments are integrated; changing a cell value on one template may change values on other templates. We also have a "change log" tab. It is a good practice to keep the latest versions of these planning templates and document the changes. These templates provide structure and discipline, but they are not fixed, rigid, one-size-fits-all templates. The MacroCharter and MicroCharter are usually modified to better fit the specific needs of a particular client environment.

Keeping Systematic Plans Aligned and Living

Keeping systematic plans aligned and living is a key practice of global Kata. The MicroCharter and its associated matrices provide the identical Kata-based functionality to adaptive systematic improvement. This subprocess identifies the problem statement, the objectives and scope, improvement targets, and much more detail than Toyota Kata. It puts associates through the same plan-do-check-act (PDCA) and plan-do-standardize-act (PDSA) cycles of improvement and continuously generates new target improvement opportunities. Every improvement activity has obstacles, gray zones, and boundaries of unclear territory; this is simply the wilderness of new improvement opportunities. There is nothing new here; this is basic

Industrial Engineering 101 and the essence of continuous improvement. The differentiator is how organizations deal with these situations, and Toyota has chosen a much more successful approach than most Western organizations have. Kata *does* require systematic planning. Kata is impossible with shotgun, train the masses, bizz-buzz approaches to improvement, the same approaches used in Western organizations in previous improvement programs.

Living laser-targeted improvement on the front end is the key to success in sustainable adaptive systematic improvement. The MacroCharter and MicroCharter planning templates have found more use in organizations beyond what we have presented in this chapter. One thing that we have not mentioned yet is that these templates are Excel spreadsheets with their appropriate tabs and pivot tables. It is simplified hoshin kanri intended for daily use. Some have used these templates more as an ongoing project management system where they are able to close out improvement activities, document the validated savings, and capture lessons learned from the teams. Others have figured out how to use these templates as a mini business analytics application for adaptive systematic improvement and performance measurement.

MacroCharter and MicroCharter Synchronization

At the risk of redundancy, it is important to mention that the aligned improvement strategy and the living deployment plan are both living and directly linked. These subprocesses identify and maintain the status of released improvement activities, and the hopper or inventory of planned, assignable-ready improvement activities. These subprocesses are kept current by the executive core team and the XYZ business system organization. The MacroCharter is reviewed monthly or on demand, and the MicroCharter is reviewed on a weekly (or also on demand) basis. Changing business conditions, organizational scan updates, and performance to plan all create the need to adjust and resynchronize a systematic process of improvement. The living deployment plan should never become the trash compactor of unqualified or irrelevant improvement ideas, and it should never be empty. When organizations let this happen, they are admitting that they no longer need to improve and quickly lose their *continuous* in continuous improvement.

Keep in mind that the location, maintenance, and level of detail of the MacroCharter and MicroCharter are a function of the deployment organization. In smaller and midsized organizations these roles will be more centralized, and in larger organizations these roles will be more decentralized to divisions or business units. However, there should always be alignment within business units and also to broader corporate goals and objectives. The Lean Business System Reference Model provides a design guide; executives, architects, and their organizations must design how the aligned improvement strategy and living deployment plan work best within their organizations.

Improvement Analytics and Measurement

Data in the MacroCharter and MicroCharter planning templates are easy to analyze because the design had this intent in mind. The purpose of this analysis is to provide closed-loop feedback to the executive core team, the XYZ business system organization, and the CEO and his or her executive leadership team. The purpose is for performance and future requirements. Here are a few examples:

▲ Identifying the highest and lowest value contributors in the organization; measuring the level of engagement of executive sponsors, functional or key business process areas, or individual associates. It is also simple to identify the types and functional areas of improvement activities completed by individual associates and to gauge the degree to which the organization is providing the opportunity for growth through exposure to different parts of the business.

▲ Sorting and displaying released and planned projects by business unit, key business process or functional area, and anticipated benefit timelines to determine how the organization's adaptive systematic improvement activities will contribute to the operating plan and financial plan. For example, if supply chain management was identified as an improvement theme and there is little-to-no improvement activity (and there are several improvement activities released but not linked to an improvement theme), our systematic process is out of alignment. These data can also reveal the functional areas that are aggressively stepping up as well as the areas that are barely in the game. As we mentioned earlier, it is becoming more commonplace for organizations to build the planned savings into their budgets.

▲ Analyzing projected and cumulative rates of improvement over a specified timeline, and making adjustments to the living deployment plan to maintain or improve the rate of improvement. The rate of improvement is a great metric. Organizations maintain or increase the rate of improvement by new thinking, innovation, new boundaries, new higher-talented associates, and continuously *improving how they improve.*

▲ Evaluating the relative value contribution of launched and queued-up projects by business unit, functional area, or as a baseline to measure actual performance to plans. Again this is another check to validate the segment of improvement activities across business units that may need to improve the most. This is also another check to make sure that adaptive systematic improvement is enterprisewide and focused on the improvement themes and highest-impact opportunities, rather than a manufacturing or quality initiative. It is not unusual to exceed the anticipated benefits of improvement because true root-cause problem solving reveals opportunities that were hidden and unknown to the organization.

▲ Evaluating current and planned professional and talent development needs, developing backstop organizational skills and capabilities or input to a formal recognition and rewards system.

▲ Providing a knowledge-sharing repository for completed, launched, and planned improvement projects. For completed improvement projects, a directory with a search capability is set up so that other business units or future efforts can reference completed improvement activities.

These and other analytics are particularly useful to the executive core team and XYZ business system organization. Lean and continuous improvement in general is not an exact science. It was treated that way in the days of Taylor's scientific management, but the notion of process is much different and more complex today. Therefore, the approaches to improving processes and measuring results have also become more difficult and complex. The Lean Business System Reference Model and its subprocesses provide a better and more robust means of dealing with these complexities successfully.

Formal but Not Bureaucratic

Our Lean Business System Reference Model and its subprocesses provide a formal architecture for adaptive systematic improvement. We want the reader to understand that this architecture is not another attempt to create the next modern-day complex and bureaucratic improvement plan. Nor is it a conduit where every improvement activity needs to be scrutinized by some central authority before acceptance. Adaptive systematic improvement requires a precise, formal architecture to address the evolving complexities of improvement in high human and technology content environments. In practice, the architecture is very simple and effective. There are improvement opportunities that do not require this level of formalization but just a quick, *Get R' Done* action.

Earlier we mentioned a MicroCharter matrix that includes *above-the-line* and *below-the-line* improvement activities. Above-the-line items become fully characterized, prioritized, assignable-ready improvement activities. These activities are either in an assigned or planned status. Every improvement idea within the universe of the organization does not need to flow through the formal architecture. We are referring to the below-the-line improvement activities.

There are two different below-the-line categories:

1. *Potential improvement activities where there are questions about feasibility, benefits, or even if it is real or a symptom of another opportunity.* Project ideas in this section need more fact finding and data analysis to verify feasibility with evidence. Improvement activities in this category may either make their way up the list, fall off the list, or become consolidated into the scope of another above-the-line improvement activity.

2. *Potential Kaizen improvement activities.* For these opportunities, resolution is more of a legitimate quick strike or Kaizen opportunity, and they are assigned to the area manager or supervisor for further investigation and resolution.

Adaptive systematic improvement promotes a culture of openness, engagement, and empowerment. To this end, we do not want every improvement idea flowing out of the Operations Excellence Due Diligence. Organizations want and need free flowing ideas from associates: bottom-up, middle-out, and lateral improvement. We have incorporated a talent development initiative called basic improvement skills (BIS) for associates. BIS provides an introductory level of skills and structure training for these local Kaizen events or quick-strike improvements, implemented as part of the Lean Business System Reference Model but following simplified practices to achieve the guiding principles. BIS uses a compatible Kata-based approach to improvement with several iterations of improvement through local engagement, and it enables a faster involvement of the organization in adaptive systematic improvement. The area manager and supervisors work with the business unit improvement leaders to focus on the next targets and go through the continuous PDCA and PDSA cycles of improvement. The broader purpose of BIS is to develop and mentor the organization's widespread problem-solving skills and to remove the fear of improvement and change. Engaging all associates where they work with problem-solving skills and no fear enables people to achieve what they once thought to be impossible through autonomous means.

Managers and supervisors maintain a standard quick-strike log, a simple spreadsheet of planned, in-process, and completed Kaizen activities. The quick-strike log captures the names of the individual(s) assigned to the improvement activity, the area, the improvement, and the benefits. These area quick-strike logs can also be consolidated and used as a mini business analytics applications for Kaizen activities, and also be rolled into the aggregate Lean Business System Reference Model. The point here is that the quick and easy improvements may evolve from many sources, and it is acceptable to bypass the complete formality of our Lean Business System Reference Model. Improvement is encouraged and accepted from all sources in the organization. However, organizations should capture and consolidate the quick-strike benefits and other statistics into their formal Lean Business System.

Achieving the 6Fs of Systematic Planning

Success in every organization is not 100 percent dependent upon adaptive systematic improvement. Strategic directives include new markets and product concepts, growth through acquisitions, outsourcing to low-cost countries, reinventing end-to-end customer delivery models, or financial value creation. Organizations must have a great strategic plan and a great way to execute and achieve or exceed their strategic plan. Often these annual exercises are empty rituals and abstractions. The strategic plan is loaded with initiatives and supporting market and financial data. The operating plan becomes a numbers game with little attention paid to the details of execution.

Systematic planning is not a business strategy; it is an enabler of business strategy because it can aid in the processes of execution—how these strategic initiatives are achieved. For example, we have been involved with improving the new product development process, creating an acquisition evaluation and integration process, rationalizing outsourcing, streamlining and reducing complexity in global supply chains, and better understanding the factors that most influence revenue growth and profitability. Execution through systematic planning is the key to superior execution.

We often talk about the *6Fs* of systematic planning:

1. *Fast.* Simple, nimble, and rapid deployment; translation of strategic and operating initiatives into quick executable actions.

2. *Fervor.* Operating with the passion, energy, and positive enthusiasm to become the best.

3. *Factual.* Fact-based and data-driven, supported by analytics that get at causes of poor performance.

4. *Fluid.* Capable of flowing freely with change, adjusting to change, accepting change as the norm, and recognizing that planning is much more important than "the plan."

5. *Focused.* Meticulous attention to details, and keeping oneself on the road to success.

6. *First.* Planning with the best in mind, planning to be the best, and achieving what one expects to achieve with great execution.

The Finale on Systematic Planning

Systematic planning in our Lean Business System Reference Model is where the rubber meets the road. Organizations that have simply renamed Lean as their business system and are lacking an aligned improvement strategy and a living deployment plan are flying by the seat of their pants. Living laser-targeted improvement and its subprocesses include thinking, analytics, and execution plans for breakthrough improvement and superior operating performance. The MacroCharter and MicroCharter planning templates are moving scrolls of opportunities over time. Execution is what moves their content into a completion status. *Complete* in this case means that a team has solved a problem and has turned the responsibility over to the process owner. Resources can now be redeployed to other improvement activities. Continuous improvement is never complete.

In the past organizations skated their way through poor operational planning and execution, pleading for additional time and complaining about tough business conditions. Business conditions are now tougher and will continue in that direction for the foreseeable future. Organizations no longer have years to change—the timeline is 6 to 18 months in this *improve or get beaten* economy. Organizations must continue this cycle with a consistent rate of improvement with perfection (i.e., no birth-death cycles). Adaptive systematic improvement has only two outcomes: performance and excuses. The requirements and risks of adaptive systematic improvement are very definable, predictable, measurable, manageable, and controllable. A buyer, stockroom clerk, billing coordinator, financial analyst, design engineer, or customer service representative has excuses because these individuals are the victims of the processes and poor execution that leadership provides for them. Their performance is only as good as the capability of the processes and cultural environment within which they work. For the CEO and other executive leadership, there is no more room or time for excuses. It is time to get serious and radically change the mind models in the leaders of many organizations. Too many leaders continue to encourage their organizations to copy the Toyota Production System in their manufacturing operations rather than leading their entire organizations down a renewed road of success with true adaptive systematic improvement. One frustrated executive commented to me, "All I'm trying to do is hurry up and finish our Lean improvements." It's time to engage or develop the strong cultural resolve in organizations. Executives and their organizations must find *the right stuff* to make adaptive systematic improvement an autonomous cultural norm, or they will sit passively and become the victims of competitors who have found *the right stuff*.

Bibliography

Burton, T. T. 2012. *Accelerating Lean Six Sigma Results: How to Achieve Improvement Excellence in the New Economy.* J. Ross Publishing, Ft. Lauderdale, Florida.

Burton, T. T., and Boeder, S. M. 2003. *The Lean Extended Enterprise: Moving Beyond the Four Walls to Value Stream Excellence.* J. Ross Publishing, Ft. Lauderdale, Florida.

Burton, T. T., and Moran, J. T. 1995. *The Future Focused Organization.* Prentice Hall, Upper Saddle River, New Jersey.

Christianson, D. 2014. *Eight Real World Realities Not Taught in Business School.* LinkedIn blog. https://www.linkedin.com/pulse/article/20141029133217-1408860-8-real-world-business-realities-not-taught-in-business-school?trk=object-title.

Collins, J. 2001. *Good to Great: Why Some Companies Make the Leap … and Others Don't.* Harper-Collins, New York.

Collins, J. 2011. *Great by Choice.* Harper-Collins, New York.

CHAPTER 5

Communication and Cultural Evolution

Communication is the means or set of deliberate activities to convey information to the organization. It involves the exchange of ideas, strategy and vision, plans, intentions, and expectations. Communication has the most direct influence on defining, nurturing, and reinforcing the right improvement Kata. This is another area that organizations have given little thought to in previous improvement programs. The potential for miscommunication was bad enough when its simple form was face to face with people around a conference room table. Evolving technology, the Internet, mobility, virtual meetings, and other means of communication are making this topic much more immediate, confusing, and challenging.

Executive communication is an area that I have become particularly interested in, especially as it relates to adaptive systematic improvement and evolving culture. Communication that strives to change behaviors and culture requires much more than banners and slogans, symbolic storyboards, an all-hands meeting, an e-mail blast, a monitor in the cafeteria, or a ceremonial videoconference. A fully functioning Lean Business System requires much more time, effort, and concentration on continuous, open, meaningful, *two-way* communication. It is the means of building awareness and a sense of urgency, renewing associate commitment, disseminating information about plans and progress, and reinforcing the need to stay on a particular track. It is the foundation for building honesty, trust, loyalty, respect, commitment, unity of purpose, and the right desired behaviors in order to achieve the right desired results. It is the means of proactively engaging and dealing with associate questions and/or barriers to success. Communication has also been accomplished *matter of factly* or by mimicking the actions of other organizations in previous improvement programs.

Walk into most organizations and ask associates about communication, and they typically give it a *needs improvement* grade.

This chapter provides guidance about communication in an adaptive systematic improvement environment. Embedded within this subprocess is also an improvement role for evolving the *invisible* behaviors and cultural development needs of a Lean Business System. In its simplest terms, adaptive systematic improvement requires leadership, planning, organization, resource management, controls, and communication. The architecture of our Lean Business System Reference Model™ includes various formal subprocesses that are used to perform these essential roles. Leadership and communication are the largest inducers for setting behavioral patterns (Kata) and cultural norms. They are also the most difficult subprocesses because they include the highest human content and are the most difficult to systematize and evolve to a higher state. In our reference model, the *integrate, adapt, systematize* functions really involve observing and evolving behaviors and culture over time with the right, authentic situational leadership. Great organizations invest their thinking, time, and resources in communication because it provides the means for shaping the desired culture of the company. Adaptive systematic improvement requires well-designed and delivered communication; there is no such thing as too much communication when the messaging is adding value to the organization. Poor communication can poison the atmosphere for improvement and change as well as the morale of associates. When associates perceive communication as an insincere gesture, it can do more harm than good.

Purpose-Driven Communication

The purpose of communication is to create awareness, commitment, trust, inspiration, engagement, and other positive behavioral attributes of change. Communication also helps to evolve cultural values and beliefs, and brings the best-practice leadership behaviors (Adaptive Leadership) to life. This represents the human and emotional foundation for adaptive systematic improvement. Communication creates unity and constancy of purpose and strengthens organizational relationships with that end in mind. In terms of adaptive systematic improvement, communication conveys the *what, where, when, why, who,* and *how* of the aligned improvement strategy.

Why is the most important question to answer for the organization. Associates need to understand and embrace why the organization needs to move away from its current as-is state and the consequences and risks of staying the same. When leadership fails to answer this question, the members of the organization answer it for themselves—often based on fears and false perceptions. The common fears include fear of failure, ridicule, rejection, disappointment, exclusion, the unknown, and a perceived loss of freedom and the status quo. *Why* creates a shared understanding and demolishes fear, pure and simple. Purpose-driven communication helps associates to better understand the external market and competitive pressures that are driving the need for continuous adaptive systematic improvement and to internalize the emotional sense of urgency for improvement.

Can You Hear Me Now?

A good place to begin with purpose-driven communication is to understand current conditions. This does not require a lengthy study, it involves talking with and engaging associates, and it involves active listening. This is a competency in itself. Beyond listening to the words, it is important to understand the unspoken messages such as behaviors, facial expressions, attitudes, and body language. The *five whys* are another useful approach when evaluating the state of communications and the barriers. Some of the typical current communication barriers in organizations include:

▲ Lack of respect between leadership and associates, between functions within the organization, or between individuals. Executives cannot avoid these situations; they must deal with them head on if they expect to create a positive, collaborative, team environment.

▲ Failure to clearly define the purpose and objectives of communication. Communication is often delivered on the fly with the best of intentions, but the message is disorganized and confusing to the listener. Communication is missing the basic rules of *what, where, when, why, who,* and *how.*

▲ A one-size-fits-all media strategy (e.g., letter with payroll check, e-mail blast, signage, cafeteria monitor, etc.). Associates in the organization receive messaging much better by customized media strategies, and it requires multiple hits to stick.

▲ Leadership assumes that the organization fully understands and accepts the message. Presenters usually have much more background and understanding than the recipients of the message. It requires thought and planning to deliver a clear message. And presenters should be prepared to answer questions. Never assume that a message is received positively and is well understood. Also, put the message at the listener's comfort level of understanding.

▲ Unintended, one-way communication is common. This approach disengages and intimidates listeners because it leaves all their questions and concerns unanswered. People always seem to navigate more to the negative than the positive aspects of change because they fear the unknown. Recognize that the cause of fear is always much larger than reality.

▲ The hollow monthly review. These reviews are scheduled with the same agendas, but they often leave associates wondering how the message and numbers are related to what they do every day. Communication must be meaningful, purposeful, and value-adding to all.

▲ The wrong or mixed message. A good example of this is having a meeting about quality defects and then telling people that they must try harder, as if they are intentionally creating the defects. That's not the root cause; it is insulting. Wavering and inconsistent direction and priorities are other examples, like doing Lean for the first three weeks of the month and then focusing 100 percent on shipments during the last week of the month.

Communication becomes extremely challenging in organizations with a Lean program on the rocks or a track record of failed fad improvement programs. The mention of *systematic improvement* is received as the next new flavor and leaves people with the feeling of, *"Here we go again. It won't last long."* Associates in many organizations have lost all faith in improvement programs. A common theme that we have observed is that leadership is not authentic, committed, and serious. Stop right here: Another hasty communication effort is not what is needed in these situations. Executives must come clean with their people, whether it was *their* previous improvement program or not. People generally embrace an honest explanation of what happened in the past. No excuses, no blame, but an honest explanation of the facts followed by an apology for bad performance and how it may have negatively impacted the organization. This is now a perfect place to begin communicating about the future and, in particular, why the organization must get improvement right this time, and what will be done differently to get improvement right. History is a huge contributor to culture and the status of an organization's behavioral attributes of change. History may have created a negative grapevine and invisible resistance to change. Simply ignoring previous experience with improvement initiatives is a sure way to keep these undercurrents of resistance alive.

Communication Kata

This section provides prescriptive guidance for the communication subprocess of our architecture. Much of this guidance is known but not rigorously practiced as an integral part of adaptive systematic improvement—or leadership in general. Also, it is important to factor in Western attributes and values when developing a communication plan. American culture can be assertive, individualistic, tending toward questioning authority, and standoffish, yet it can be very personable, friendly, and accommodating. When it comes to change, associates are not always willing to reveal what they are really feeling. Effective communication brings their emotions out so they can be dealt with.

Figure 5.1 provides a simple map of purpose-driven communication, with the Kata style of thinking embedded within its structure.

The first step in communication is thinking through the purpose of the communication and what the organization desires to accomplish. Evolving culture to a higher state of excellence requires deliberate thinking, deliberate planning, deliberate execution, and deliberate evaluation. Following is a checklist of the multiple purposes of communication:

▲ To convey and share relevant information about the business.

▲ To engage and interact with associates about various challenges, issues, and general *what's on their mind* topics.

▲ To build awareness and persuade associates to align with a specific direction or initiative.

▲ To motivate associates through a positive work environment possibly with recognition and rewards, and to create the inclusive *emotional experience* of being part of the team.

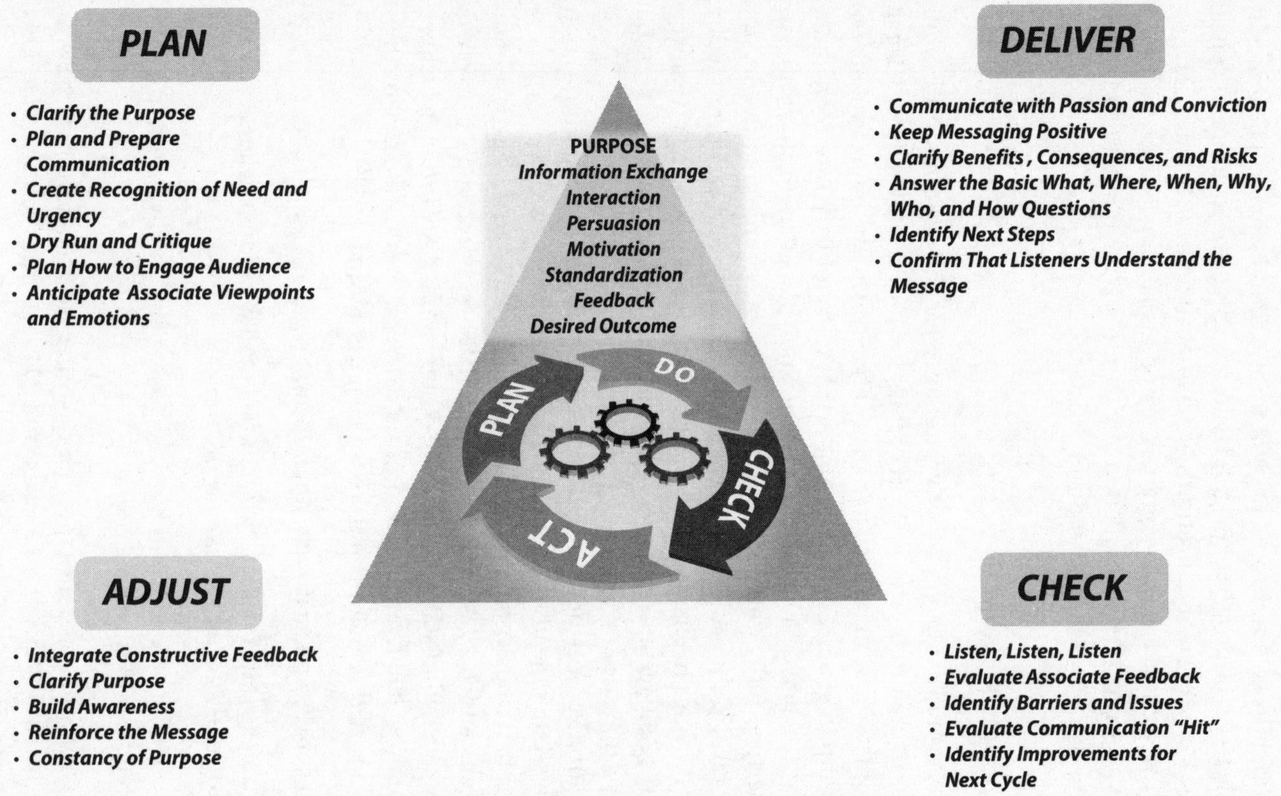

Figure 5.1 Purpose-Driven Communication Map
Copyright © 2015, The Center for Excellence in Operations, Inc.

PLAN

- *Clarify the Purpose*
- *Plan and Prepare Communication*
- *Create Recognition of Need and Urgency*
- *Dry Run and Critique*
- *Plan How to Engage Audience*
- *Anticipate Associate Viewpoints and Emotions*

DELIVER

- *Communicate with Passion and Conviction*
- *Keep Messaging Positive*
- *Clarify Benefits , Consequences, and Risks*
- *Answer the Basic What, Where, When, Why, Who, and How Questions*
- *Identify Next Steps*
- *Confirm That Listeners Understand the Message*

ADJUST

- *Integrate Constructive Feedback*
- *Clarify Purpose*
- *Build Awareness*
- *Reinforce the Message*
- *Constancy of Purpose*

CHECK

- *Listen, Listen, Listen*
- *Evaluate Associate Feedback*
- *Identify Barriers and Issues*
- *Evaluate Communication "Hit"*
- *Identify Improvements for Next Cycle*

PURPOSE
Information Exchange
Interaction
Persuasion
Motivation
Standardization
Feedback
Desired Outcome

PLAN
DO
CHECK
ACT

▲ To achieve a unity and constancy of purpose and to reinforce the organization's core values and expected code of conduct.

▲ To continue to work toward a desired outcome through total stakeholder engagement and empowerment.

This is not an all-inclusive checklist, but these elements represent targets of communication—targets that people do not always think through when they prepare their presentations. Before communicating with the organization, it is often very useful to make planning notes as an executive team around this checklist of purpose points.

The figure provides a brief outline of activities in the communications Kata cycles. This is as much common sense as it is Kata. Nevertheless, if it takes a catchy phrase for an old practice to provide a more disciplined approach to communication, then so be it. The disciplined approach includes:

▲ *Plan:* This includes clarifying the purpose of communication with a very crisp and clear message. Adaptive systematic improvement requires precision, not a rambling, confusing ad-lib story about improvement. Planning also includes determining how the organization will communicate to different associate groups with which type of media or approach. Another important aspect of plan is the *what ifs*—how might associates react to the message, and what questions might they ask? Be prepared!

▲ *Deliver:* This is the actual delivery of the message. A very positive, upbeat, and passionate message is the first step in recruiting the organization's support. In parallel, the message must be crystal clear and justify itself with facts. Do not assume that everyone understands and embraces the message. We have conducted a train-the-trainer exercise with communication where every executive, manager, and supervisor is capable of providing the same consistent message to associates and soliciting more detailed feedback. Associates are very comfortable about opening up to their peers and direct supervisors.

▲ *Check:* This includes listening to and capturing associate feedback and concerns, evaluating their responses, and developing plans to resolve any barriers or detractors to improvement. An important part of check is reflection and lessons learned, and how to improve the next cycle of communication.

▲ *Adjust:* This is the integration of feedback, lessons learned, additional clarity, examples and success stories, and other elements to build awareness and stimulate the desire to join in. Adaptive systematic improvement is *systematic* because it involves a continuous integrated process of reinforcement, eventually leading to autonomous improvement. It's what the Kata principle is all about.

Executives must remain super-conscious and uniform when it comes to communication, especially in the less formal signals in their behaviors, choices, and actions. It is always much easier to undermine communication than it is to keep it on a track. Executives are always on stage, where associates are interpreting the meaning of their behaviors, choices, and actions. One unintended comment can send a signal that improvement is no longer a priority. Associates are the first to observe inconsistencies in the message. A few years ago I was involved with a major quality improvement initiative with a company. Its communications strategy was well-thought-out and perfect. Monitors were installed in high-traffic areas to reinforce the message. The IT department scrounged up whatever flat screens it could find, and apparently a few were severely scratched and installed with snowy resolution. The standing joke with a particular group of associates was, "They're committed to Six Sigma, but they hang up Two Sigma monitors." Associates are always testing commitment and sincerity behind the communication.

Expect Resistance; It's Evident

Resistance to change occurs when there is a perceived threat to an individual. The two key words here are *perceived* and *threat*. In most cases the basis for resistance is imaginary, and the risk of change is always much lower than the risk of staying the same with a solid adaptive systematic improvement process. It is very common for members of an organization to listen to a communications session and then return to business as usual. Some of the fault may lie in the message itself, but there is always some degree of resistance to change. While this resistance is evident, it is also a leadership growth opportunity.

Communication is very similar to strategic selling. It requires thought, planning, and multiple hits to a broad base of associates. At the end of the day, communication is about change management: removing fears; building confidence, acceptance, and internalization of change; and mentoring the right actions to achieve the right desired results. A favorite resistor comes from individuals who proclaim that they do not have time to improve and do their regular jobs. They are too busy doing all the wrong things and cannot see that a little investment in improvement could actually result in less firefighting and more value-added time. Yet they can always find the time to do things over. The problem is that so many forms of hidden and unknown wastes are buried in cost of poor quality (COPQ) and other financial variance accounts. Regardless of any claims about Lean, waste is institutionalized in these organizations. They can explain away the *what,* but they never address the *why,* so the same problems continue to recur. Many leadership behaviors, choices, and actions build and promote this cultural muddling. Perception is reality to these managers and associates, and it must be addressed by communication and other critical success factors of our Lean Business System Reference Model. The best decision in these situations is to replace the insanity with *autonomation* (line shut-down practice from TPS) and send associates off for a disciplined and uninterrupted team improvement exercise. This is the most effective means to break this damaging vicious cycle of incoherent thinking.

Seek Out the Signs of Resistance

Organizations respond to change in several different ways once the message of change is delivered. Some of the common responses include:

▲ *Joining in:* This is the best situation. The segment of associates have listened to the message and wish to get on board early (the "GOBEs"). They want to be part of the solution, not part of the problem. They are generally open to change because they trust leadership and thrive on challenges. Although they are missing the details, they envision the benefits of change and view their participation as a career-expanding opportunity. Many of these associates convince their peers to step up and commit to change. Occasionally an individual may join in to appear that they are on board. Joiners and hedgers are easily spotted by their behaviors and performance.

▲ *Hedging:* This is a condition in which associates are not for or against change. They are merely holding out with the thoughts of change on their minds. These people become preoccupied with the perceptions of change, just when they should focus and commit to change. These people are indecisive and waffle about commitment. Most in this segment are the "I'll believe it when I see it" crowd. Others will hedge until the risk of hedging is higher than the risk of boarding the improvement train.

▲ *Kibitzing:* This segment of associates is not convinced of the benefits of change because there are many unanswered questions about the details of change and how it will affect them personally. They legitimately seek the truth through socialization, but stir up opinions, perceptions, fears, and imaginary concerns. These associates require continuous communication to achieve clarity, remove fears, and increase their acceptance of change.

▲ *Holding out:* This is the tough segment of suspicious associates who are not committed, but wish to hide their true feelings for political reasons. Their reasons are influenced by personal beliefs, values, career goals, previous experiences, or simply bad attitudes. This is the *make-believe* and *can't* crowd that keeps a low profile but often opposes initiatives under the radar. Some of these associates must go because they are undermining the good work of other associates. Others may be brilliant individual contributors where adaptive systematic improvement requires a much higher degree of innovative adaptation (e.g., research scientists, medical and clinical staff, etc.).

These and other responses to change are to be expected. Adaptive Leadership and communication get executives and their organizations through these ripples of change. These subprocesses grow and nurture full stakeholder engagement. Keep in mind that the above responses to change are at a symptomatic level; that is, executives cannot mandate 100 percent commitment and acceptance although it has been attempted many times in previous improvement programs. There are many stories of Toyota leadership's ruthlessness in implementing the Toyota Production System. It worked in that culture (respect for authority, allegiance, harmony, working together, reserving opinions, etc.), and it was also a matter of human survival. Western organizations require more TLC (tender loving care, for lack of a better name) and want a voice in how things are done. Intimidation and coercion do not build trust and loyalty; a more collaborative and empowering approach is required. Communication must go deeper into the root causes of these initial responses to change and take into account the *why why why why why* below the surface. Some of this may be identified through the Operations Excellence Due Diligence cycles or by the multiple cycles of communication. It is important to understand the idea of *systematic process* and *integrated system* because our Lean Business System Reference Model and all of its subprocesses are interconnected and interrelated. This is the differentiator between just another improvement program and a robust systematic process of improvement.

Address the Root Causes of Resistance

Recognizing the root causes of resistance to change is important in developing an effective ongoing communications strategy. Many of the root causes are opinion- and perception-based because associates need more information to fill in their blanks. Be prepared that some resistance may be a reflection of poor leadership and substandard cultural norms that have been allowed in the past. Overcoming the human drama and root causes of resistance is the core of leadership. Dealing with these root causes head-on and continuously with an effective communications strategy will establish strong underpinnings for adaptive systematic improvement.

There may be hundreds of reasons why associates initially refuse to accept change. Typically these reasons fall into the following categories:

▲ *Associates are happy with their current situation.* People who have served in the same capacity for a long time find comfort in familiarity and routine. Change introduces the perceived fear of failure.

▲ *Associates are heavily invested.* Some people have spent time building their career in a stable social and organizational dimension. The social investment has created a sense of identity, individualism, and power and influence (i.e., healthcare physicians and clinicians). The combination of cross-process systematic improvement, process thinking, empowerment, and teaming is at cross-purposes therefore and rejected by these individuals.

▲ *Associates are metric-bound.* Some people are committed to achieving a specific objective, and they think that involvement in change will disrupt or jeopardize success and individual performance. Individual metrics play a crucial role in adaptive systematic improvement.

Many metrics are too immediate and localized, creating conflicts with the broader vision of adaptive systematic improvement.

▲ *Associates view systematic improvement as additional work.* The first reaction of change with many people in organizations is that there will be more work—with no additional compensation and requiring efforts that far exceed the perceived benefits. They cannot fathom that improvement can actually simplify and eliminate many frustrations from their daily work.

▲ *Associates see change as hollow.* People do not see the *what's in it for me* attraction of change. Their reactions might be shaped by previous experiences with improvement programs and can be turned around only by regaining trust and credibility.

▲ *Associates are confused by the journey.* The grand plan of systematic improvement is introduced, but it is missing the *what, why, where, when, who,* and *how* details. Unanswered questions invite fear, speculation, and resistance to change. Commitment requires a much better understanding of change and the individual roles of people in the process.

▲ *Associates do not trust leadership.* Whether imaginary or real, justified or not, perception is reality when it comes to managing change. It is certainly worth taking the time to better understand the root causes of resistance and build the right countermeasures into the communication strategy.

▲ *Associates have been there, done that, got the T-shirt.* This is a culture where people are just waiting for another improvement program to stumble so they can pull out their "See, I told you so" script. Skipping this fence-mending and renewal effort leaves the organization full of skeptics who will visibly pretend to go with the flow but will not be emotionally committed.

▲ *Associates are allowed to reject and/or obstruct change.* Some organizations have perpetuated this condition by their leadership behaviors, choices, and actions. These people fall into two categories: Passive and obstructive. Passive people go about their business and pocket-veto change. Obstructive people reject and undermine change. There are *no exemptions* from systematic improvement.

Understanding the root causes of resistance to change involves patience for sure, and more awareness and common sense than science. Management consulting involves constant communication and dialogue with many people in different functional roles and levels of organizations. This communication involves understanding current business conditions, analyzing and reviewing current performance, working through business challenges and improvement needs, and understanding leadership and cultural barriers to change. The process involves a very detailed *peeling back the onion* of organizations—like a first time through Operations Excellence Due Diligence. Working with people and listening to their issues and concerns builds trust very quickly. Often it feels like the first time associates have been given an opportunity to discuss their issues and other things on their minds. Many associates express fear of sharing knowledge and concerns with their own management groups, but they open up when an outsider makes the effort to listen and show interest and empathy. Leadership, culture, and the associates' need for continued employment suppress many issues that are necessary to integrate into a rock-solid communication strategy.

Purpose Requires Patience and Compassion

Change is inevitable in this world, and so is the need for continuous adaptive systematic improvement. This statement is a no-brainer in my profession, but I always remind myself that my passion for improvement does not always translate to those around me. And I would be lying if I said that I never resist change. Everyone resists change at some point for many reasons. Executives contract with our firm to help them change their business, and often they are initially the greatest resisters to change—especially when they understand that *they* and their organizations need to change too. This is not a criticism, but a fact of major change and breakthrough improvement. It requires a momentous and continuous amount of patience and compassion to master the gift of change leadership. Actually it is never mastered; it is continuously developed through interaction with the diverse group of individuals in organizations. It also requires lots of head bumping and knee scuffing along the way because change management is an abstract topic in textbooks. My personal change leadership skills come from interacting with tens of thousands of people in hundreds of different organizations around the globe. I certainly do not have all the answers and am always eager for the next learning and leadership development experience.

Purpose-driven communication is the leadership art and science that transforms fear and confusion into trust, understanding, and acceptance. This is a simple statement but represents an ever-challenging endeavor. Before an organization hurries up and launches systematic improvement, have the patience and compassion to address current communications conditions in the organizations. Take the time to conduct a thorough organizational scan: the business scan and cultural scan via the Operations Excellence Due Diligence. Beyond this, listen to the voice of the organization and understand the multiple audiences. Be accessible and take advantage of face-to-face communication. Explore and use whatever means of communication possible to flush out the root causes of resistance to change—e-mails, monitor messaging, videoconferences, town hall meetings, the hallway power hits ("Great job on X"). Communicate often and with a great plan, not as a scheduled trivial exercise. Answer all the *whys*—and never assume that associates understand, internalize, or are committed to an idea. Have the patience to shape expectations over time by frequent and well-constructed communication. Demonstrate to associates that leadership is listening by integrating their feedback and addressing their concerns into future communications plans. Help associates to proactively engage in and internalize the end in mind. Remove the fears and open up the door to no-limits thinking. And do not forget widely publicized successes and recognition and rewards. These are the critical factors of purpose-driven communication that help to deliberately build a high-performance culture.

Culture Is Not an Accident

Every organization has its own unique culture—its values, vision, mission, and expected codes and standards of conduct. Culture is the personality of the organization, its shared belief system. The only certainty about culture is that "culture happens," for the better or for the worse. The characteristics of culture are shaped by collective behaviors, choices, actions, experiences, and other accepted norms and events over time. Culture is also influenced by leadership and constancy of purpose and is disrupted by several transient leaders with their different styles, agendas, personal goals, and organizational expectations. Culture plays out in a variety of ways. Culture is reflected in the way the organization is structured, whether work is conducted cross-functionally or within individual silos, how the hierarchical levels are set up, and how the chain of command and span of control work. Culture is often defined by the type of industry, the backgrounds of the executives, the discipline of systems and processes, and the less formal symbols, conduct, values, and behaviors in the organization. Culture is even reflected in how and why meetings are held in an organization. Often, there is a big difference in culture between the mission statement on the lobby wall and the actual behaviors and practices behind the lobby doors. "Culture happens," either through *structured means and deliberate actions* or through inattention.

From a practical perspective, culture is what it is; executives cannot wish and hope for a change in culture or flip a switch and change it overnight. Culture is, however, the largest enabler of or obstacle to change. Culture is simply about individuals in a group sharing expected patterns of behavior. There is no cultural absolute because culture is both relative and dynamic to the organization's strategy and mission. Left on its own, culture is not sustainable. Culture is not some natural evolution in business; it is formed by the right intentional cascading best-practice leadership behaviors, choices, and actions. Executives have the power and responsibility to deliberately design, create, and nurture a culture that is the best fit for an organization's future direction.

An Improvement Culture Is Cultivated and Nurtured

Let's look at Ahrens, Flextronics, Lincoln Electric, Avery Dennison, General Cable, Audi, GE, Harley Davidson, Bosch, Motorola, IBM, BMW, Deere, Lockheed Martin, Raytheon, Dana, Boeing, Porsche, Johnson Controls, Visteon, Honda, Daimler Benz, Emerson Electric, Caterpillar, Honeywell, and dozens of other great global organizations (Toyota is a given). All these organizations continue to face the same or greater operating obstacles as everyone else, yet they continue to evolve winning cultures and be the benchmarks of improvement. What is it about these organizations that sets them apart? Although they might not call it by the name, they have a very precise and well-integrated Lean Business System and all the subprocesses in place, and they position the overarching philosophy of improvement front and center as the cultural standard of excellence throughout the enterprise. They have thought through and implemented all the critical success factors of adaptive systematic improvement. They have the elements of the architecture and subprocesses of our Lean Business System Reference Model implanted in the governance, implementation, and cultural foundation of improvement. They continue to win and define best-in-class performance because they deliberately design, create, and nurture improvement-enabling cultures.

How do your executives and organization weigh in on deliberately designing, creating, and nurturing an improvement-enabling culture? In terms of adaptive systematic improvement, what is the difference between an improvement-enabling culture and an improvement-dysfunctional culture? Part of the answer lies in reflecting on the traditional Western *process* of improvement with its tools focus and flavor-of-the-month programs. A stream of fad improvement programs and Lean *manufacturing* tools do not change culture; in fact, it's just the opposite. Adaptive Leadership creates an environment and shared belief system for success (i.e., for the program and tool content to work effectively). Culture is a deliberate and defined goal that positively influences the organization's shared values, belief system, and code of conduct. The role of Adaptive Leadership is to continue to evolve culture to higher standards of excellence by understanding and realigning behaviors and values. This has within it a continuous Kata-like process that includes the following cycle of learning:

▲ Creating a learning and development environment for associates (e.g., center of excellence and other professional development opportunities).

▲ Applying new knowledge and skills, often in situations that may be viewed initially as unlikely or impossible to improve.

▲ Mentoring and helping associates to experience success and personal discovery (from being intellectually to emotionally committed—the believers).

▲ Reflecting and solidifying personal beliefs through continuous efforts (e.g., communication, involvement in other improvement activities, pride of accomplishment, formal recognition, etc.).

▲ Growing incremental talent and evolving cultural values, standards of conduct, and expectations to higher levels of autonomous excellence.

Shaping culture is not rocket science, but it does require rigorous leadership attention, planning, and involvement. When leadership chooses not to assume this deliberate and proactive role, culture is accidental and improvement is limited. Let's discuss the signs of improvement-dysfunctional cultures. Improvement is not systematic at all. Wavering leadership, token agreements (rather than true commitment), constant disruptions, and changes in priorities are the norm where improvement is the first casualty. High-anxiety executives are always under pressure to make their numbers. In such organizations, improvement is an activity composed of *wishes* and *hopes*. Executives are seeking out programs like grabbing at straws, wishing for the big home run from a tool or single point program and hoping that everyone in the organization embraces change without asking questions about all the unknowns. Brute force and firefighting receives more recognition than improvement, and improvement is viewed as *in addition to* rather than an *integral part of* daily work (the separation disorder of improvement). This vicious cycle of overhyped and shoehorned improvement programs ultimately fail because they lack strategy, deployment planning, execution, accountability, widespread organizational credibility, authenticity, and substance. They continue to be undermined by ongoing executive behaviors, choices, and actions. Hence, these organizations create improvement-dysfunctional cultures. The problem with this concept is that it is extremely difficult for organizations to look in the mirror and recognize that this situation is a major barrier to future success. "We'll deal with it as we go forward" is not an acceptable approach unless an organization wishes to remain in this malfunctioning and maladaptive state. "We will" and "we already know how to" usually do not change much in these organizations.

Great improvement-enabling cultures do not view improvement as a magic box of improvement tools or a quick, emergency response to changing business conditions. They do not copy and paste tools applications, and they do not follow along with the next "in-vogue" program that everyone else is implementing. These organizations do not dwell on individual tools or the merits of Kaizen compared to Lean compared to Six Sigma. Adaptive systematic improvement is a living best practice and critical enabler of strategic and operating performance. Executives and their organizations focus on improvement every minute of every day intuitively, without even thinking about a buzzword or a tool. In these organizations it is difficult to tell the difference between executives, managers, and the workforce because great ideas for improvement are coming from everywhere. Everyone is engaged and empowered to make decisions about improvement and corrective actions, and they understand the dynamics of collaboration and always get the right people involved. The organizational hierarchy and silos are replaced by interactive networks of people working together. Adaptive systematic improvement is built into individual performance via recognition and rewards and direct compensation. Adaptive systematic improvement is fully internalized, which we discuss in more detail later.

Cultural Evolution Requires Total Stakeholder Engagement

Cultural evolution is the systematic improvement of culture. Moving the culture needle is the most difficult aspect of change. This is a deliberate and planned leadership effort that evolves by leaders continuously checking the organization's cultural vitals, and making the right leadership adjustments with the right momentum. Culture is never steady state and is always being transformed through both deliberate and unintentional means. There is positive momentum from the right executive behaviors, choices, and actions; and there is negative momentum from the wrong executive behaviors, choices, and actions. Negative momentum also comes from inaction, or action without communication, or disengagement. The objective is to deliberately define, design, and shape culture and not allow it to accidentally shape itself. A major cultural norm needed in organizations is the expansion of associate engagement and collaboration. Today the majority of organizations is losing ground because it is not developing and tapping into its vast talent pool. Associates are also unhappy because their work environment is not allowing them to engage and realize their full potential. Engagement and collaboration of all talent is a must in this fierce global economy. A major objective of adaptive systematic improvement is to find new ways of unleashing the tremendous human imagination, knowledge, experience, skills, and other capabilities that exist in every organization. Previous improvement programs have talked a good game about engagement and empowerment, but many organizations are in the infancy stages of associate participation.

Our integrated Lean Business System Reference Model architecture creates both the substance and momentum needed to evolve culture to higher levels of excellence. The goal is internalization where executives and their organizations reach constancy of purpose in terms of their shared beliefs, values, goals, and assumptions about systematic improvement. These values are evident in the behaviors of groups or individuals and are visible in how people think and work every day. Systematic improvement becomes embedded in culture, and executive behaviors, choices, and actions further amplify and reinforce the importance of systematic improvement. The process of internalization not only represents superiority, but it also ensures the longevity of systematic improvement through continuous cycles of positive cultural evolutions.

Internalizing Adaptive Systematic Improvement

Internalization is a process of transforming culture through critical mass acceptance. Internalization is the deliberate, human-focused process of installing shared beliefs, values, assumptions, attitudes, and organizational best practices about improvement into the consciousness of individuals, groups, and the organization as a whole. Over time, internalization becomes the acceptance of a set of norms, strategies, and expectations established by and maintained by leadership. The process begins with defining, communicating, and learning the desired cultural values and attributes. Then people go through a process of understanding why these values are critical to success and why they make sense. Finally they accept the norm as their own created viewpoint. In effect, internalization is the *interpretation process* of formal and informal communication that creates cultural conditions and shapes Kata.

With adaptive systematic improvement, internalization begins with individual egos in a manner that is integral to one's sense of self, usually through their personal discovery moments. It is one thing to believe in improvement conceptually or intellectually. Individual beliefs become much more powerful through engagement, empowerment, and the success of their eureka moments. When this happens over and over, the external world of improvement as a corporate operating philosophy is brought into the internal belief systems of individuals, thus creating individual ownership for improvement and at the same time filling in the separation anxiety of improvement (from "in addition to" daily work to a "normal integral part of" daily work). Internalization always begins with individuals or individual improvement teams. One important lesson about improvement in organizations is that nothing changes until associates are willing and ready to accept and physically support change by their actions. Culture change is the aggregate of associate change.

Figure 5.2 provides an overview of the internalization of adaptive systematic improvement. Note that the diagram represents a single cycle of cultural evolution, which is a continuous, never-ending role for executives. Discussing culture and how to cause it to evolve to higher standards of excellence may sound a bit Zen-like and Freudian, but it is more common sense than anything else.

This deliberate and longer-term process of internalization is achieved through proactive management of four specific cultural conditions:

▲ Projection

▲ Introjection

▲ Identification

▲ Incorporation

These cultural conditions are dynamic and easily influenced by real and perceived events. They require continuous attention and management so that they can continue to transform culture in a positive direction. When the gurus of the past 30 years talked about continuous improvement as a relentless, never-ending process, they meant what they said. Continuous improvement is not easy; it has taken Toyota 70 years and counting to get to where it is today. Like everything else it becomes automatic and routine (Kata) at the mastery stage. The remainder of this section provides additional information about each cultural condition of internalization.

Projection

Projection is the initial defense mechanisms that occur in response to improvement and change. Fear is the major driver of projection because individuals are afraid of all the perceived loss, effort, commitment, discipline, sacrifice, risk of failure, and disruption to their established norms. When individuals do not understand the *what, when, where, why, who,*

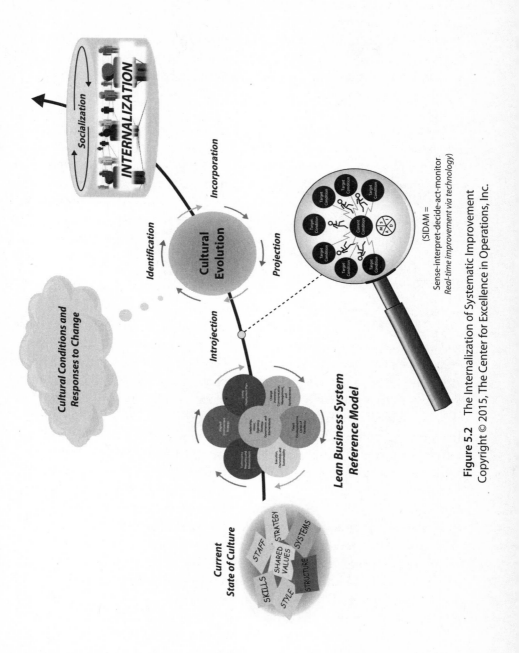

Figure 5.2 The Internalization of Systematic Improvement
Copyright © 2015, The Center for Excellence in Operations, Inc.

165

and *how* of improvement, they fabricate negative thoughts. The more people think about change, the perceived losses, and their unanswered questions, the larger their initial barriers grow. The signs of resistance are obvious: silence, deflection, criticism, confusion, denial, easy agreement, pocket vetoes, excuses, or *"whatabout-itis."* Projection is the attempt people make to put space between the inner self (norms) and the external environment (change).

Projection is also positive. Every organization has the initiators and early enlistees of improvement. These associates generally have positive attitudes and see the glass as half full instead of half empty. They may have similar concerns as others, but they see more good than bad in improvement. Leadership, communication, and education are the means of dealing with projection. This phase is the early stage of the next cultural condition called introjection.

Introjection

Introjection is a group version of projection. As associates begin talking with each other about their individual perceptions of change, the exchange (positive or negative) becomes a collection of data points that shapes the perceptions and visions of improvement and change. Associates are drawn into beliefs or are influenced by others internally by the communication that they are receiving from the external space. Through this cultural condition, individuals replicate in themselves the behaviors, decisions, actions, attributes, or other fragments of associates around them, especially leadership or lack thereof. Introjection occurs through rumors, political motives, the stronger personalities of others, or the real data and facts. Associates cannot decide whether to jump on the train or hang around and get run over by the train. If the perception of the messages is negative, it creates pockets of naysayers and dogmatic cults, but an effective adaptive systematic improvement initiative exposes these folks rather quickly. Introjection is a dynamic process that continues to be influenced and shaped by communication and direct engagement in the improvement process. The shared beliefs, values, and assumptions about improvement are influenced by inconsistent versions of improvement, wavering leadership, a perceived or actual change in commitment, and other leadership behaviors, decisions, and actions. This in turn can change the behaviors of groups or individuals positively or negatively and the organization's ultimate commitment to improvement. Constancy of purpose, effective communication strategies, and "walk the talk" best practices leadership behaviors are the best methods for dealing with introjection.

Identification

Identification is the cultural condition in which individuals seek to become an integral part of the larger group in terms of shared beliefs, values, and assumptions about improvement. Many of these associates are the "Show-me, I'm from Missouri" people in the organization. This is actually a favorable condition because it increases the attention to and desire to demonstrate success. Once they either experience or understand improvement, they jump on the train. Through this cultural condition, internalization occurs through the transformation of individuals, groups, and the organization, wholly or partially, after the role models of leadership and other champions of change. It is in this phase that the new personalities of individuals, groups, and the organization are formed. This is the phase where, with enough participation, cultural transformation is visible in the way associates think and work every day.

Incorporation

The final cultural condition of internalization is *incorporation*. This is the psychological and social ingestion of the philosophy of improvement as well as the systemized process of improvement. Incorporation is undeniably a cultural standard of excellence—in improvement strategy, deployment plans, values and code of conduct, individual behaviors, education, performance expectations, decisions and actions in associates' own daily work, and their interactions with the entire organization. Cultural transformation is extremely visible in the way associates think and work and how they are intolerant of the mediocrity of those around them. Incorporation implies permanence in shared beliefs, values, and assumptions about improvement that are glued into culture—and that lead to the rhapsody level of continuous improvement. Remember that this is all a state in time; culture and adaptive systematic improvement as a whole require continuous renewal and nurturing to continue the positive evolution cycles.

Socialization: The Operating System of Internalization

Socialization is not a cultural condition in itself, but it is an important part of every cultural condition of internalization. *Socialization* is the ongoing transfer of information and nurturing of the organization's mission, vision, shared beliefs, values, expectations, and standard code of conduct. The goal of socialization is to manage and minimize the disruptions of the various cultural states, to grease entry of internalization by whatever means necessary. Cultural evolution is simplified when executives have the full trust, loyalty, and commitment of their entire organization. Socialization helps to establish this unity of purpose between the organization and its associates, but it goes beyond communication. Socialization develops knowledge, skills, and personality characteristics within individuals so that they can function successfully within the broader context of the organization. This occurs through many directions: from leadership and/or organizational development to employees, from older employees to newer employees, exchanges between individuals in a department, exchanges between functional areas, from an experienced improvement resource to a new team, from a formal buddy or mentoring process, from interactions with champion employees, through a center of excellence in the company, and from many other directions. These are common practices at Toyota and within our small sample of great organizations mentioned earlier in this chapter.

Culture Change and Frogs in Boiling Water

There is an old story about dropping a frog in boiling water. If you drop a frog in boiling water, it will leap out immediately. However, if you put a frog in a pot of water that's at room temperature and slowly bring the water to a boil, the frog will die. I have never validated this claim in my own kitchen, and do not intend to in the future. The story provides a relevant metaphor about how many organizations deal with culture change. Many organizations are operating like a frog in boiling water mode. They procrastinate or postpone improvement in favor of more (perceived-to-be) immediate problems. Slow cooking and the frog dies. Another viewpoint is that when faced with a crisis or need for instant gratification, they themselves leap out of hot water like the frog. First, they are not dealing with the root causes of problems; they are dealing with symptoms of problems. Second, waste is like a living organism; if you are not uncovering and eliminating waste continuously, it is growing and keeping itself well hidden. These behaviors create an anti-Kata culture, the opposite values and code of conduct necessary for adaptive systematic improvement. Executives are smarter than frogs, and it is healthy to unplug and observe occasionally and check the vital signs of culture.

Culture is a frequent topic of discussion, but it is often within theoretical and abstract space. We provide a systematic means of changing culture, and we have also been advising our clients to improve the intangible qualities of their culture. The *soft stuff* is the *tough stuff* that you cannot observe with your natural senses. Nevertheless, creating the right cultural competencies is much more important (and difficult) than developing competencies around the tools of improvement. Let's add a little *boots on the ground* detail to our discussion. How does an organization create a Lean Business System culture? Here are a few summary points:

1. *Communicate! Communicate! Communicate!* There is no such thing as too much communication when the message is purpose-driven and well targeted. Executives can use their interpersonal skills to attract associates to the mission and create the call to action.

2. *Plan-deliver-check-adjust.* Communication can be a positive reinforcer, a negative reinforcer, or a neutral reinforcer of change. Executives and managers must make sure that there is constancy and unity of purpose in the message. If associates were to talk with any executive or manager, they should hear a consistent story and messagie about their XYZ business system. Trickle-down communication is important; organizations must make a special effort to clarify questions before issues become misinterpreted, distorted, or blown way out of proportion.

3. *Walk the talk.* When executives and managers communicate to their organizations, they must keep in mind that this is not the end. They are on a perpetual stage where people in the organization are observing their behaviors, choices, and actions. If leaders desire a certain change in behaviors, they must be prepared to change their own behaviors and demonstrate constancy in direction. Never allow associates to feel that they are being asked to do something that executives and managers are not willing to do themselves.

4. *Implement all the operating philosophies, subprocesses, and content of our Lean Business System Reference Model.* As a whole, a well-architected and well-maintained Lean Business System creates a very positive environment for associate success.

5. *Practice proactive engagement.* This includes the engagement and participation of associates through a deliberate outreach best practice. Don't wait for volunteers; proactively recruit associates and use communication, mentoring, education, professional development experiences, and many other elements of the Lean Business System to build confidence and drive out fear.

6. *Develop talent continuously.* Great organizations are always in learning mode. This is encouraged by coaching and mentoring, and often it is through the personal initiative of an associate. This point is not suggesting that the organization spend 50 percent of its time in classroom education. There are all kinds of different ways to develop talent in people which we discuss in further detail in Chapter 6. People can develop significantly through continued mentoring and reflecting on events, root causes, and corrective actions.

7. *Help associates at all times.* One of the reasons change does not stick is that people fail and there is not a "help desk" function to get them out of trouble. In Toyota Kata this is the strong coaching and mentoring practices. These fundamentals apply to all organizations. Don't allow associates to remain in a wheel-spinning or failure mode. Provide support, and help associates succeed and experience their eureka moments. They become believers very quickly from these positive experiences. They develop the courage to change and to not fear change.

8. *Do it! Live it! Breathe it!* I am certain that these points are not new to most readers. What *is* new is developing the capability to evolve culture through a holistic, for-real Lean Business System. Most organizations have not been able to develop a culture of *continuous* improvement. For decades organizations have spent too much time on the *technical* (fad programs and tools) side of sociotechnical elements and not enough effort on the *socio* (behaviors, values, cultural development) side of sociotechnical elements. When one visits Toyota, GE, Honeywell, Harley Davidson, and other great organizations, one finds

that they are literally oozing with constancy of purpose and enthusiasm to improve. One can sense this commitment and enthusiasm before talking to anyone.

The Tenth Waste

Most Lean practitioners are familiar with the standard waste categories of Lean. Some call them the seven wastes, the eight wastes, or the nine wastes. We use ten wastes in our practice. They include:

1. Waiting

2. Overproduction

3. Transportation

4. Overprocessing

5. Storage

6. Motion

7. Defects and rework

8. Underutilized human capacity

9. Safety

10. Inadequacy of human initiative

The eighth waste, underutilized human capacity, is often discussed in terms of management's failure to engage, involve, and leverage employees and their tremendous wealth of knowledge. Since the 1980s organizations have talked a good game about employee engagement, involvement, and empowerment. But it quickly vanishes when there is a frog in the pot of boiling water. The eighth waste is definitely an immense loss for many organizations, and as a result, there are many dormant improvement opportunities—and *defective* improvement opportunities as well.

The tenth waste we discuss with clients relative to the Lean Business System Reference Model is the other side of the eighth waste, and it's called—inadequacy of human initiative. Too often, organizations wait for their executives to step up, give their commitment and proactively lead an effective improvement initiative. Executives are the most overloaded resources in organizations; they are always in situations where they need to make decisions or nothing gets done. They are distracted by many issues that run counter to systematic improvement or that they wish they did not have to deal with in the first place. They are not always in a position to have all the knowledge, skills, and facts to organize and launch a well-designed and planned Lean Business System. What happens to systematic improvement in these situations? It becomes easy for executives to underestimate and oversimplify all the elements of a Lean Business System and what is required for lasting success. What might have started out as a commitment becomes a temporary token agreement. The above comments are not a criticism or a defense for their behaviors, choices, and actions. I am certain from my experiences that at least 95 percent of executives (and their associates) are for the most part acting with the best of intentions. When organizations hang around waiting for or complaining about executive direction, commitment, engagement, and endorsement, it does not change the status of things much. Think about the five why answers to this dilemma.

Many successful Lean initiatives have begun by grassroots activities of energetic practitioners and associates. This is what inadequacy of human initiative is all about. If something is not working well, take the initiative to jump in. Always ask for forgiveness, not permission. Create a community of managers and associates interested enough to demonstrate success. Organize a few pilot activities. Engage both managers and associates; it will make the story more compelling down the road. Get associates talking and engage them. Put the extra effort into pilots and create a few impressive local successes. Publicize the financial benefits and positive experiences of participants. Lay out the pilot experiences and lay out the details of how to scale the pilot successes across the enterprise. Results matter; numbers get executives' attention. Plan-do-check-act! "Pull" executives into systematic improvement through the success stories. Earn the commitment and engagement.

There is no disagreement that a Lean Business System requires unwavering commitment, engagement, and ongoing endorsements from the CEO and executive leadership team. Period. End of story! But when an organization is missing these ingredients up front, it needs to begin somewhere. Senior and middle management, supervisors, and associates have a professional obligation to engage themselves in systematic improvement—with or without executive commitment. In other words, all people in organizations need to step up and accelerate their own human initiative. Executives are intelligent people. In these *middle-out* situations, I have never seen an executive deny Lean or any other initiative with well-documented, impressive results. Again, this is not the end all, but it is a start when all the stars of systematic improvement are misaligned.

Inadequacy of human initiative applies to executives and managers as well. Not that they do not have enough to do already. We encourage executives to become directly involved in a major improvement activity, gain additional familiarization with the overall process, principles, and methodologies, and most important of all experience the success on their own. This creates enormous benefits (Kata contributions). First of all, it demonstrates that executives have not asked their organization to do something that they would not do on their own. Second, it develops the Adaptive Leadership competency because executives are leading from direct engagement and experiences, not at some intellectual level. Leading at an intellectual level can also create disconnects during communications activities. Last, it helps develop leadership into better (informed) executive mentors and coaches.

Kata is a behavior that comes from within. It starts with a single person or a few individuals, and it evolves to the *religion* of conducting business. It is developed over time through the right patterns, routines, and work ethics. It takes time, patience, effort, and people—all people to build these invisible competencies in organizations. Four major elements missing in the Western translation of Kata are *learning to learn, learning to observe, learning to coach,* and *learning to develop culture.* Many people who are serving as coaches today have been thrown into those roles and are missing the complete skill set to coach effectively. Coaches must be motivated to expand their learning; they also need continuous learning and development and coaching from vertical, horizontal, and lateral sources in the organization.

Create a No-Limits Culture

Culture is the invisible energy field in organizations. We have provided guidance concerning the subprocess involving communication and cultural evolution. Evolving culture is, in itself, a race without a finish line—it's not an event. It is the most challenging role of being a CEO and a member of his or her executive team. Culture is difficult because it is an abstract topic requiring strong interpersonal and communications skills. It involves the right messaging with the right interpretations, and persuading people to change their ingrained habits and embrace new thinking, behaviors, choices, and actions. We have chosen the word *evolution* because it requires many small, consistent steps over time. It also requires that executives set the example by modeling and mirroring the desired cultural state. In particular, this means finding a balance between numbers and short-term performance (which is a must-do), and strengthening the organization's capacity to eliminate detractors to performance (wastes) and continuously exceed the numbers. Following are a few key summary points:

▲ The CEO and his or her executive team are responsible for defining, designing, and creating cultural evolution. Culture cannot change through an empty message or delegation to human resources or an outside consultant or by continuing to mimic the cultures of other organizations with a tools-based approach to improvement.

▲ The subprocesses of our Lean Business System Reference Model are inseparable. All play an integral role in evolving culture. It is not just about changing performance metrics or communicating a vision. It is about the complete and repetitive follow-through of fully integrated adaptive systematic improvement as a whole.

▲ Constancy of purpose is critical. The CEO and executive team must become capable of delivering a consistent message to their respective organizations and provide consistent leadership and mentoring to move the culture needle. Additionally, constancy of purpose must become an adaptive and well-communicated step-down practice. Managers, supervisors, and peer associates must also reach the point of consistent thinking, behaviors, choices, and actions. The organization needs to remain on a consistent course of adaptive systematic improvement and not be distracted by some new flashy program.

▲ Controversy and confrontation must be dealt with head on. Executives should expect resistance, get down to the root causes, and plan the right response strategies. Most associates will come around, and a few iterations will lead to more associate acceptance. Executives cannot change culture overnight. Evolving culture is never ending, and a single evolution might take years. It also requires patience and persistence and investing enough time and effort to make a difference. Adaptive systematic improvement brings out the best in most people. I have personally turned individuals who their executives were ready to write off into the greatest improvement champions in the company. Culture change includes many unknown challenges. Finally, look for the players who undermine progress and cannot be turned around; send them on their way.

Reason and logic do not always work when it comes to modifying behaviors and reducing the fears of change because the emotional elements are not addressed properly. These include fear, perceived loss, mistrust, conflicts, and confusion to name a few. Additionally, most cultures are not wired to embrace change without question. People are individualistic, enjoy freedoms and space, become comfortable with the status quo even if it is not so good, and reject being forced to change. However, there is a powerful resolve to perform beyond expectations and win when the invisible energy behind engagement is drawn out and nurtured. Organizations must begin their systematic journey with their present culture and deliberately evolve this culture to a more desired state. The experiences of Western organizations provide a good example. Imposing the values of other organizations through a mass implementation of tools and programs has not worked, and the Western culture excuse is garbage. Maybe these approaches worked for a while, but they did not stick because organizations failed to evolve *their own* culture as an integral foundation of continuous improvement. Culture is what it is and can be changed to a higher order of improvement Kata. It's time for all global organizations to dig deep into their souls of improvement and leverage their cultural resolve to create a superior adaptive systematic improvement process in the near future and beyond.

Bibliography

Hillman, O. S. 2011. *Change Agent: Engaging Your Passion to Be the One Who Makes a Difference.* Charisma House Book Group, Lake Mary, Florida.

Horwath, R. 2013. *Elevate: The Three Disciplines of Strategic Thinking.* John Wiley & Sons, Hoboken, New Jersey.

Kotter, J. P. 2008. *A Sense of Urgency.* Harvard Business School Publishing, Boston.

Lawler, E. E. 2008. *Talent: Making People Your Competitive Advantage.* Josey Bass Publishing, San Francisco.

Liker, J., and Hoseus, M. 2008. *Toyota Culture: The Heart and Soul of the Toyota Way.* McGraw-Hill, New York.

Thean, P. 2014. *Rhythm: How to Achieve Breakthrough Execution and Accelerate Growth.* Greenleaf Publishing Group, Austin, Texas.

CHAPTER 6

Creating a Center of Excellence

This chapter provides guidance on how to create a center of excellence capability, a subsystem and an integral part of our Lean Business System Reference Model™. A center of excellence is the core competency and capability center for a Lean Business System. It can be either a physical or virtual center of knowledge that concentrates existing expertise and resources in a discipline to attain and achieve continuity of purpose and optimize value contribution throughout the enterprise. This function promotes collaboration, guidance, shared learning, homogeneity, and best practices for enterprisewide adaptive systematic improvement. The purpose, scope and content, organization, and service delivery are driven by business requirements, talent development needs, and the degree of special support required throughout the enterprise. There is not much published about the design and architecture of an *improvement Kata* center of excellence. We share insights from our reference model as a guide for your progressing with your own Lean Business System. Keep in mind that it is a reference model and always evolving as new information is discovered. It is very possible and acceptable that organizations add to this reference model based on their own special requirements.

In our reference model, a center of excellence is a hybrid entity that provides thought leadership, technical improvement applications knowledge, education and talent development, implementation support, benchmarking and best practices information, and uniform integration of the Lean Business System across the enterprise. This last point is important because it means that there is a uniform architecture and systematic process of improvement across the organization. The other element of integration is cross-pollination: making sure that best-practice successes and lessons learned are leveraged to the max across various business units and other key processes. It is important that the center of excellence function as a resource center and not a direct responsibility center for improvement. Its resources are usually the most highly skilled and experienced, *crème de la crème* improvement resources in the company. A center of excellence provides a terrific professional development and career exposure stop for the organization. Working alongside other professionals in the center of excellence expedites learning and development and facilitates continuity when individuals return to their business units.

Key Roles of a Center of Excellence

The roles of a center of excellence are designed around business requirements, priorities, and cultural needs. The purpose of this entity is to take advantage of scale and scope in terms of developing, supporting, and nurturing a common Lean Business System across many business units or divisions. These roles can be fulfilled through a combination of internal and external resources, through a corporate functional role, or through a Lean Business System leader role in smaller organizations. We mention earlier that the right proven external experts can add significant value early on in designing, integrating, adapting, and systematizing a true, enterprisewide Lean Business System. The remainder of this section outlines the typical roles found in a center of excellence.

Thought Leadership and Development

A center of excellence includes highly skilled, well-versed, and experienced improvement leaders. Sometimes these individuals are called lead architects, an appropriate name for their role. They act as the lead architects and implementation experts of a holistic, enterprisewide Lean Business System. These individuals have significant implementation experience in a variety of industries, global business units, operating environments, and cultural settings. They are highly experienced in executive mentoring and development, change leadership, and all of the subprocesses in our Lean Business System Reference Model. They are well versed in Kaizen, Lean, Six Sigma, ERP (enterprise resource planning), enterprise cloud architectures, and all other improvement methodologies. They understand how to adapt various improvement methodologies to special operating environments, and they innovate their way through wilderness improvement situations by developing new approaches to improvement. They are experts at anticipating obstacles and barriers to success and proactively preventing them before they occur. This is the lead role for designing, integrating, adapting, and systematizing the organization's Lean Business System and building out the support roles of the center of excellence to support and ensure its success.

Technical Applications Support

Developing a strong core competency of improvement is not as easy as getting a black belt or Lean Sensei certificate. It requires years of experiences and hundreds of improvement activities before an individual gains expertise in *all* the various improvement methodologies. This role provides technical support to business units and/or improvement teams on how best to approach their improvement activity. Ideally, this is accomplished through the local improvement team. The reality is that teams get stuck and become very discouraged if left in that state for too long. This is the "go-to" role relative to any complex, subject matter questions that cannot be resolved by resident improvement resources. Technical applications support is more of a help-desk function for improvement. This type of support is usually responsive and incident-based. It can involve very senior mentoring support to help teams through their assignments, working with business units and teams to remove obstacles and provide assistance about how to use a particular improvement methodology. Lead architects are often requested to help business unit executives increase the momentum of their local Lean Business System efforts. They may also be requested for their technical expertise in problem solving, such as how to set up and run a design of experiments (DOE), or how to adapt the right concepts and methodologies to unique, nonstandard applications. Sometimes, the lead architect does not have the answers but has the competency to pioneer his or her way to a solution to the problem as well as a more defined approach for continuing on with improvement. Technical applications support is often needed in the complex interconnected network of transactional processes. These efforts are often *improvement forensics* efforts, trying to replicate (through historical sampling plans, modeling, and analysis) the conditions that generated the problems. Often it is difficult to define the problem and differentiate the multiple causes from the multiple effects. One cannot *see* these types of problems. It's much more complicated than constructing a value stream map or a visual board.

Education and Talent Development

In a Center of Excellence the role of professional education and talent development involves developing and delivering relevant and uniform educational materials to build the core competency of improvement. The specific content and scope is not a standard curriculum, nor is it modules of generic improvement tools. Lead architects tailor education to the specific needs and applications of the organization, including the applicable improvement concepts, company examples with real data, tailored participation exercises and instruction, and specific guidance and instruction about how to apply these methodologies to the business. Generic education on basic manufacturing improvement tools is out. Education and talent development are definitely about designing, integrating, adapting, and systematizing. Herein lies a very challenging issue: The labels of Kaizen, Lean, TPS, theory of constraints, Six Sigma, ERP, emerging technology, and the respected approaches and tools are no longer stand-alone initiatives. Training the masses in a batch mode is also out. It must all be viewed as adaptive systematic improvement. This is another good example that underscores the importance of a Lean Business System as an integrated architecture. It will require significant thought to design and construct an educational curriculum and its content. It will require significant communication for it to gain acceptance. And it will require robust implementation best practices to transform the educational knowledge into results and positive cultural experiences.

A center of excellence plays an important role in developing the improvement competencies of an organization. The scope often includes improvement-related education on change leadership, manager and supervisor development, the body of knowledge of various improvement methodologies, team and group dynamics, how to define and quantify benefits, performance management, basic improvement skills (local Kaizen activities), training within industry (TWI), training in safety and environmental (green), and specific job skills development. Other important considerations of education and talent development include:

▲ *Adaptive.* Custom-tailored education to an organization's requirements and operating environment (e.g., job shop, hospital, defense contractor, automotive, utilities, oil refining, services provider, etc.).

▲ *Application-directed.* Education that is delivered in smaller *just-in-time* increments and directly applied to an improvement activity (learn-apply-succeed-believe).

▲ *Achievement-based, not attendance-based.* Education followed by a requirement to implement a successful improvement activity while demonstrating the proper use of the methodology and tools.

▲ *Refresher and reinforcement.* Creating the means to strengthen talent competencies with existing improvement knowledge or new developments. Other means might include boot camp time at the center of excellence, or an instructor or mentoring assignment where individuals sharpen their improvement and change leadership skills.

Successful execution is dependent upon *active learning and talent development* through a combination of personal and group development planning, tailored education, instructional delivery, coaching and mentoring, technology, and a wide variety of work experiences. The ultimate goal is to become self-sufficient with your own education and talent management offerings, and also to be capable of expanding and continuously internalizing the improvement body of knowledge. Later in this chapter we discuss the possible scope and content of improvement education as well as alternative delivery and reinforcement approaches. While it may be obvious, it is worth mention that a center of excellence is a resource, facilitation, and integration center and not a command and control center for all improvement activities in the organization.

Implementation Support

Implementation support is similar to technical applications support, but it entails a broader and longer duration of support to a business unit. This might include mentoring business unit lead resources through the planning and early stages of their Lean Business System start-up. Lead architects help business units and divisions with the details of how to install the capabilities of the subprocesses of Lean Business System architecture. Examples include:

▲ How to launch and communicate the vision and strategy

▲ How to conduct a business diagnostic

▲ How to define, prioritize, and align specific business unit improvement needs

▲ How to organize and staff the resident Lean Business System

▲ How to prioritize and initiate improvement activities and teams

▲ How to define the right metrics

▲ How to provide local education and talent development

▲ How to apply basic project management

In smaller and midsized organizations, lead architects are more involved in supporting implementation within the business units. The organization is not large enough to justify a dedicated resident staff of improvement resources, but the need for improvement still exists. In these situations it makes sense to appoint a site improvement leader and leverage the center of excellence and lead architect resources. I know of several organizations in which the lead architects work out of their home and travel to where they are needed at a specific time. Very large organizations can justify their own business unit improvement leaders and a small staff of improvement resources. In these situations a corporate lead architect is less involved in longer-term implementation support.

Business, Process, and Technology Integration

Another important role held in a center of excellence is the integrator of adaptive systematic improvement. From a business perspective, it is the bringing together of all the critical success factors of systematic improvement. It is the enterprisewide quality assurance function, making sure that all business units are concurrently and collectively improving with constancy of purpose and continuity. In essence it is the integration of the Lean Business System to produce breakthroughs in corporate performance and evolve culture to higher standards of excellence.

From a process perspective, the integrator role involves knowledge sharing of improvements at the process level with other business units and divisions of the organization. In the transactional processes, for example, the experiences and successes of a team improvement activity are easily leveraged to other business units with the same or similar process issues.

An effective way to accomplish this is through a scheduled monthly meeting of company business improvement leaders. During this meeting, information is exchanged about improvement activities through a formal peer review session. These sessions include questions and answers and often have requests for a team leader to assist a team in another business unit that is just getting started on the same improvement activity. Effective exchanges around new product development and supply chain management can generate megasavings quickly while adding standardization to these complex processes.

From a technology perspective, this involves the integration of systematic improvement and technology. Organizations should plan for technology competencies to exist in the center of excellence. Organizations have talked about this idea for decades, especially in the realm of business process improvement (BPI) and business process reengineering (BPR). Historically technology has been viewed more from an information technology (IT) perspective than a business integration perspective. In practice these two elements have functioned independently in many organizations. Y2K and ERP implementations are two examples—organizations signed up to implement their ERP architecture and business process improvement (BPI) at the same time. Then in the interest of time they focused more on implementing the software while pledging to come back to BPI at a later date. Many organizations never found the time to come back. People quickly found nonstandard work-arounds, kluge spreadsheets and databases, shortcuts, and other means to perform their work. Because these large architectures are so integrated, organizations flooded themselves with hidden, non-value-added work everywhere!

Today the need for technology integration is critical because technology is evolving at a faster rate than organizations can assimilate and benefit from. Technology can enable or disable organizations exponentially. Data warehousing, mobility, virtualization and the cloud, business analytics, visualization, and other emerging technologies are pushing decision makers toward immediate reason and instant gratification and away from root-cause problem solving. Life was simple when organizations had their conference room war rooms of manually maintained metrics. Today technology can instantly display a thousand times more information on the walls of people's minds. Technology by itself undermines systematic improvement. The integrator role of a center of excellence must accomplish the proper balance between improvement and technology and ensure that there is a seamless integration of improvement and technology. In this economy, each enables the other.

Benchmarking and Best Practices

Benchmarking and best practices research have been a legitimate means of improvement in the past, especially the *within-industry* scans. A center of excellence needs to continuously scan competitor and industry best practices and also the *outside-industry* best practices. Benchmarking is an asset to adaptive systematic improvement if conducted and used correctly: to scan, learn, stimulate thinking, adapt, and improve best practices to the organization's business requirements. Benchmarking can create the temptation to blindly copy, and this practice must be avoided. The cycle of *scan, learn, think, adapt, improve* is critical to the purpose and ultimate success of benchmarking.

Here is a bit of caution regarding benchmarking: Many benchmarking activities tend to be treated as one-time events rather than as a continual journey for excellence. Other benchmarking efforts have expanded their scope and inadvertently replaced the original objective of improvement. Best in class is a moving target in this global economy. It is a fact that the organizations that gain the most are those that continue to innovate and adapt best practices before their competitors do. In other words, they are the inventors and leaders of best practices. The problem with searching for and copying the best practices of others is that the practices are often dated, commoditized (already copied by others), misinterpreted, oversimplified, or obsolete by definition.

Best practices are typically conceived via the following approaches:

▲ *Radical discovery.* These are best practices that are discovered when executives of organizations open their minds to new possibilities that enable them to redefine their traditional business models. Visioneering and mind mapping about how a hospital might operate like Amazon, FedEx, Boeing, or Toyota and no waiting rooms are sure to create a lively discussion of potential healthcare innovations with the right people in the room.

▲ *Adaptive.* These are best practices that represent a departure from known customer and market needs by adapting an existing or new process to a new prospective but unproven/unknown market need. The ideas may come from benchmarking, customer collaboration, or internal process innovation. Many retailers are implementing adaptive best practices to get closer to customer and market opportunities, reduce fulfillment cycles, and improve cash to cash.

▲ *Technology.* This involves creating new processes and practices through evolving technology solutions plus process rationalization that have not been previously feasible or possible. Many organizations are creating new best practices through the correct deployment of technology.

▲ *Incremental.* These are best practices that continue to build upon an organization's best practices and continuously *improve how we improve* current processes to higher levels of achievement and benchmark performance. This is the most common approach to sustaining existing best practices in many organizations.

One final word of advice is to find the right balance in benchmarking. Benchmarking is not improvement. Benchmarking time takes away from improvement time. Remember that from the customer and market perspectives, "best" is relative in time and space and at any transactional or reputational moment in time. The only way to deal with this challenge is to continuously strive to be the best through innovation and origination. Unexpected circumstances happen even to the *best-of-the-best* practice organizations, but their recovery is superior because they are always on their *best* game.

Managing Evolving Roles and Scope

A center for excellence is a resource and competency. It is not a centralized command and control center for improvement, nor is it a central group of resources that assumes the responsibility for improvement from other business unit and/or functional managers. The most recent example is Six Sigma. One of the objectives of Six Sigma was to create a structure and tsunami of dedicated master black belts, black belts, green belts, and yellow belts throughout organizations. In all fairness, sometimes it takes a tsunami to create momentum for change in organizations. They used an unofficial center of excellence way of thinking and built this competency through a large, centralized education function that acted as the traveling certification center within companies. Six Sigma advanced the science and discipline of improvement with its mandated leadership engagement, structured DMAIC gate-keeping process, fact-based and data-driven approach, deep-core root-cause problem solving, achievement-based (rather than attendance-based) education, technology (Minitab), and a strong focus on execution. It attempted to introduce many attributes of the Lean Business System Reference Model into improvement, but in retrospect it became an *immersion* strategy and a ritual of *belts*. There were several executives like Jack Welch of GE, Larry Bossidy of Honeywell, Jim Owens of Caterpillar, and Anne Mulcahy of Xerox who kept their organizations on a path of success with Six Sigma. Most organizations ended up with large, dedicated corporate groups of black belts that supported the organization's Six Sigma needs. We visited with several of these organizations that were concerned about not enough getting done for the investment. We observed a common practice among all these organizations. When managers were asked about problems, they always responded, "I have a black belt working on it." By creating these large, centralized Six Sigma departments, organizations allowed their management to throw the responsibility and ownership for improvement over the wall to an outside corporate group. Then these managers went back to business as usual. They would often reject the recommendations of these large central groups unless they coincided with what the managers had already decided to do. There was a perpetual problem of an outsider recommending changes that people did not understand or were not engaged in. Eventually these large central black belt departments were dismantled and decentralized into functional areas where they belong.

A center of excellence is a resource and competency center. It is also the innovation center and constancy of purpose center for a Lean Business System. A center of excellence is always evolving; there are always emerging needs that require adjustments to the roles and scope of a center of excellence. Organizations want to avoid the mistake of allowing the scope of a center of excellence to include responsibilities that should be within the realm of other functions within the organizations.

Lean Crossroads

The Lean Business System Reference Model is a composition of concepts, an architecture of integrated processes, best practices, metrics that stimulate thinking, and an organization-specific architecture for adaptive systematic improvement. Since the reference model is enterprisewide in scope, organizations need to rethink the concept of Lean and improvement in general. This is a prerequisite for proceeding further with the design of a center of excellence. The reference model can be used as a foundation on which the professional development competencies will be configured and delivered to the organization.

With respect to education and talent development, the past decades of improvement have been full of well-intentioned efforts, but also full of unintended consequences. Let's look at the ground that many organizations have covered with improvement: SPC, IE, OR, MTM, MODAPTS, SIS, ZBB, QCC, TQM, PDCA, little mrp, MRPII, ERP, CEDAC, GT, QFD, TPM, SMED, TOC, JIT, PACE, ME, Kanban, WCM, QRM, Pull, SCOR, ECR, BPI, BPR, BPM, TPS, 5S, ABC, 4Ms, 3Ms, OEE, Lean, Six Sigma, Lean Six Sigma, VSM, operational excellence, hoshin kanri, TRIZ, DMAIC, and a few others that I missed. Now think about all the next level of terminology and acronyms behind each initiative. (The key to all these acronyms is at the end of this chapter.) Have a look at your own organization's experiences, and then put yourself in the shoes of associates who have been exposed to these improvement initiatives for the past 20 years. What's wrong with this picture? Is there any question that this *wonks-and-wizards* approach to improvement might have caused a little confusion? All these initiatives incorporate improvement philosophies, methodologies, tools, and terminology for improvement. They also represent advances in the principles of scientific management, and their specifics are very relevant to the entire spectrum of improvement challenges in organizations today. The problem is that all of these initiatives have been pursued as single-point improvement programs. A closer look reveals the overlap in philosophies and methodologies of improvement repackaged and rebranded under a different name. Organizations have been on a journey of continuous improvement via *a box with a different colored ribbon* strategy, where the content of the box remains basically the same. In retrospect, this is a fragmented, suboptimization strategy of improvement. The journey has not been a holistic, constancy-of-purpose strategy like that of Toyota. No single-point improvement program or fragmented set of tools is all inclusive or all exclusionary. In Western organizations, for example, the Toyota Production System (TPS) is the current popular methodology of choice.

A continuation of a *mimic the tools* strategy is limiting the potential of Lean in these organizations.

Lean *is* at a crossroads. It's time for organizations to put the Aristotle spin on Lean and think very deeply about how to evolve Lean *manufacturing* into a true, holistic Lean Business System. Over 2,000 years ago Aristotle spoke of actual versus potential motion (improvement), reasons for causality (root-cause analysis), criticizing regimes with their empty words and poetic metaphors (tools), and giving greater weight to empirical observation (experimentation and evidence-based practices) than pure theories (*canned* approaches). The reference to Aristotle is not an accident, for his wisdom is very relevant today. A Lean Business System represents a *defrag* of individual improvement principles and methodologies. Organizations must now expand the notion of Lean beyond the Toyota Production System tools. A Lean business is about improvement, regardless of the principles and tools. From a center of excellence strategy, organizations need to think about consolidating all these methodologies into a unified body of knowledge and powerhouse version of Lean. Additionally, organizations need to increase their competency efforts significantly on behaviors and cultural development. The Lean Business System Reference Model essentially suggests that organizations need to evolve to a Lean strategy where there is one all-inclusive box of competencies and capabilities, well thought through, and customized for the organizations' specific business requirements and cultural development needs. A good name for the box is the XYZ business system because it implies a broader and more holistic model of adaptive systematic improvement.

Integrating Talent Development Requirements into Education

A center of excellence is always driven by business requirements and cultural development needs. This is also true for all of the resources and services offered within a center of excellence. One area worth discussing is education related to talent development. In the past, education has been structured in a vanilla batch, train the masses mode with generic content in many organizations. Beyond all of the maladaptive dynamics in organizations, this *throw it at the wall and see what sticks* approach to education and talent development is not the right approach for a Lean

Business System. Adaptive systematic improvement requires precision; so too does the education that creates the talent inventory to keep the best practices best. The following points provide guidance about how to customize education and talent development in a Lean Business System. When developing the specific education content, organizations should keep the following best practices in mind:

▲ *Cascading.* Education designed to deliver a uniform base of skills and knowledge to people at different levels in the organization and to deliver specific injections of skills needed for success in their specific organizational roles.

▲ *Integrated.* Replacing single-point tools thinking with a "toolbox and master craftsman" approach to improvement. This is the integration of Kaizen, Lean, Six Sigma, and all other methodologies and a means of improvement that contributes to success. This also involves integrating other factors into continuous improvement, such as enabling IT, the human elements of change, regulatory and compliance considerations, communication, and performance and rewards.

▲ *Needs driven.* Curriculum design based on the organization's business improvement requirements. The goal is to provide education that goes deep into the true needs of specific organizational areas and avoids unnecessary and confusing education that is unlikely to be used in an operating environment.

▲ *Environment specific.* Infusing education with real-life pilots, examples, and data from the client's environment. The availability of real-life examples connects theory and practice and reinforces the feasibility and applicability of improvement.

▲ *Holistic.* Recognizing that all improvement properties are not addressed by the tools alone. Education may be required in soft skills development such as leadership development, teaming fundamentals, team dynamics, change management, project management, cost/benefit analysis, implementation planning, selling, support-building skills, and performance management.

▲ *Participative.* Incorporating hands-on participatory exercises with relevance to real-life issues. This may include waste walks, role playing, and custom-designed simulation exercises. Participants learn how to apply the improvement tools with success and see an immediate connection to their workplace.

▲ *Achievement based.* Educating followed by successful application to a real improvement opportunity, followed by teaching and mentoring others. This was one of the best characteristics of Six Sigma because black belt certification required that candidates demonstrate their new knowledge and expertise through successful completion of a large and successful project.

▲ *Concurrent.* Learning in small doses, immediately applied to a real situation with specific goals and expectations. The objective of concurrent education is to tighten up the "learn-apply-improve-realize success" cycle.

The benefits of incorporating these customization attributes into education and talent development offerings are obvious. The ability to apply, learn from the experiences, acquire new knowledge, coach and mentor others, and continuously strive for professional growth is extremely valuable in terms of developing natural behaviors and a superior cultural code of conduct.

Architecting a Professional Development Center

We mention earlier that a major role of a center of excellence is that it act as the professional and talent development resource for a Lean Business System. This role enables the acquisition of associates' skills and knowledge for personal development, career advancement, and organizational development. When architecting a Lean Business System, this is a good time to think through various professional development options and how best to provide different types of facilitated learning opportunities to the members of the organization. It is also a good time to scan the organization for its current skills inventory and needs. There is a variety of approaches to professional development, including classroom study; mentoring and coaching; individual and teaming implementation experiences; associate shadowing; simulations and participative exercises; self-study; on demand, Internet-based communities of interest; communities of practice; consultation and technical assistance; conferences, professional society participation; formal education (college courses); and many other approaches. The traditional approach of training the masses and mandating compliance is not recommended. A solid professional development strategy integrates a tailored combination of these approaches that is customized to an organization's specific needs and requirements. Another effective approach is just-in-time, achievement-based education in small increments that can be directly applied rather than the plain vanilla, batch-all inclusive workshops. Smaller increments can be structured easily to accommodate specific education and talent development needs, and they are less disruptive than a consecutive five-day workshop. In practice this may include basic essentials offerings, followed by additional intermediate and advanced education based on situational needs. These practices enable associates to accelerate the connection between concepts and execution.

Lean Business System Educational Content

The following discussions present a suggested outline or checklist of educational content in the professional development center role of a center for excellence.

Leadership Development

- ▲ Executive roles in a Lean Business System
- ▲ Change leadership
- ▲ Behavioral alignment and culture change
- ▲ Management and supervisory skills development
- ▲ Mentoring and coaching
- ▲ Organizational infrastructure and key business processes
- ▲ Performance management essentials
- ▲ Basics of financial management and cost
- ▲ Executive coaching and instructor development

(Continues)

▲ Management and peer coaching development

▲ Facilitating communities of excellence

Lean

▲ Basic Lean principles (deeper "how-to" instruction on value stream mapping, pull and kanban methods, one-piece flow, quick changeover analysis, visual management, waste elimination, synchronization, 5S, work cell design, structured gemba walks, A3s, rate-based scheduling, POU stocking/replenishment techniques, five whys, 8 wastes checksheets, etc.)

▲ Kaizen

▲ Toyota Production System (TPS) structure

▲ Theory of constraints (TOC)

▲ Factory physics/production analytics

▲ Training within industry (TWI)

▲ Lean services and transactional process improvement

▲ Transactional stream mapping

▲ Lean product development

▲ Lean supply chain

Six Sigma/Analytics

▲ Basic quality fundamentals

▲ Root-cause problem solving

▲ Basic analytics (graphs and plots, Pareto, checksheets, cause and effect diagrams, FMEAs, sampling plan design, control charts, SIPOC, MSA, C_p & C_{pk})

▲ Intermediate analytics (multi-vari, regression and correlation, hypothesis tests, ANOVA)

▲ Advanced analytics (DOE, Taguchi, EVOP, reliability/MTTF/MTBF, simulation modeling, game theory, risk analysis)

Teaming and Engagement

▲ Standard structured problem solving (e.g., PDCA, DMAIC, SIDAM)

▲ Project management, PMI body of knowledge

▲ Leveraged mentoring, coaching, and facilitation

▲ Team leader development

▲ Principles of high-performance teaming

▲ Group dynamics

▲ Barrier reduction practices

▲ Communication for teams

▲ Understanding X&Y metrics

▲ Packaging and selling improvement

Finance/Accounting

▲ Basics of cost accounting

▲ Baselining current performance

▲ Calculating financial value contribution of improvement (growth, cost reduction, avoidance, cash flow)

▲ Budgeting for improvement

Technology Essentials

▲ ERP architecture fundamentals

▲ Business analytics

▲ Digital visualization

(Continues)

▲ Data warehousing

▲ Technology-enabled improvement

Complex, Nonlinear Improvement (Innovation)

▲ Mind mapping

▲ Affinity diagrams

▲ Freestyle mapping

▲ Worth factor analysis

▲ Prioritization grids

▲ Dialogue mapping

▲ Abstraction factor analysis

▲ Risk analysis

Miscellaneous (On Demand, Need)

▲ Microsoft Office basics

▲ Basic ERP architecture skills, user education (APICS body of knowledge)

▲ Root-cause analysis

▲ Hoshin kanri

▲ Management and supervisory development

▲ Quality, ASQ body of knowledge

▲ Minitab education and quantitative analysis

▲ Compliance and regulatory (FDA, DOD MIL-STD, AHRQ, EPA, OSHA, etc.)

▲ Specialized refresher, reinforcement, and advanced education

This is not an all-inclusive list of concepts by any means, but it provides an effective starting point. Additionally, the list is displayed as is for communication and creativity, and organizations will need to evolve this list of content offerings over time. In practice an organization should give thought to, and *pick and choose* from, the core topics. Then it should customize the content to the organization's requirements and deliver education under the broader name of XYZ business system. For example, an organization may need to develop additional depth around how to implement work cells. There are all types of design options for work cells depending on the characteristics of the manufacturing environment. Work cells can be repetitive, job shop, mixed model, reconfigurable, one-off, universal, adaptive to changes in volume and mix, engineered configurations, virtual, or transactional in nature. The education around this topic should be customized to the intended end use, with real company data and relevant examples.

Avoid Doing It All

One important point related to creating a center of excellence is to allow the offerings to be driven by business requirements and cultural development needs. This seems so obvious, but it is easy to lose sight of these parameters when a group of practitioners begins developing PowerPoint decks for education. Six Sigma certification was notorious for this, taking candidates through four grueling months of statistical engineering techniques. Most black belts will openly admit that they have never needed to use 80 percent of what they learned through the certification process. There is some intrinsic value to "nice to know, nice to have experienced" development, but it wastes valuable limited resources. As our friend *Monsieur Tallpole* points out, a center of excellence should not attempt to do everything provided in the guidelines of this chapter. Organizations that attempt to do it all spread their critical resources too thin, and it becomes difficult to offer services and construct professional development offerings with the levels of excellence they deserve. A center of excellence should focus on the core requirements that can be delivered to the organization with economies of scale. Those working in the center of excellence should consider engaging outside resources for both initial development needs and specialty or advanced development needs that evolve over time. This is not a discrete boilerplate education project but a longer-term collaborative relationship to provide uniform and custom-tailored specialty education and other service needs. Proven external resources can accelerate the design and development of a center of excellence. The goal is to develop talent on demand, build the right mix of development competencies internally, and deliver these development competencies in as much of a distributed and localized means as possible.

A center of excellence is a resource and support center, but it should never become the *doer* center. Responsibility, accountability, and ownership for improvement has not worked well when managers of organizational units can throw their problems over the wall to a detached central organization and then sit in meetings saying that they have a Lean sensei or black belt working on *their* problem. Responsibility, accountability, and ownership for improvement belong within a business unit or department. The center of excellence role is to support talent development and improvement Kata needs throughout the enterprise by integrating the right improvement skills and behavioral competencies throughout the organization.

Coaching and Mentoring

Coaching and mentoring are important competencies in a successful Lean Business System. Yet organizations have viewed these as more of an osmosis skill of improvement or an on-the-job phenomenon. In sports, coaches and players have very well-defined roles, and all are needed for success. The same is true in a Lean Business System. These skills take years of diversified experience to develop and do not come with a black belt or a Lean sensei certificate. Many people in organizations are mentoring teams with a narrow Lean *manufacturing tools* focus, a "one company deep" experience level, undeveloped leadership skills, light business and process knowledge, and a "within industry" perspective. This is in addition to their stretched workloads. These factors combined with constantly changing priorities are often the reason why structured and disciplined improvement becomes either suboptimized or the first casualty. Organizations cannot expect to turn systematic improvement on with weak coaching. Continuous improvement simply does not work that way.

The coaching process itself must be backed up by clearly defined and shared talent development objectives. We are not insinuating long-term goals here but an on-the-spot, clear understanding of what the coach and coachee are trying to accomplish. The other half of coaching is keeping the coachees focused on their initiatives, and also to keep the coachees accountable for results through formal measurement and feedback. Too many organizations have treated coaching and mentoring competency development with much less attention than it deserves. This is a good time to share an executive's quote that has always stuck with me. He said, "You can't just throw a group of people in a room with a little training on a tool, a pad of sticky notes, an easel and markers, and expect them to be a high-performance team." Fact is, all employees can benefit from a higher level of structured and disciplined coaching. One of the best practices of our reference model involves the development of super-coaches. These individuals are highly skilled coaching and mentoring resources who also develop the coaching and mentoring capabilities in organizations. We refer to this as *leveraged mentoring* because these resources have much broader and deeper coaching skills, and they facilitate coaching and mentoring skills within other associates. The whole idea behind Kata is widespread coaching and knowledge sharing.

Leveraged Mentoring

One of the best practices in our Lean Business System Reference Model is called *leveraged mentoring,* an advancement of traditional individual/team coaching and facilitation. The idea behind leveraged mentoring is to accelerate adaptive systematic improvement through a more seasoned and deliberately developed coaching and mentoring resource. Leveraged mentoring includes five important core competencies that accelerate improvement and internal talent development. These include:

1. *Proven continuous improvement implementation expertise.* This includes mentoring on the specific structure, disciplines, and methodologies of improvement (e.g., DMAIC, Kaizen, Lean, TPS, Six Sigma, technology-enabled improvement, etc.). An important factor in this area is the ability to help improvement teams understand opportunities well enough to evaluate various options and make the right data-driven and fact-based recommendations. Improvement teams waste valuable time and resources in their inexperienced journey through some structured problem-solving process with an inexperienced

mentor or trainer limited to the mechanics of the tools themselves. Knowledge and proven expertise of the methodologies and tools are essential, but the more important ability in mentoring is adapting and deploying the right improvement approaches to the highest-impact opportunities. Exposing mentoring and coaching resources to a wide variety of experiences over time is the best way to develop this element of leveraged mentoring.

2. *Business process improvement knowledge.* This includes deep expertise and knowledge of the integrated ERP architecture and key business process knowledge and experience in analyzing and improving these complex, integrated transactional process networks. This includes areas such as supply chain management, new product development, marketing and advertising, IT and software development, distribution and logistics, finance and cash-to-cash management, warranty and returns, sales and operations planning, and other key business processes. This experience is invaluable in mentoring and managing associates and teams to a successful conclusion while understanding the upstream, downstream, and interrelationship impacts on other parts of the organization. In fact, this competency of leveraged mentoring ensures that residual improvements will actually be realized in other process areas. In a Lean Business System the professional, knowledge-based transactional process offers significant opportunities for improvement. These opportunities will never be realized by creating blind–value stream-map wallpaper, a dash of 5S, and confusing terminology. Leveraged mentoring involves adapting the philosophies of improvement to these highly complex integrated process networks.

3. *Knowledge of best practices.* Expertise in the knowledge of best practices also helps to avoid *wheel spinning* and accelerate improvement down a proven positive path. Competitive benchmarking—especially outside of one's own industry—is a great approach to learning more about best practices. Often, the right seasoned outside experts have gained voluminous and continuously evolving knowledge and experiences through working in a variety of organizations. They are familiar with best practices and are often the architects of best practices in other client organizations. Best practice knowledge can also be acquired over time via professional societies or firms that specialize in providing

subscription-based benchmarking data. Today best practices are relative and temporary; the best Lean organizations use benchmarking as a learning channel but adapt and innovate their own best practices. By the time an organization identifies and copies a best practice in this economy, the practice may well be obsolete. As we suggest earlier, find the balance between benchmarking and *execution*.

4. *Multi-industry executive experience.* The most important competency of leveraged mentoring is multi-industry executive leadership and implementation experience. When an organization embarks on developing a true, enterprisewide Lean Business System, there is always the false sense of executive confidence in deciding how best to proceed with the effort. It's the *don't know what we don't know* attribute of improvement at play. Our Lean Business System Reference Model reveals many potential issues and details in adaptive systematic planning. Architects, coaches, and mentors who have successful *experience by doing* from other environments can add significant value to executives and their organizations in terms of powering up the learning curve quickly.

5. *Technology-enabled improvement expertise.* This competency has to do with new and emerging technology that can frame improvement in more of a near real-time mode. We have presented this structured thinking as SIDAM (sense, interpret, decide, act, monitor). It is predicted that 50 percent of the workforce will be virtual in the next 10–20 years. Associates need to become familiar with, and not fear, technology. Data warehousing (a single version of the facts), predictive and preventive business analytics, digital *multilayered* performance dashboards (production, quality, improvements in progress, etc.), virtualization, mobility, cloud technology, data visualization, and so on, will have a significant impact on the speed and quality of improvement in the future. Technology is a huge game changer for a Lean Business System because it transforms the traditional wave (batch), project-based linear waterfall approaches of improvement activities of the past into living, real-time rapid execution improvement.

Embedded in the Lean Business System Reference Model is a philosophy that states, "If you are not improving, then you are falling behind." There is a lot of truth behind this statement. It is a huge challenge to build a culture that can improve systematically and continuously—and autonomously. It is much easier to lose progress when organizations allow their improvement resources to remain in *hit the wall* mode, fail to integrate all potential resources and methodologies of improvement, or push aside improvement altogether for more important priorities.

Leveraged Mentoring Accelerates Kata

Figure 6.1 is an illustration of leveraged mentoring. In practice, improvement activities are nurtured through coaching and mentoring. Frequently, mentors and their mentees *hit the wall* in practice. This is a common condition, and some obstacles cannot be managed solely by an immediate coach. In fact, if an organization is improving without the presence of these larger complex obstacles, then it is leaving many improvement opportunities on the table.

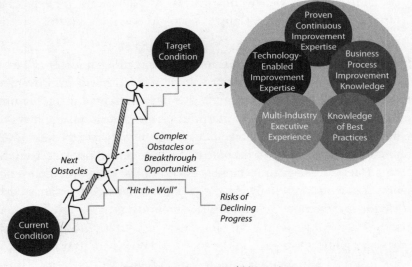

Figure 6.1 Leveraged Mentoring
Copyright © 2015, The Center for Excellence in Operations, Inc.

When improvement hits the wall, a leveling in progress begins to occur. Another condition is an opportunity to introduce breakthroughs in performance through the injections of additional talent and skills beyond the capabilities of an individual coach (e.g., technology-enabled improvement, broader cross-functional improvements, adapting an external best practice, adapting Lean to very complex, nonstandard situations, etc.). Failure to act on these conditions puts improvement in a flatline mode and often leads to a slippery slope of declining progress. Leveraged mentoring views these conditions as new opportunities for improvement through positive intervention. These conditions not only boost improvement, but they act as *mentor the mentor* experiences.

The big plus of leveraged mentoring is that it provides the ability to accelerate an organization's progress with a Lean Business System, not only in sharpening Lean technical skills but particularly in the areas of behavioral alignment and cultural development. We use the words *structured* and *deliberate* throughout the book. These are the differentiators in leveraged mentoring. Coaches and mentors must also improve how they improve through deliberate means and structured talent development.

Another best practice that works well is creating a *community of practice* composed of coaches and mentors in the organization. These resources may meet monthly on a peer review basis and exchange information about their own experiences, successes, and challenges. A community of practice forum is an effective way of *sharpening the saw* of coaches and mentors. The next generation of Lean requires that coaches and mentors expand their bandwidth of knowledge and support. Working within a true, enterprisewide Lean Business System is much more challenging and complex than working just on Lean *manufacturing.* This is not a lessening of Lean manufacturing or TPS as it is an integral part of a Lean Business System. The fundamental purpose of our reference model is to get executives and practitioners thinking about the larger potential of Lean through expanding the existing body of knowledge and evolving Lean to a higher *adaptive systematic improvement* state in all organizations.

A Few Insights from Mark Twain

The collective works of the great Mark Twain teach us many profound lessons about humanity, morality, and courage. One of my personal favorites is *The Damned Human Race*, a collection of essays and topical writings, mainly and most eloquently concerned with the themes of American civilization and social justice. In his wisdom, Twain talks about the behaviors of dogs, cats, birds, and many other animals and then draws comparisons to human beings. He also draws the distinction in morals between these animals and humans in his witty, humorous style. Mark Twain's underlying message is that from birth, animals all understand and assume their natural role in life. Humans on the other hand possess intellectual capacity at birth but are totally unaware of their natural role in life. Humans spend their entire lifetime searching for who they are, who they want to become, and how to evolve this potential into a higher role in life. Mark Twain's wisdom is timeless; therefore, it provides one of many elements of the different kinds of talent development needed today and into the future.

In a Lean Business System this journey is a partnership. One thing with a Lean Business System that must be avoided at all costs is when practitioners and associates gain a defined set of improvement skills and then live out the same routine. If improvement is continuous, then talent development also needs to be continuous. The approach to professional development in our reference model is to become more holistic and driven by business requirements and cultural development needs. The interpretation of Twain's message is that one trains animals because that is what works for animals. One must continuously educate, mentor, and develop the talent, the intellectual capacity, and full potential of people. It is both a moral responsibility and a business requirement to fully develop the intellectual capacity and talent in organizations so that the collective entity reaches new levels of achievement and superior performance over and over again. All organizations are entitled to and must make a profit. The largest opportunity to become best in class is through behavioral alignment, talent development, and cultural evolution.

Acronym Key for Page 187

SPC: statistical process control

IE: industrial engineering

OR: operations research

MTM: methods time measurement

MODAPTS: modular arrangement of predetermined time standards

SIS: short interval scheduling (a *pull* and *TOC* approach)

ZBB: zero-based budgeting

QCC: quality control circle

TQM: total quality management

PDCA: (Deming's) plan-do-check-act cycle

little mrp: material requirements planning

MRPII: manufacturing resource planning

ERP: enterprise resource planning

CEDAC: cause and effects with the addition of cards

GT: group technology

QFD: quality function deployment

TPM: total preventive maintenance

SMED: single minute exchange of die

TOC: theory of constraints

JIT: just in time

PACE: product and cycle time excellence

ME: manufacturing excellence

WCM: world-class manufacturing

QRM: quick response manufacturing

SCOR: supply chain operations reference model

ECR: efficient customer response

BPI: business process improvement

BPR: business process reengineering

BPM: business process management

TPS: Toyota Production System

5S: short-straighten-shine-standardize-sustain

ABC: activity-based costing

4Ms: man-machine-material-methods

3Ms: muda mura muri

OEE: overall equipment effectiveness

VSM: value stream mapping

TRIZ: theory of inventive problem solving

DMAIC: define-measure-analyze-improve-control

Bibliography

Burton, T. T., and Boeder, S. M. 2003. *The Lean Extended Enterprise: Moving Beyond the Four Walls to Value Stream Excellence.* J. Ross Publishing, Ft. Lauderdale, Florida.

Twain, Mark, 1962. *The Damned Human Race.* Hill & Wang Publishing, New York. Originally published in 1905.

CHAPTER 7

Systematic Execution

This chapter discusses the execution subprocess of our Lean Business System Reference Model™. Let's return to our partial list of great organizations: Toyota, Ahrens, Flextronics, Lincoln Electric, Avery Dennison, General Cable, Audi, GE, Harley Davidson, Bosch, Motorola, IBM, BMW, Apple, Deere, Lockheed Martin, Raytheon, Dana, Boeing, Porsche, Johnson Controls, Dell, Visteon, Honda, Daimler Benz, Emerson Electric, Caterpillar, Honeywell, and dozens of other great global organizations. All these organizations have superior competencies and capabilities in execution and superbly get things done. All these organizations know how to systematically expose reality and act on it to their competitive advantage.

Execution is without a doubt, the weakest link in Lean and other continuous improvement initiatives. There are three major factors that detract from successful execution:

1. First, execution is seen as the tactical side of Lean that executives need not be involved with. Execution is delegated to practitioners and associates while executives focus on more *perceived to be* important issues. Their actions make execution a less *perceived to be* priority for practitioners and associates. It is difficult to implement systematic improvement while firefighting because the two are often at cross purposes.

2. Second, execution of Lean has been focused on training and implementing TPS tools, in the absence of a logical plan that solves specific problems for specific reasons. Reconfiguring equipment into cells, hanging up production boards, value stream mapping, or implementing a pull system are the *means*. In many of these situations the problem is unclear and has not been calibrated with data and facts. Execution lacks a purpose, a plan, clear goals and outcomes, focus, authority, and accountability. The results of Lean are transparent to

customers and illusive to executives. Criticism over the gap between expectations and actual results stimulates more change, but what kind of change? No one really knows—*they don't know what they don't know*—but they change anyway. A Lean Business System is an oxymoron in these environments.

3. Third, execution is attempted with a weak infrastructure. Planning and implementation management are often very fuzzy, so there are many versions of Lean and many ideas about what is going to change. Communication is not well planned with a consistent and repetitive message. Education is generic, narrow, and focused on a limited set of tools for the production floor. Team leadership, coaching, and mentoring are weak, so it becomes difficult for organizations to turn Lean strategy and principles into concrete executable steps on a path to success. Execution is a confusing free-for-all of principles and tools going in many different directions. Lean becomes a lengthy, drawn-out process with questionable commitment, poor results, and a confused organization.

When organizations fail at Lean, the old excuses get dragged out: lack of leadership commitment, poor implementation strategy, scope and magnitude issues, wrong projects, insufficient education, conflicts with other day-to-day priorities, wrong metrics, serious customer issues, lack of executive and process owner support, lack of employee acceptance, short-term financials focus, Japan versus U.S. culture, complexity and differences of the business, lack of time to improve and perform regular real jobs, workforce skill limitations, and several other excuses. What happened? Either the executives misjudged and misguided the Lean philosophy, principles, and methodologies (Lean strategy), or the organization is not capable of implementing and sustaining Lean successfully (Lean execution), or both. It is usually both. Without strategy and planning, execution becomes an *Alice in Wonderland* trip—"If you don't know where you're going, any path will take you there." Without strong execution, a Lean Business System is a mirage. Learning adds no value, people become confused and cannot engage properly, and Lean stops dead in its tracks. Lean without execution and success is change for the worse, because failure drains energy and enthusiasm from the organization. The repeated failure of Lean and all the improvement programs that preceded it destroy the interest and potential for future improvement initiatives.

Structured Means and Deliberate Actions

Execution is a systematic set of behaviors, disciplines, and techniques in a Lean Business System that translates plans into the right deliberate actions that deliver the desired results of improvement. It is not limited to a Lean Business System; it is a competency that must be built into the organization's strategy, goals, and culture. Executives must be directly engaged in execution, and it must be practiced uniformly by all leaders at all levels of the organization. Execution requires much more than teaching and implementing tools and putting one's faith in employee involvement and empowerment. Execution in a true Lean Business System is proactive, where leaders are always searching out problems and barriers, synchronizing plans and actions, asking tough questions about milestones and timing, verifying where the improvements will come from, checking that the right people are involved, clarifying accountability and expectations, looking for places where coaching help is needed, and paying attention to other details that influence the achievement of successful results.

The architecture of the Lean Business System Reference Model demonstrates the systematic nature of execution. In the model it is highly integrated into strategy, improvement planning, change management, and performance management. The executive core team is engaged in the improvement activity details of the organization's major improvement themes. Team leaders and process owners are engaged in execution monitoring. We share a simple green-yellow-red execution chart used to track progress later in the chapter. However, the discipline of execution goes much deeper in our reference model. Execution as a stand-alone activity is called *firefighting*. In our reference model execution is a systematic process of rigorously discussing the *what, why, when, where, who,* and *how* of a Lean Business System at a lower level of detail as reality is exposed. Since execution is integrated into the Lean Business System architecture, there are mechanisms for adjusting assumptions and tactics as business requirements change, keeping adaptive systematic improvement well aligned with strategic and operating needs. There is a continuous "closed-looping" between execution and all other subprocesses in our reference model architecture. Communication and talent development are of the utmost importance in a Lean Business System. Success with Lean is a direct function of how effective associates communicate and work with each other as a cultural norm. Adaptive Leadership creates this environment for success by putting a Lean Business System architecture that incorporates the processes, practices, and cultural development needs in order to develop a strong execution competency. Widespread coaching is an important element in execution. This is more than the old vanilla facilitation process. It involves knowing enough about the business and the process to ask the right questions of improvement teams and keep them on the right path to rapid deployment and rapid results. At the same time, coaching develops the behavioral side of improvement through personal associate observations and feedback about internalizing change. Finally, organizations must integrate execution into their recognition and reward systems. Changing culture involves positive recognition and gainsharing to develop and reinforce a strong execution culture. (Gainsharing is a system of management used by a business to increase profitability by motivating employees to improve their performance through involvement and participation. As their performance improves, employees share financially in the gain [improvement]. Gainsharing's goal is to improve performance and eliminate waste [time, energy, and materials] by motivating employees to work smarter as a team rather than just working harder. Gainsharing should not be confused with profit sharing. There are many differences between gainsharing and profit sharing. Gainsharing is also called "gain sharing, gainshare, and gain share." It could also be called "savings sharing." In other words, a company shares with employees the savings from improved performance.)

There are several other essential requirements and practices needed to develop a strong Lean execution competency in organizations. We introduce these in the next sections.

Best Practices in Execution

The Lean Business System Reference Model (and particularly the execution subsystem) incorporates several best practice concepts. They serve as a checklist for evaluating the effectiveness of execution in organizations. Like all other elements of the reference model, the purpose is to stimulate thinking for the design, architecture, and implementation of (your own) XYZ Lean business system. Figure 7.1 provides an overview of execution best practices. They are in a conceptual state and require specific customization and detailing for an organization's specific business requirements and cultural development needs. The following sections provide more guidance about these execution best practices.

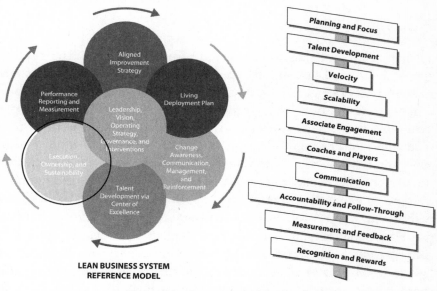

Figure 7.1   Execution Best Practices
Copyright © 2015, The Center for Excellence in Operations, Inc.

Planning and Focus

Execution is most efficient when there is a well-thought-out and scoped plan for improvement. In Chapter 4 we cover the living deployment plan subprocess of our reference model. This element details the what, why, when, where, who, and how of improvement. It defines and scopes improvement activities where there is no question about the problem, objectives and scope, baseline performance, improvement goal, anticipated benefits, milestones and expectations, and a get-started plan. This subprocess also ensures that there is prioritization and alignment, and a controlled release of activity based on the capacity and capability of teams and associates to execute the plan. It provides focus through the planning process. Living deployment planning creates the clarity and focus that makes execution effective (doing the right things) and efficient (right the first time). Many of the barriers and resistance issues are dealt with and resolved up front in the planning process; therefore, they do not show up as unanticipated surprises during execution. Planning and focus enable rapid deployment and rapid results, which in turn influence culture positively by putting associates in low-risk, winning situations.

Talent Development

Talent development is discussed in Chapter 6 in connection with how to create a center of excellence and all its competency services including education and talent development strategies. This point is really simple: Organizations cannot execute with the wrong people in the wrong places, or with people lacking talent and/or fearing change. The center of excellence provides a solid foundation for execution via thought leadership, technical improvement applications knowledge, education and talent development, implementation support, benchmarking and best practices information, and uniform integration of the Lean Business System across the enterprise. Talent development encourages open dialogue between teams and associates relative to present experiences and lessons learned that can be leveraged to the max across various business units and other key processes. No Lean Business System begins with an abundance of talent to make it successful from the start. There are too many unknowns, and therefore talent development must become a continuous process of growing people skills and capabilities based on emerging business needs. Other less popular aspects of talent development are talent outplacement and talent acquisition. Organizations need to maintain the right mix of current skills and encourage low performers to find a more compatible career situation. This is a common routine in large organizations seeking to develop their talent base with the right mix of skills and capabilities. This practice is much needed in talent development because it has positive or negative influences on execution.

Velocity

Velocity is really related to planning and focus. Executives are eager to achieve results in this economy, and they have a low tolerance for another long-term, top-down improvement program. Much of the proven methodologies throughout this book were spawned from executive discussions about expediency. I have met with many executives who said something similar to, "I know about Lean, I've read about the tools and what it takes to be successful. I have read several case studies. But we're not Toyota. Is there something that we can do that is more simplified and streamlined but that will produce the same dramatic results?" I thank these executives because they threw down a gauntlet. They put the challenge out there to *improve how we improve.* I admire Toyota and am a big proponent of the Toyota Production System. But I have found that the principles and tools are not enough. Improvement requires creativity and innovation and development of reusable methodologies and analytics of improvement. My point here is that many of the elements of our reference model will facilitate velocity in execution. However, often (especially in the professional transactional process areas) one must step out of the box and achieve velocity through more customized approaches to improvement. The most senior architects of a Lean Business System can be very helpful if this becomes the chosen method of improvement. Velocity is important in execution. Organizations cannot afford to let their valuable and limited resources flounder for too long. People lose interest, results are either delayed or missed completely, and it becomes an overall bad experience that impacts behaviors and culture negatively.

Scalability

Scalability is about planning and organizing improvement activities so that they can be rapidly executed and then scaled to other potential improvement opportunities or moved to other business units and/or functional areas. We have had great success with this concept in multiplant and multisite business units and divisions with very similar issues and processes. When the subprocesses of our reference model are working synchronously, scalability and fast execution are very achievable. Later in this chapter we introduce our Scalable Improvement Methodology™, an adaptive practice using Pareto thinking to target a Lean Business System at the highest impact opportunities while aligning talent development efforts on the same opportunities. A large part of scalability is synchronization and a laser-targeted focus. The positive impact on execution is leverage: creating the opportunity to achieve even more with less at a quicker pace.

Associate Engagement

Execution in a Lean Business System requires widespread involvement of the organization. But it goes further than involvement or bringing a group of people together. And for leaders it means much more than a ritual gemba walk to check up on people and their issues. People need to understand the challenges and their roles in execution. Communication, planning, structure, and discipline all play a major role in the associate engagement part of execution. Execution is the ideal time to develop and bring out the best in people by coaching, mentoring, asking the right questions, and encouraging discussions—not barking orders. Leaders can do this casually with some success. But changing culture requires *pulling* people into execution emotionally, providing the authority to act, and the accountability for results. Organizations cannot command great execution; it is a cultural competency developed over time. Execution happens through a strong coalition of people focused on the same goals. Of course they can't do this in a vacuum. This is where strong execution leadership and the other elements of our reference model help associates to experience the victory of success, change individual behaviors, and develop a culture of excellence.

Coaches and Players

Coaches and players are another important aspect of execution. Coaching and mentoring are necessities for an associate's personal and professional growth. Education just by itself does not cut it in a precise Lean Business System. Coaching and leveraged mentoring bridge the gap between conceptual learning and learning by doing. When we talk about associate engagement above, one must recognize that organizations cannot really engage associates without coaching and mentoring. This is a big discovery of Toyota Kata, and it is common sense. A true Lean Business System deals with a wide spectrum of improvement issues ranging from simple to very complex. Also, because we are dealing with cross-enterprise processes, it requires a portfolio of the right skill sets and competencies in the right places at the right times. The player side of this concept insinuates real first-string players— playing from the heart—not just dressing for the game or occupying a seat on the bench. High-performance execution requires engagement of the organization's top performers. At the same time it involves adding deeper bench strength through talent development. One mistake organizations tend to make is always calling upon the same champion employees because management is comfortable that they can get things done. The problem is that executives overlook that they have called on their champions for a dozen assignments (in addition to their normal work). Even the best champions can become overloaded and ineffective if their time and efforts are not managed. This is even more reason to focus on developing more first-string players. Regarding the undesirable players, don't immediately exclude them—listen to their story; they all have one. I have personally coached several second- and third-string players who everyone had previously written off. Sometimes these people have been beaten down by previous management and have lost all confidence. They need coaching and a voice that helps them to recover their confidence and sense of belonging. I have developed several of these so-called undesirables into the champions of Lean. Some of these folks may not be salvageable, but do not base your decisions on historical perceptions and opinions: Coach, and then decide. Again, several elements of our reference model aid in this aspect of execution.

Communication

We cover communication in great detail in Chapter 5. The point here is that associates need a clear understanding of the objectives and their role in improvement. At the point of execution, people shouldn't be wondering what problem they are solving or what their objectives and expectations are relative to an improvement activity. On the associate side of things, they should always be encouraged to speak freely and speak their mind. There is no room for formality and one's relative position in the organiza-tional hierarchy when it comes to communication. Everyone has a voice, and it is leadership's job to engage those voices. Leave the formal one-sided PowerPoint presentations behind and use the less formal on-the-spot A3 thinking. Frequent positive dialogues during execution energizes people and boosts self-confidence, optimism, and ownership. Effective two-way communication exposes reality. It will without a doubt make people tempo-rarily uncomfortable, but they get used to working through uncertainty and become stronger implementation resources. Organizations cannot fix their problems if they don't know what they are or deny that they have them.

Effective, consistent, repeatable communication throughout the organization smoothes the path of execution—for technical content and a behavioral and cultural content.

Accountability and Follow-Through

Accountability for results is critical to the success of execution. This involves more than a hollow statement. People must be very clear about their objectives for improvement and the expected outcomes. We have not mentioned it in the book but the Lean Business System Reference Model uses a chartering process up front in the living deployment plan. No, it's not the lengthy Six Sigma project charters of the past. It is a very simple but precise process of sitting people down and going through the details of a planned improvement activity. It is at this point that the expectations and accountability for results are initially communicated and agreed to by all. Then all relevant information is added to a customized A3 template and used through the implementation. People act very differently when they are keeping their own score and are directly in charge of determining what the score should be. Here is an example: For one client a digital performance dashboard was developed and placed in the center of a cell. The dashboard was a collaborative design of the Lean crew and the cell employees. It included three panels: one for performance to the rate schedule, a second for quality performance and defects, and a third as a workmanship troubleshooting reference. Everything was maintained by the cell. Management always made comments about how perfect the cell operated. Fact is, the cell experienced productivity and quality issues every day. Who do you think was watching the dashboard first? Who was making the right corrective actions before anyone else noticed? That's accountability in execution.

Measurement and Feedback

Execution requires constant closed-loop feedback for evaluating the effectiveness of activities. Performance metrics are the formal part of this concept. Today through technology and business analytics, it is possible to measure performance in near real-time mode. One needs to be careful with the use, interpretation, and response of near real-time feedback. A mechanic, for example, can introduce process shifts and more variation by constantly making adjustments based on immediate conditions. If one is looking at making changes to the Internet orders process, this is less likely to occur. Feedback is the other component of this concept. This goes back to two-way communication. Feedback is multidirectional and is a necessary part of execution. When everyone has a shared story of what is going on, execution has fewer surprises. Feedback can be hard variables data or attribute data based on some evidence. Measurement and feedback develop a data-driven and fact-based culture of improvement.

Recognition and Rewards

The final component of execution is recognition and rewards. Recognizing and rewarding employee contributions and accomplishments are an important part of creating a Lean Business System culture. When employees know that their efforts are appreciated, it increases their self-esteem and satisfaction with Lean and continuous improvement. Recognition and rewards go a long way toward changing behaviors and developing a stronger culture of excellence. Keep in mind that different employees will respond to different types of rewards. Some employees, for example, respond better to rewards with financial value. While we cannot cover sharing profits in detail, it is worth mentioning. For many employees, the value of a reward is not as important as the fact that they know that their contributions are valued. Organizations have found numerous creative ways to recognize and reward their employees for incremental value contributions to improvement.

The Lean Business System Reference Model is an integrated architecture of subprocesses and practice that brings all the critical success factors together. It should be obvious by now that the reference model is an interconnected framework, the parts of which cannot be separated if success is to be achieved. When the reference model is firing on all cylinders, the architecture and its subprocesses are enabling each other's success, thus creating a big bang effect for improvement. A true Lean Business System *is* a big bang improvement over the various initiatives and programs of the past.

A Structured Uniform Language of Improvement

The Lean Business System Reference Model promotes the use of a standard protocol for problem solving. A standard structured protocol for problem solving creates a shared language and approach to improvement and builds disciplined, repeatable, and scientific behaviors into an organization's culture (Kata). Deming introduced us to his PDCA (plan-do-check-act) cycle, and many organizations have adapted their own variations of this disciplined cycle of continuous improvement. DMAIC (define-measure-analyze-improve-control) was popularized by the recent Six Sigma approach to improvement. Earlier in the book we introduced SIDAM (sense-interpret-decide-act-monitor) which was born out of our collaborative work with SAP on the adaptive enterprise relative to technology-enabled, near real-time improvement. Regardless of the acronym, these protocols (when deployed correctly) direct people to understand, calibrate, and solve *real* business problems and find *real* improvement opportunities with the right principles, methodologies, and tools. The tools are part of the protocol and an important *means* of success. The absence of a protocol leads to informal and scattered symptomatic improvement with tools. The important point here is that structured problem solving works best with a universal language and standardized approach. This requirement goes hand in hand with the precision of adaptive systematic improvement.

PDCA? DMAIC? SIDAM?

Many organizations continue to use Deming's PDCA cycle in their Lean initiatives. The benefit of PDCA is that it provides a structured methodology and common thought process about improvement. In practice, PDCA is usually used in a team environment where much of the results tend to be *compensating improvements* based on brainstorming around group experiences and perceptions. This is fine for the more obvious "low-hanging-fruit" opportunities. In our practice we noticed a real boost in Lean results when we adapted Lean Six Sigma (integrated Lean and Six Sigma) back in 2001. We treated Lean and waste reduction as the primary focus but added the powerful analytics of Six Sigma to the approach. We also standardized on Six Sigma's DMAIC problem-solving structure because it provides a data-driven and fact-based structure and gatekeeping process of improvement with formal and deliberate checkpoints. We believed that it would impact culture by developing a more structured, analytical, data-driven, and evidence-based problem-solving way of thinking, and it has worked very effectively at influencing behaviors in this direction. These decisions significantly improved the design, flexibility, predictive and preventive actions, and results of Lean with our clients.

The specific elements of each DMAIC phase are not all used all of the time, but they exist for practical application when their use is warranted. In the case of an atlas, not every page of the atlas is used for every trip. The pages used depend on the destination in mind. Likewise in DMAIC, the specific steps and tools applied depend on the specifics of the particular problem. In addition, similar to taking a trip, the secret to completing the journey successfully is first to understand where it is you want to go (*define*). Once the starting point is established, it becomes critical to characterize the problem and the process (*measure*). At this point, improvement teams define potential root-cause diagrams, value stream mapping, and other analyses that quantify the current process and its associated baseline performance.

Moving further into the DMAIC process, teams perform root-cause analyses and other analytics to diagnose and analyze the current process (*analyze*). At this point, the problem is better defined and understood than ever before. The onion has been peeled back, and the true root causes are known and calibrated. Next is the point at which improvement alternatives and options are evaluated (*improve*), and the best improvement course of action is decided on by the team. Finally are the implementation of recommendations (*control*) and the handoff to process owners.

The DMAIC process is logical and is the lifeline of strategic improvement. Unfortunately, DMAIC and structured root-cause problem solving are the first casualty in times of crisis. It takes strong, unwavering, and seasoned leadership to take DMAIC from a novel concept for a few teams to an accepted standard of behavior in organizations. Some criticize DMAIC for its linear, waterfall approach to problem solving. This is not a problem of DMAIC; it is a problem of an inexperienced improvement practitioner trying to fit every problem into the standard recipe (like stand-alone TPS principles and tools). DMAIC is not a simple recipe, and it should not be followed blindly for every improvement opportunity in every functional area of the enterprise.

DMAIC has become our protocol of choice because we have experienced success evolving client cultures to a very disciplined, repeatable, and fact-based way of thinking about and solving problems. Remember that the content of this book is providing a reference model, and in that regard an organization can adapt PDCA, DMAIC, SIDAM, or whatever acronym best fits its own (deliberately designed) standard problem-solving protocol as long as it helps to develop the right thinking, patterns of behavior, and culture in a true Lean Business System.

Wicked Problem Solving

There are serious limitations to mandating DMAIC or any other improvement methodology across the board in organizations. Adaptive systematic improvement recognizes this fact. The experienced Lean Business System architect and practitioners recognize and adapt many implementation factors outside the standard DMAIC process (e.g., nonlinear problem solving). Many of the more high-complexity/high-impact improvement opportunities in organizations, particularly the technology-related projects, are about dealing with what is referred to as *wicked problems*. These challenges are typically characterized by significant ambiguity and uncertainty, no single correct and fixed definition of the problem, multiple views of the problem with conflicting solutions, lack of information, different participants with different motivations, multiple connections to other problems, and a situation-based workable solution rather than *the* permanent solution to a problem. Some examples of these complex improvement opportunities include research and development (R&D), technology development, concept engineering of new products, software development, advertising and promotional effectiveness, and global product development and commercialization. The common thread is innovation and many unknowns. Indeed, it is this *social complexity* of these problems, not their technical complexity, that overwhelms most current problem-solving and project management approaches. At a philosophical level, DMAIC *thinking* (not the rigid linear structure) can also be applied to these totally nonlinear creative and innovative process improvements. We have used what we refer to as a *randomized DMAIC* facilitation process (e.g., IDAMIDCIDMA) using the nonlinear problem-solving methodologies. The fundamental link in these situations is fact-based, data-driven root-cause analysis (without locking creativity and innovation in a box), which actually enables more effective levels of creativity and innovation. Once innovation is translated into a more well-defined development project, DMAIC *thinking* is very relevant to this process.

Scalable Improvement Methodology™

A large element of waste in the traditional approaches to continuous improvement is that people end up either forgetting, or wind up applying much less of the content that was covered through the expensive and exhaustive education and certification processes. This type of batch education and development is obsolete. In today's economy there exists an urgent need for rapid identification of high-impact opportunities followed up by rapid deployment of solutions and rapid results. If executives and practitioners follow Monsieur Tallpole's advice and apply Pareto thinking to the design of their Lean Business System architectures, there are some very interesting (but not necessarily surprising) conclusions:

▲ 20 percent of the improvement opportunities yields 80 percent of the benefits.

▲ 20 percent of the wide array of improvement methodologies and tools are used to achieve 80 percent of the benefits.

▲ 20 percent of the organization becomes the outstanding champions for improvement, and attempting to make this 100 percent is a game of diminishing returns.

▲ 20 percent of the supply base creates 80 percent of the sourcing and procurement issues.

The traditional top-down, executive-mandated, train-the-masses model of improvement force-fits organizations and their cultures to a rigid, one-size-fits-all recipe with its very stringent compliant processes and boilerplate education. It is the shotgun approach to improvement, hoping that something sticks. Historically we all know how much overhead, cost, time, and resources it takes to keep these improvement programs alive before they eventually fizzle away. Dozens of fad programs have passed through this model of improvement with their respective birth-death cycles during the past decades, and then organizations slide back into their inefficient norms. The real issue is that organizations do not take the time and effort to think through how best to architect their Lean and other continuous improvement initiatives. The traditional model has identified business issues based on perception and opinions (not through a rigorous diagnostic and vital signs check). Then widespread improvement is delivered, and the improvement initiative becomes more of a wish and hope exercise rather than a precise architecture plan.

Figure 7.2 provides an overview of the Scalable Improvement Methodology™. This is the integration of planning and deployment with education and talent development. The purpose of this methodology is to guide the Lean Business System architecture, while simplifying and laser-targeting the planning, deployment, talent development, execution, and sustainability. Scalable Improvement Methodology is a best practice in the Lean Business System Reference Model.

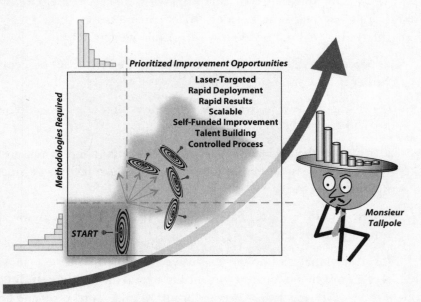

Figure 7.2   Scalable Improvement Methodology™
Copyright © 2015, The Center for Excellence in Operations, Inc.

This methodology is a more adaptive "middle out" model of improvement. Our Scalable Improvement Methodology *adapts the process of improvement* to the organization, its culture, and mission-critical success factors. It's all about defining the organization's 80/20 sweet spot of opportunities and then navigating through the barriers to success while developing very laser-targeted plans, internal talent, and "internalized" participation and momentum. This approach evolves Lean to a cultural standard of excellence in how people think and work. Scalable

Improvement Methodology is a laser-targeted, rapid deployment, and rapid results model that eliminates all of the non-value-added waste in traditional approaches to improvement—the wastes and overhead in prior improvement programs that kill improvement initiatives and make it nearly impossible to keep the word "continuous" in continuous improvement.

This is very different from the scattered, "improvement for improvement's sake" approach of traditional improvement programs. Scalable Improvement Methodology is a "low-risk, surgical, high ROI, bull's-eye" approach to improvement. The strategy behind Scalable Improvement Methodology is to ensure that a Lean Business System is a solid investment in the right mission-critical areas with a significant ROI, and not a sunk cost or another fad, check-the-box program.

"Scalable" implies a living cycle of targeting highest-impact improvements and then developing improvement talent in small increments giving people just what they need at the right times to achieve success, and then repeating the cycle at a higher order of learning. The methodology is also designed to position organizations quickly in a self-funding mode with their strategic improvement initiatives.

Is Lean or Six Sigma certification no longer recommended? Of course not. Scalable Improvement Methodology views certifications as a longer-term professional development endeavor based on demonstrated achievements and successes rather than a prerequisite to improvement. The methodology promotes rapid injections of new knowledge followed by engagement in a never-ending cycle of professional development and growth. By the time individuals become certified, they are much more technically qualified and experienced through several improvement initiatives, and they are also much more likely to develop into super-champions and super-coaches. Let's face it, the traditional approaches to improvement are irrelevant in this challenging economy. What do organizations do when their processes are not working? They improve their processes. Scalable Improvement Methodology is a best practice in our reference model because it represents an improvement to the overall process of how improvement is designed, architected, implemented, and sustained with a high impact and a high ROI. The other aspect is that Scalable Improvement Methodology structures specific improvement activities to the quick response realities that executives find themselves in today.

Green-Yellow- Red Execution Grid

One of the templates in the Scalable Improvement Methodology is called a *green-yellow-red execution grid*. This is a very simple visual display of the status of improvement activities in process across two dimensions: execution and behavioral development. The grid is not an exact science but a helpful guide in terms of allocating mentoring and coaching resources to the right teams and improvement initiatives. The objective is to mentor and coach teams and improvement initiatives toward the northeast corner of the grid (see Figure 7.3). As shown, the progress is interpreted in the following manner:

▲ Red-Red: Low execution and behavioral development progress. These are typically teams and initiatives that are wheel spinning and require extensive attention, mentoring, and coaching support.

▲ Yellow-Red: Average execution progress and low behavioral development progress. These teams and initiatives require constant mentoring and coaching to push them in the northeast direction on the grid.

▲ Green-Red: Great execution progress but the entire team is not engaged. These teams and initiatives require extensive mentoring and coaching.

▲ Yellow-Yellow: Average execution and behavioral development. Requires a lesser degree of mentoring and coaching but these teams and initiatives should be monitored closely.

▲ Red-Yellow: A team is working well together and advancing their behavioral skills but not making much progress with execution. These teams and initiatives require extensive mentoring and coaching.

▲ Green-Yellow: Great execution but need more behavioral development mentoring and coaching.

▲ Green-Green: These teams and initiatives are making great execution and behavioral development progress. They require a minimum level of "check-in" mentoring and coaching.

The grid can present the status of larger Lean improvement activities, and it is used at a departmental level for Kaizen events. The executive core team uses the grid containing the larger, complex, higher-involvement improvement activities in its weekly reviews. The team also reviews the grid for localized Kaizen events. For the quick Kaizen events, the grid is not used because the administrative task might take longer than the Kaizen event. However, the Kaizen results are captured on the local MicroCharter so that the benefits and other details can be consolidated organizationally. The grid not only displays status, but it also provides insight about what interventions and coaching are required to move these activities to a successful status. During the week there is a healthy amount of dialogue and communication in the gemba through coaches, mentors, team leaders, and other executives. The grid is updated weekly by the executive core team leader with help from other executives, coaches and mentors, process owners, managers, and supervisors. The updates are not an exact science but are based on known, existing conditions of each improvement activity. It is posted visibly on the appropriate performance dashboards (*digitally* is the preference). Figure 7.3 provides a picture of the grid.

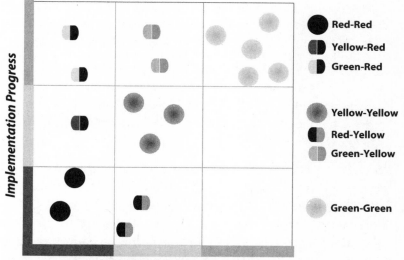

Figure 7.3   Green-Yellow-Red Execution Grid
Copyright © 2015, The Center for Excellence in Operations, Inc.

The green-yellow-red execution grid may appear to be complicated, but it is a simple template in practice. Here is how the executive core team, business improvement leaders, managers, and supervisors interpret the template:

▲ *Green:* This is the space where one would like all improvement activities to be. Teams in this space are progressing well with their improvement activities, and they are acting as high-performance teams. People are emotionally invested, and they are developing professionally from their experiences. A quick coach check-in is adequate for these activities.

▲ *Yellow:* Teams have made some progress but are struggling. Usually there is some type of barrier, and the team is working cohesively through it. Mentoring is needed—maybe technical or political—to help these activities progress to the green space.

▲ *Red:* This is the danger zone. Teams may have formed, but there is total confusion and complete disagreement among associates. It may be a definition and scoping issue, a communication issue, or a personality clash of associates. Nevertheless these situations need to be turned around quickly or things will become much worse— and difficult to turn around. A large, continuing amount of technical and behavioral mentoring is needed until progress and continuity of behaviors are visible.

▲ *Yellow-red:* This space of the grid represents improvement activities and associates that are making some progress but are a dysfunctional team. They need technical coaching and mentoring to improve their progress, but they need more behavioral alignment and group dynamics help to become a more cohesive team.

▲ *Red-yellow:* In this space, the improvement activities have not made much progress, but the associates are beginning to function as a cohesive team. Allowing associates to remain in this stuck mode will result in no implementation progress and will eventually frustrate associates. These activities require coaching and mentoring on both: more on technical implementation progress, a little less on behavioral alignment.

There are nine sectors in the grid. In practice, improvement activities fall into only five of the nine sectors. It is not impossible but it is very rare that improvement activities are great at implementation progress with a totally dysfunctional group of associates—or that wonderful behavioral alignment and culture change occurs through failed assignments. Furthermore, it is difficult to advance into the next respective levels with either of these existing conditions.

Complete the C in DMAIC

The *C* in DMAIC, which stands for control, is the most important phase of the DMAIC cycle. It is also the most important component of the execution infrastructure. This is the actual point of implementation, the realization of improvement, and process owner handoff for sustainability. Over the past several years, we have observed some organizations that make their way through the DMAI phases of their Lean Six Sigma assignments and then fall down on *C*. It almost appears as if their continuous improvement efforts end with the PowerPoint presentation of *what they are going to do*. Again, whether an organization chooses to use DMAIC, PDCA, or some other acronym for its structured problem-solving protocol, the last step and its content are always the same. In other words, Items 1 through 6 are best practices in the Lean Business System Reference Model.

In the case of DMAIC, control includes the following six major elements:

1. *Validation of improvement:* This element verifies that the recommended actions have actually improved the process. For some organizations, their approach is sufficient if someone says, "Oh yeah, things are much better now." That is simply not good enough. Validation occurs through measurement of the key process metrics before and after the changes. Sometimes, validation is achieved by positive and negative replication of results (shifts back and forth from old to new processes, demonstrating oscillations in performance). Improvement should be demonstrated by a positive movement in the metrics. Finally, the benefits derived from improvement must be validated by the financial organization.

2. *Sustaining measurement systems:* This element defines performance ownership, which metrics will be monitored by the process owner, corrective action guidelines for slippage in improvement, periodic audit and validation plans, and integration into the overall performance measurement process. This includes tracking of both primary metrics and critical root-cause metrics, and practices to expose and prioritize ongoing root cause of problems.

3. *Process owner transition:* This element includes all activities that must take place (e.g., new procedures, checklists, templates, visuals, education, IT modifications, knowledge transfer, etc.) to transfer ownership of the improvement initiative to the process owner and his or her organization. This element addresses all questions related to transfer and continuation of improvement, dismantling of an improvement team, and freeing up resources for new improvement initiatives. Process owner transition includes both the hard process improvement details and the behavioral alignment issues of improvement and change.

4. *New improvement opportunities:* This element has to do with defining additional improvement opportunities that are either directly or indirectly related to the current improvement project. The team members are in a great position to comment on further improvements from their existing assignments or other unrelated observed opportunities that may inhibit further improvements. These ideas go into the hopper for future consideration relative to the existing content of planned improvement projects. Some of these may also go directly to a functional manager or supervisor for additional Kaizen events. The other piece of this element is asking each team member to identify and commit to an independent improvement activity in his or her immediate area, using the methodology and knowledge gained in the team assignment.

5. *Knowledge repository:* This element is twofold. First, the executive core team officially closes the larger improvement activities in a formal team meeting. The purpose of this meeting is to capture any additional lessons learned firsthand and integrate them into the overall Lean Business System planning process. Second, the executive deployment team must build a formal approach to archive the knowledge, experiences, analyses, and other relevant information for future reference. This repository of knowledge is available and accessible for future improvement activities as both living and learning references and to reduce redundancy in improvements (e.g., using value stream maps, analytics, or FMEAs [failure mode and effects analyses] from previous improvement activities). One bit of caution here is that things change. One should use the repository as a reference; using and updating previous analyses is fine if conditions have not changed.

6. *Celebration:* The final element of control is celebration, which incorporates much more than a few token pats on the back for the team members. One important aspect of celebration is organizational reinforcement through the showcasing of success. The other aspect is recognition and reward for the team and extended participants. Celebration must also become a deliberate formal process because this is an opportunity to leverage successes and expand the behavioral alignment beyond the direct participants of an improvement activity.

Control is the most critical part of DMAIC. Treating the tasks of control casually and haphazardly is a sure way to fail at improvement. In the short term, process owners and their people will have difficulty repeating and sustaining the results of the team, and they will slide back into business as usual when leadership becomes focused on another issue. In the long term, the right Lean business improvement architecture and its subprocesses are not in place to sustain gains and improve the process further. The consequence of wavering leadership and lack of sustaining infrastructure is that there will be a gradual backslide in gains until people are back to their routines as they existed before improvement. The journey of improvement is difficult because people are only human and are susceptible to human error and variations in consistency, perceived expectations, and performance.

Expand the Thoughtware in Lean Thinking

What is "thoughtware" in Lean thinking? It is the patterns of thinking and behaviors that enable people to observe, anticipate, prevent, or proactively deal with expected deviations from the norm. Thoughtware is the basis of Kata. The famous Murphy's Law that "anything that can go wrong, will go wrong," is inevitably met in every journey of Lean execution. The differentiator is in how one thinks, faces, and acts in these situations. In today's competitive universe, organizations must execute with the thinking like there are no second chances, failure is not an option, no improvement left behind. The Lean Business System Reference Model and the execution subsystem enables executives and their organizations to mitigate or outright avoid these missteps, mishaps, and mistakes that often cause costly and failed outcomes of many Lean initiatives. Unknown is not always bad; in fact, it is these unknown opportunities that often create the most value contribution and competitive advantage from Lean. Some additional behavior best practices of execution include:

▲ Confirm stakeholder engagement through constant dialogue, outreach, and communicating the facts. In a Lean Business System environment, organizations make sure that everyone involved has a clear and current understanding of the challenges in execution. Always present the current facts. Never hide or postpone the communication of problems or make and present opinions and assumptions—it's the mother of poor execution.

▲ Identify and escalate risks and barriers early on. In a Lean Business System organizations cannot execute by *hiding the bacon*. Execution fails when organizations make believe that bad performance is good or acceptable performance, or when they procrastinate or postpone dealing with potential and real showstoppers. Organizations that communicate these situations and assign responsibility for mitigating risks and preventing potential barriers are usually great at execution.

▲ Think through things that can go wrong. We call these TGWs. Map out the risks of certain unplanned, unexpected, or unforeseen events and their repercussions. Develop a plan to either head off or manage these risks. Lean is very simple in the planning, education, and analysis stages because nothing has changed yet. Execution is the *reality moment* stage where people suddenly realize that change is real. Engagement and communication prepare the organization for change. Planning identifies many of these issues, but one can never anticipate all the obstacles of execution.

Visualize the obstacles. Let the organization know that there is a well-defined and logical plan for dealing with the obstacles and that Lean is coming soon. As new obstacles pop up, deal with them immediately. Build the principles of *Jidoka* and *Andon* into execution. *Jidoka* is one of the two pillars of the Toyota Production System along with just-in-time. *Jidoka* highlights the causes of problems because work stops immediately when a problem first occurs. This leads to improvements in the processes that build in quality by eliminating the root causes of defects. *Andon* is a manufacturing term referring to a system to notify management, maintenance, and other workers of a quality or process problem. *Andon* is used in conjunction with *Jidoka* as a signaling and communication mechanism—there is no "We'll deal with this later when we have more time" allowed. Great execution has no limits when it comes to mitigating risks and knocking down the barriers to success. With great execution, the risks of change are much lower than the risks of hanging around and doing nothing.

Is It Strategy, Execution, or Luck?

Some experts have claimed that execution is more important than strategy. In our reference model, strategy, deployment planning, and execution are interdependent subprocesses. Strategy, deployment planning, and execution are further supported by the remaining interconnected subprocesses. The reference model architecture is not an accident. Strategy without execution is a failed Lean Business System; execution without strategy and planning is irresponsible and leads to a terribly inefficient and ineffective Lean Business System. There may be some degree of luck in improvement without these factors, but luck has no place in a Lean Business System. The benefits from a Lean Business System are planned and deliberate, not luck.

Wanted: Creativity, Innovation, and Critical Thinking

There are many executives and practitioners out there who are not engaging their full potential of Lean. We have talked throughout the book about the mimicking tendencies of organizations, while others subscribe to and learn a limited set of TPS principles and tools and then are content living out their daily routine of Lean. Some practitioners refuse to accept that Lean and continuous improvement require creativity and innovation. Fact is, creativity and innovation are critical when Lean evolves from a *production* system to an *adaptive, systematic, enterprisewide business system*. We use a formula about this topic in our practice:

$$\text{Same People} + \text{Same Thinking} + \text{Same Process of Improvement} + \text{Same Principles and Tools} + \text{Same Information} = \text{Same Results}$$

An enterprise wide Lean Business System is much more complex, but the hidden opportunities for improvement are mind-boggling in many organizations. Mining these opportunities requires nonstandardized approaches to problem solving. A principles-and tools-focused slice of the Toyota Production System without the invisible behavioral and cultural development underpinnings is *improvement-limiting* and will not produce *for-real,* continuous improvement that positively impacts the business and its people. The left side of one's brain is overrated when it comes to systematic, continuous, and sustainable improvement. Creativity, innovation, and critical thinking involve the challenge and the evolution of habits and behavioral patterns in the minds of practitioners and those around them. It opens the door of improvement to new and unexplored opportunities. There are many situations where we have stepped out of the TPS or Six Sigma boxes and created special methodologies and analytics for improvement. This is critical especially in the unknown, nonstandard wilderness of professional, knowledge-based transactional processes. We share a few of these experiences and examples with you in Chapter 9.

Execution brings out the best in many Lean and general continuous improvement practitioners. Execution is the point at which all those involved need to develop the skill of listening to the voice in their own minds instead of listening to a recipe or orders from a remote executive. Execution is the most challenging element of a Lean Business System, but it is the point where plans are translated into results. There is no recipe or standard set of tools for execution; often it requires creativity and improvisation, creating methodologies and best practices, innovating one's way through a complex challenge. A Lean Business System and its subprocesses are always evolving to meet new business challenges and/or cultural development needs. It requires creativity, innovation, and critical thinking to make this evolution a successful reality.

Bibliography

Bossidy, L., and Charan, R. 2002. *Execution: The Discipline of Getting Things Done.* Crown Publishing Group, New York.

Burton, T. 2001. *Is This a Kaizen, Lean, or Six Sigma Project?* Originally published in 2001 on the iSixSigma.com website. http://www.isixsigma.com/new-to-six-sigma/how-is-six-sigma-different/six-sigma-lean-or-kaizen-project/.

McChesney, C., Covey, S., and Huling, J. 2012. *The Four Disciplines of Execution.* Free Press, New York.

CHAPTER 8

Performance Reporting and Measurement

This chapter discusses the final subprocess in the Lean Business System Reference Model. Performance reporting and measurement include collecting, analyzing, and reporting information regarding the plus or minus gap between desired and actual outcomes in everything from profit margins to detailed process performance to the selection of associates for promotion. The Lean Business System Reference Model also incorporates four formal assessments:

▲ The Adaptive Leadership Assessment

▲ The Architecture and Operating Practices Assessment

▲ The Organizational Design and Dynamics Assessment

▲ The Improvement Kata Assessment

These assessments determine gaps and probable root causes between current and desired XYZ Lean Business System performance. These assessments also help to design, measure, and analyze how well an organization's XYZ Business System is working relative to strategic, operational, financial, technology, and cultural development needs. A key word in this statement is *gap*. Great organizations are always in the process of closing the gap and exceeding desired expectations—it's the *target value* of Kata at work behind an individual, group, organization, system, or component performance metric.

Lean is the mantra of our times. To achieve the long-term successes of Toyota and a few other organizations, the economics of Lean must *pencil out* across the board—strategic, operation, financial, and cultural development success. The purpose of this chapter is not to expound upon the subject of performance measurement in its entirety but to share some of the best practices from the reference model. Everyone knows about performance measurement. People's lives are touched by performance measurement every day—at work, driving on the freeway, or at sporting events. There are numerous reporting and measurement activities throughout organizations. Some organizations claim to have a balanced scorecard of metrics that guide their way. Many other organizations are measuring so many conflicting activities that create more confusion than guidance. The Lean Business System Reference Model includes this subprocess for obvious reasons. However, the purpose of its existence is to guide organizations to think about their portfolio of performance reporting and measurement.

A Common Performance Dilemma

Let's go back to the basics. What is performance measurement? It is a critical process of helping organizations understand, manage, and improve their business. Performance measurement provides financial feedback about how well an organization is performing with respect to goals. It lets organizations know if their customers are satisfied. It provides quantitative data about products, services, and all the processes that produce them. It highlights where the major gaps exist between current and desired performance. Most important of all it provides a variety of information necessary to make the right decisions about improving performance. Is that all there is to performance measurement? Absolutely not. Organizations can have all these attributes in their performance measurement system and fail miserably at performance measurement. Performance measurement also drives the right (or wrong) behaviors to take the right (or wrong) actions to achieve the right (or wrong) results. Performance measurement has a major impact on improvement Kata.

Consider the typical organization. It is measuring the right metrics and the wrong metrics and has set up a process of conflicting metrics between functional areas. Associates in sales are working very hard during the last week of the month trying to sell anything and everything available in inventory with deep discounts in order to hit their quotas.

Order entry is making unrealistic commitments to customers to get the order delivered. Purchasing is using premium freight to ship materials from China. Engineering is looking for the cheapest suppliers because its designs must hit a unit cost goal. Following executive directives, sales and operations planning (S&OP) is loading offshore suppliers way beyond their demonstrated production capacity and process capability. Manufacturing is jumping through hoops to ship unplanned products with negative margins, while the planned products and their respective inventories sit on a contractor's production floor, a warehouse, or a ship. How is the leveling working out in the Lean manufacturing system? Engineers, buyers, and production managers are flying around the world every week attempting to resolve these issues. Finance is pointing out missed targets, returns, warranty problems, high inventories, and operating costs that are over budget. Sales representatives are paid commissions for creating part of this mess.

Think about all the waste of people sitting in hot-list meetings, doing things over, the nonstandard workarounds, and other activities and behaviors that metrics can set off. Functional areas are undermining the metrics of other areas at different times of the month and quarter. Somehow the monthly financial performance numbers are met, but at significant cost, waste, and pain. This is not intentional; it is a dysfunctional measurement process that evolves over time. This probably does not occur in your organization but it is very common, especially at month end—and it destroys Lean! As a Lean practitioner, when was the last time your organization initiated a major effort to improve the *process* of performance reporting and measurement? When an organization runs with a measurement system that is counterproductive, it creates a *chaotic, immediate reason* culture that does not think and does not evolve to a higher level. Instead, these organizations operate in vicious cycles of insanity and hyperinsanity. In terms of PDCA (plan-do-check-act), people are always in A mode. These measurement systems create bad improvement Kata. Organizations require strong Adaptive Leadership to pull themselves out of these vicious cycles. More specifically, leadership must create the environment for success, including the right metrics that drive the right desired behaviors, achieve the right desired results, and create the right thinking and behaviors to repeat the process no matter what.

Think Causes and Behaviors

In a Lean Business System organizations need to rethink their complete infrastructure of performance reporting and measurement. Performance measurement must be deliberately designed as a cascading process of defining the right causal metrics that drive the right behaviors and achieve the right desired results. Every organization knows this intuitively, but they fall down in daily practice. Performance measurement is not just about short-term financial performance; it is also about aligning behaviors and developing a culture of excellence. Performance measurement is about creating the right Kata in organizations. For many organizations this is a departure from classical performance metrics and a mindset change for the positive. Organizations must step back and think deeply about the most influential factors of a more holistic performance management system. Figure 8.1 provides an overview of this initial process.

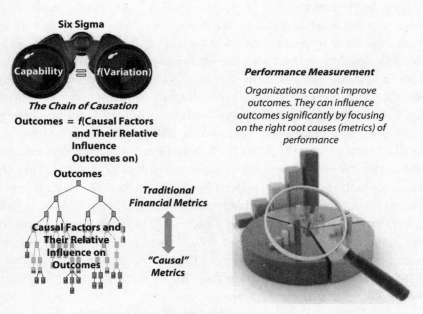

Figure 8.1   Performance Measurement—Lean Business System Reference Model
Copyright © 2015, The Center for Excellence in Operations, Inc.

In Six Sigma one learns a very important principle about variation that applies well to performance management system design. Process capability is a function of variation. One cannot improve process capability without understanding and eliminating, reducing, or managing to their advantage (i.e., a designed sigma shift), the root causes of variation. In practice this involves chasing down the most influential root causes of variation based on Pareto thinking. The final part of this principle is that organizations cannot improve outcomes, especially by edict. Organizations can and should measure top-level outcomes because these metrics are very important to the health and well-being of organizations. Executives can express their concerns about profitability, inventory levels, operating costs, cash flow, margins, revenue growth, and other outcomes. But the best way to improve these outcomes is by understanding and improving the underlying reasons with root-cause-oriented metrics. Mandating a reduction in inventory or more month end shipments seems to work for some executives. In effect, they are asking their people to temporarily change their logic-driven behaviors and react to their requests—often in the absence of data and facts. Attempting to improve outcomes does not address the root causes of these problems. It changes behavior for the worse—because it is constantly changing behaviors in every direction. Many variations of *brute force* are applied and usually create other larger problems and *whack-a-mole* behaviors. There is no constancy of purpose. One manager recently explained his role to me this way: "My job has deteriorated to the point where I come to work every day thinking about how I can get myself in the least amount of trouble." It just is not fun working in environments where performance measurement systems place people in a *damned if you do, damned if you don't* position and compromise any chances for real improvement. It destroys every principle of Lean and structured and deliberate continuous improvement. It also drives behaviors and culture backwards. Yet it is easy for organizations to drift into this mode when organizational anxieties run high and the focus is on instant acceptable financial results.

Avoid Metric Mania

Metric mania, which is described below, is another situation to avoid. Have you ever worked in an organization that had a war room with a hundred charts covering the walls? Again, these are well-intentioned efforts at creating a performance-minded culture. This can lead to several serious performance issues:

▲ First of all, these displays tend to be overwhelming, conflicting, and confusing in terms of where and how to begin corrective actions. Organizations measure too many irrelevant activities. It can become a game of *cover one's back side* or pick the metric that best supports one's position.

▲ It is difficult to distinguish root causes and outcomes. This often leads to discussions about what happened based on intuition, opinions, and perceptions.

▲ Many performance measurement systems are tilted toward short-term financial performance and overlook the longer-term and wider perspectives of infrastructure and human capital investment, market expansion, internal core business processes, and the voice of the customer.

▲ Many performance measurement practices are ineffective at driving improvement because they report outcomes long after the path to the root causes has run cold.

▲ Too many conflicting metrics drive disconcerting behavior patterns and achieve the wrong results.

These efforts become nonactionable, non-value-added work in themselves. This condition becomes exponentially more dangerous as organizations add technologies such as business analytics and digital performance dashboard capabilities into the mix. Technology is a powerful enabler of a Lean Business System, but it can also become an inhibitor of success.

Performance Management by Design

The performance reporting and measurement subprocess of the reference model includes best practices and criteria for analyzing and improving an organization's performance management system. A robust performance measurement system is very selective in terms of identifying and aligning the right cascading metrics and encouraging the right uniform behaviors for success. Performance measurement systems must support the organization's strategy and purpose from the highest organizational level downward to the various performance points of origin. At the top of an organization are the typical financial measures. A profit and loss (P&L) statement, balance sheet, and other key financial ratios will remain because they are relevant. However, they must be broadened and balanced to include customer experience, key operating processes, learning and development, and other critical performance categories. Financial performance by itself is a misleading measure of an organization's health and well-being. Organizations that focus narrowly on financial performance are accumulating very real and hidden waste in the background.

A well-designed performance management system incorporates more root-cause metrics as one goes deeper into the organization and its processes. This design cascades more activity-based process measurements that are known (through data and facts) to influence the higher-level metrics. The design is a broader portfolio of measurements that measure both process and cultural performance. Ideally, performance measures should be expressed in units of measure that are the most meaningful to those who must use them or make decisions *on the spot* using them. The process metrics are *hard* metrics, while the cultural metrics are more *soft* metrics and will require more thought. Performance measures are developed with a *less is more* mindset and deep analysis of what factors most influence performance. Reengineering a performance measurement system is not a matter of displaying more metric charts on the walls or automating an existing manual process. It requires deep thinking and a perspective that is different from the current practices in place. There is a science to this reengineering process where organizations take the time to understand the relative influence of their performance metrics on performance. They focus on the major influencers and stop measuring trivial factors of performance. The design focuses on eliminating all the waste caused by measuring, tracking, and explaining away trivial metrics. Here are a few common examples of performance inefficiencies in organizations:

▲ Some organizations spend more time and resources on assigning, counting, moving, losing, damaging, and storing a part than the actual value of the part. It makes more sense to expense these items and treat them as point-of-use floor stock rather than treat them as inventoried items.

▲ Other organizations spend more time and resources processing more transactions on the floor than they do in building their products. The accounting department knows where every part is sitting on the floor to the nearest square inch, but is this value-added? Practices such as backflushing, phantom BOM structures, or a single transaction point simplify these situations.

▲ A new product development organization was always under pressure to meet design cost targets—its primary metric. Engineers would search for the lowest quoted cost supplier in China, often a new supplier that the organization had not previously worked with. Additionally they would choose to use through-hole versus SMT (surface mount technology) components because the cost was lower. Design projects were consistently late and over budget. However, as the product development organization met its target design cost goals, one can guess the millions of dollars of waste that was generated because of poor supplier quality and delivery issues, hand assembly and postwave solder rework, scrap, and obsolete inventory. Additionally the hidden costs were millions of dollars in airline tickets, and a design group that spent over 25 percent of its resources on ECOs (engineering change orders) and sustaining engineering after release, rather than developing the next new products.

▲ Another waste is the concise measurement and tracking of labor for cost accounting purposes. In some organizations factory labor represents less than 5 percent of labor, material, and overhead (LMO) costs. Again the cost accounting department spends more time and resources chasing down insignificant labor costs, and the numbers are typically imaginary anyway because of poor standards, unexpected supplier issues, training, design for manufacturability (DFM) issues, and the like. So everything the accounting department uses these numbers for is also imaginary. Many organizations spend too much time managing with imaginary numbers. Asking a production supervisor to explain his or her direct labor variances last month is also non-value-added. An activity-based or pooled costing approach eliminates these wastes—and the overhead to count them.

▲ A final example is a quality department that had 162 defect codes for associates to classify their quality issues on the floor. The intent was good, attempting to classify defects as accurately as possible. Some of these were redundant, and the whole process was left up to an operator's judgment. This was a measurement repeatability and reproducibility problem. An attribute gage R&R study demonstrated that the measurement system had an 82 percent error rate. To put things into perspective, a game of darts has a much lower error rate. In essence the consistency and accuracy of a single operator or group of operators to classify defects in the right categories was incorrect 82 percent of the time. The quality reports were driving people to work on symptoms and the wrong problems. We looked at the number of annual transactions and the time per defect transaction and estimated that this quality system consumed the full-time equivalent resources of 34 people transacting, adjusting, analyzing, and reporting defect data. The measurement system was reengineered to a more simplified, real-time-based system, and this particular organization increased yield performance by $15 million within the next 18 months.

There are literally hundreds of other examples where organizations are spending too much time measuring the trivial many activities and not focusing enough on the vital few activities. Their metrics are actually hiding rather than exposing problems. It is easy for these practices to become institutionalized by the wrong metrics. Also, it is very difficult for organizations to step back and *see* these wastes when they are immersed in all of it. These are a few examples to think about when evaluating a performance measurement system. No organization is perfect, and every organization has a few of these performance anomalies. There will be "must do" metrics governed by compliance or regulatory requirements that we do not just arbitrarily throw out of the picture.

Visual Performance Management

It is not surprising that the performance reporting and measurement subprocess of our reference model encourages well-designed visual performance management systems. Like several other traditional *mimic the TPS* practices, visual performance management is often a *going through the motions* activity in organizations. Storyboards display A3s, plans, and performance charts, and over time many other data elements end up on these boards. Some of the storyboards and production boards that I have observed could benefit from a 5S exercise. Please keep in mind that this condition is not intended to be a personal criticism, but to encourage managers and practitioners to think more deeply about what is going on and how it is adding value to their organizations. Many organizations can "crisp up" their visual performance management boards and use them to a much greater extent to add value to their organizations.

Rediscover Ohno's Circles

Taiichi Ohno was the Toyota executive who is credited with much of what is today known as the Toyota Production System (TPS). Toyota's advancement of fundamental industrial engineering principles and techniques over the past 70 years is nothing short of brilliant. Ohno was known to have drawn several circles on Toyota's production floor as designated process observation points. He would draw the circles at points where there was a clear view of each process. Then he would go to the gemba and stand in the circle for a short period of time (e.g., 10–15 minutes) and observe, think, and analyze what was going on in the process. During the routine he would use "the TPS 10-second rule." If he did not fully understand what was going on within 10 seconds, he would record the situation. This routine practice would provide Ohno with new knowledge and ideas to improve the process. After his observations were complete, Ohno would step out of the circle and further analyze his findings and think of incremental improvements to the process. How can one not admire Ohno's commitment, persistence, patterned behavior, attention to detail, and sheer spirit of improvement? This wonderful professional and his followers spent a good deal of their working lives standing in and out of circles for the cause of continuous improvement. Ohno's circles are but one of many testimonies to Toyota's long-term commitment to continuous improvement.

The lesson here is to rediscover Ohno's circles. Coincidentally, his practice can be found in any Western motion and time study book written in the 1950s and 1960s. A key principle is to find a perfect observation point in the process from which to conduct a study (these old references did not suggest drawing a circle on the floor). Another principle is to follow operators and discuss the process with them. Ohno's deliberate actions and structured approaches evolved this basic principle, and he made the right changes to get the processes to *talk* to him. Many organizations talk about Toyota's 10-second rule, but sometimes it takes hours to dig out the real story of what is going on. A big problem is the chosen metrics themselves, and in the design, understanding, and associates' acceptance of production boards or performance boards. The right aligned causal metrics and associate emotional engagement are the key; otherwise a stand-up review meeting is just another empty ritual of blank stares. Beyond this factor, organizations must plan on placing many new circles throughout their entire enterprise with a Lean Business System. This is more challenging in the professional, knowledge-based transactional processes, but technology is *pulling* visual management to new heights in these areas.

Good Day, Bad Day Metrics

Another practice in the reference model is called *good day, bad day metrics*. If you were to roam around the organization, how can you tell if the department where you are standing is having a good day or a bad day? This is more obvious in production because it is the early adapter of visual performance boards. Additionally, you can use your normal senses (see, feel, hear, smell, taste) to evaluate performance. But what about the transactional areas? You cannot assess performance by the normal senses because it is more concealed or hidden altogether. Walk into an engineering department, or an order entry department, or a financial organization, or an R&D laboratory. Are they having a good day or a bad day? Determining this is the objective of good day, bad day metrics.

Many large customer service organizations are experts at good day, bad day metrics. One of these is usually a great organization to visit and stand in an Ohno circle for a while. Many customer service organizations resemble a mini-stock market with real-time digital dashboards for call volumes, wait times, queues, average incident handling times, hold times and abandonment rates, number of unreturned calls, unresolved problems, calls escalated to the help desk, first contact resolution rates, number of problems resolved within an hour and within 24 hours, and other relevant metrics. These digital dashboards are being used by associates to make real-time decisions. The visualization design and built-in intelligence enables instant interpretation and response. They are beating the TPS 10-second rule. In one organization these metrics were strategically placed along the top of the walls to create a pattern and a standard place to look for certain information. For example, staffing can instantly be adjusted by channel to call volumes, which might be on the top left side of the room. This organization can avoid responding to customers with, "I don't know, it's not my job" by immediately engaging the help desk. It can flex the help desk when the incident workload display shows a dramatic increasing or decreasing trend. It coaches and develops associates constantly by scheduled *listening in* opportunities. Beyond metrics, representatives are trained to treat customers like family. It is very simple to see what is going on in these areas. This information is also consolidated into various reports used for coaching and cross-training, individual and group performance, technology upgrades, staff and resource planning, and product and channel problems as well as for engaging other organizational talent in customer service improvement needs. The entire organization operates like groups of fluid, morphing work cells, continuously synchronizing resources to different types of customer incident demand streams. Technology-enabled customer service organizations (internal and external) often provide a good benchmark for good day, bad day metrics. Large consumer products, fashion and merchandising, or retail mail order/Internet catalog industries are benchmark examples because they usually have very impressive, relevant, and actionable customer service performance dashboards.

One of the practices in the reference model is to request the transactional organizations to select and display one to three real-time metrics based on our *rule of three*: try to pick no more than three most critical metrics that instantly demonstrate to themselves and to executives and process partners if the department is having a good day or a bad day. These are one to three metrics (max) that are inclusive, and not in conflict with the organization's balanced scorecard system. Here are a few other examples of good day, bad day metric practices:

▲ An order entry department displays the number of orders, dollar value of orders, and number of "dirty" orders that cannot be released (e.g., credit hold, missing configuration information and options, etc.). The dashboard is further customized to display both daily and month-to-date information compared to goals. People inside and outside the organization visit this dashboard frequently throughout the day and discuss how to improve the situation.

▲ The sales and supply chain organizations collaborated on a broader digital dashboard. This system measures and tracks in real time actual sales performance (dollar amounts and gross margins) to the sales and operations plan (S&OP) by customer, dealer, product, geographic region and territory, sales manager, and down to the individual sales representative. It also tracks in real time planned versus actual inventory performance, bookings, backlogs, and forecasting and planning errors. This performance dashboard is not used to point fingers; it is a real motivator for *pulling* and driving the right consistent behaviors between these organizations. It is used to achieve uniformity among the S&OP, the operating plan, and the financial plan. It has substantially leveled the monthly demand streams and eliminated much of the previous end-of-month volatility. It has also been used to evaluate sales relative to sourcing topology and reshoring manufacturing back to the United States.

▲ New product development is a bit more complex than dealing with existing products and requires a variation on the standard theme. For example, a new product development organization could display just the late projects, the root causes, the corrective actions in progress, and the individual(s) responsible for getting the project out of its late status. One organization created an automated stage-gate scheduling system with due dates and responsibilities for each task of each open development project. It used cycle time guidelines and development team inputs to create the initial schedules. As task due dates approached, a yellow flag would be displayed on the dashboard. As tasks reached a late status, a red flag would be displayed on the dashboard. At any given time all product development managers, engineers, and support resources could view several cuts of the status. One display looked at individual projects and the green, yellow, and red flags (and responsible owners) that were activated. Another display could look at the number of green, yellow, and red flags by resource for either performance or bottleneck situations. Development teams used this digital visual system to better manage and *pull* shared technical resources to the most important demands and to prevent yellow flags from drifting into red status. Just like production, a red flag triggered an instant shutdown and a meeting of the development team to resolve the problem as quickly as possible.

You can see that it is nearly impossible to achieve this level of performance engagement and integration with manual charts on a storyboard. These are examples of real-time, event-driven metrics. Things change so quickly in business that it is becoming increasingly more difficult to maintain manual performance dashboards and other manual practices (e.g., manual kanbans, magnetic boards, fixed cell configurations, pull systems design, etc.). Technology is providing larger opportunities for improvement in a Lean Business System by automating and evolving key Lean principles and engaging and developing the invisible behaviors of cultural excellence.

Measuring the Performance of a Lean Business System

The architecture of a Lean Business System is the overarching *process* of improvement. How does an organization know if its Lean Business System is functioning effectively? Organizations deserve to know the answer to this question and to confirm that their Lean Business System architecture and the key subprocesses are *enabling* systematic improvement and not *detracting from* it. The reference model encourages organizations to measure architecture performance and initiate the right corrective actions to this overall *process* of improvement. A Lean business is never in steady state; there are many factors and events that introduce new challenges or drive subprocess activities and practices to slower rates or off point. In the past Lean and the Toyota Production System have been implemented in many Western organizations with a complete absence of this precision success infrastructure. When Lean initiatives drift off point, there is a high risk of continued drifting without a fully integrated systematic *process* of improvement. The Lean Business System Reference Model provides an orientation framework for architecting, measuring performance, and sustaining the gains of a Lean Business System.

A good place to start is by referring to the basic aims of the Toyota Production System:

1. Provide world-class quality and service to the customer.

2. Develop each employee's potential, based on mutual respect, trust, and cooperation.

3. Reduce cost through the elimination of waste and maximize profit.

4. Develop flexible production standards based on market demand.

5. Strive for perfection everywhere.

The reference model is not abandoning these proven aims; rather, it is both scaling and enhancing these goals across the enterprise. These aims have been practiced by other organizations more specifically in relation to manufacturing. In a Lean Business System, executive practitioners will need to think more in a *responsive-business-based-on-market-demands* goal. This includes both flexible production standards and nimble core business processes.

Organizations should avoid many of the traditional practices (or lack thereof) of the past to gauge the success of their Lean business. Statements like, "People are happier," or "Everyone likes the new process better," are nice to know, but they are not performance metrics. Some organizations have measured effectiveness by the number of teams, the percent of associates involved in teams, the longevity of teams, the number of associates trained, the number of black belts per $100 million of revenue, and other irrelevant performance metrics. Last, organizations should avoid measuring and posting the performance of everything. Measuring the effectiveness of a Lean Business System is not a simple and easy practice.

The reference model includes process-oriented metrics for improvement strategy and vision, deployment planning, execution, sustainability and internalization (see Figure 8.2). Metrics should measure improvement progress and soft behavioral alignment as well as cultural development progress. The performance reporting and measurement subprocess of the reference model is focused on Lean Business System performance and does not attempt to measure the effectiveness of business strategy directly. However, a well-designed performance management system will provide quick indications and *clue data* about the business strategy.

Improvement Strategy and Vision

There are two ways of thinking about measuring the effectiveness of improvement strategy and vision. First, the top-level metrics of a balanced

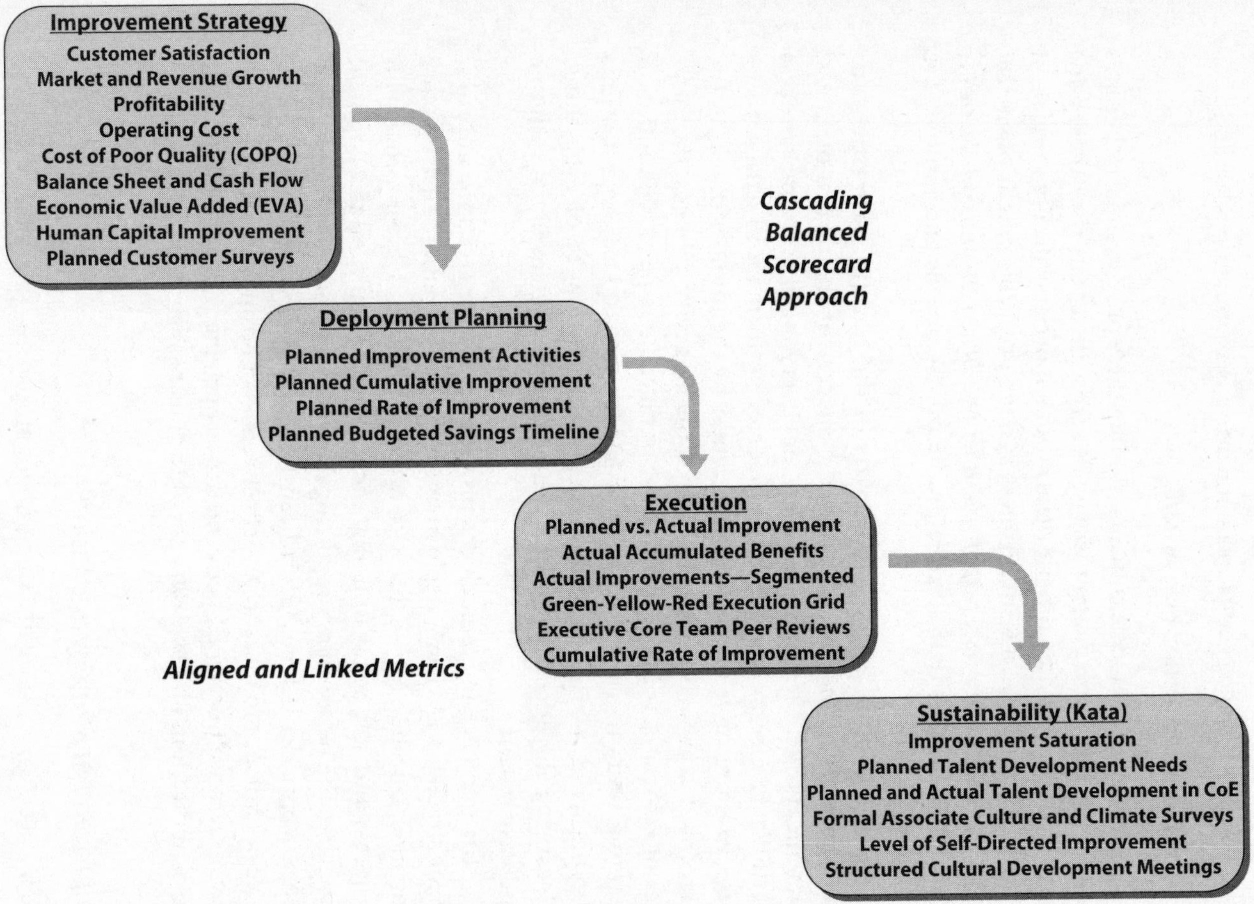

Improvement Strategy
Customer Satisfaction
Market and Revenue Growth
Profitability
Operating Cost
Cost of Poor Quality (COPQ)
Balance Sheet and Cash Flow
Economic Value Added (EVA)
Human Capital Improvement
Planned Customer Surveys

Deployment Planning
Planned Improvement Activities
Planned Cumulative Improvement
Planned Rate of Improvement
Planned Budgeted Savings Timeline

Execution
Planned vs. Actual Improvement
Actual Accumulated Benefits
Actual Improvements—Segmented
Green-Yellow-Red Execution Grid
Executive Core Team Peer Reviews
Cumulative Rate of Improvement

Sustainability (Kata)
Improvement Saturation
Planned Talent Development Needs
Planned and Actual Talent Development in CoE
Formal Associate Culture and Climate Surveys
Level of Self-Directed Improvement
Structured Cultural Development Meetings

*Cascading
Balanced
Scorecard
Approach*

Aligned and Linked Metrics

Figure 8.2   Lean Business System Metrics
Copyright © 2015, The Center for Excellence in Operations, Inc.

scorecard provide an indication of effectiveness. These might include the following categories:

▲ Customer satisfaction

▲ Market and revenue growth

▲ Profitability

▲ Operating cost

▲ Cost of poor quality (COPQ)

▲ Balance sheet and cash flow

▲ Economic value added (EVA)

▲ Human capital improvement

▲ Planned customer surveys

There is a margin for error in limiting the measurements to the above list. It is very possible that these metrics are improving or declining for reasons outside the Lean Business System scope of activities. For example, winning a new large customer(s), changing customer needs, an unknown supplier material substitution, and many other events can influence these metrics.

To measure the effectiveness of strategy and vision, one of the best practices of the reference model is called *performance pegging*. This is a process of linking benefits from improvement to the specific chart of account categories in the P&L and balance sheet that they impact. The process adds clarity to the improvement strategy and vision (i.e., are the improvement themes correct, and is the vision becoming reality). The idea is to link and analyze the value contribution for a particular improvement activity. This process requires assistance from the financial organization which conducts a rigorous evaluation of benefits before and after an improvement activity is implemented. All assumptions for calculating benefits are provided by and signed off on by the financial organization. In practice, improvements may be classified as strategic, cost reduction, quality improvement, cash flow, cost avoidance, and so on. There are also ongoing pegging activities. For example, reducing design verification spins may be viewed as strategic and may not produce an immediate financial benefit up front. But this improvement might save tens of millions of dollars in development and quality costs over the next three to five years. Performance pegging reinforces *self-respect* in teams and individuals and enables them to deliver on what they initially set out to accomplish. It also serves as a learning experience in terms of finance and benefits analysis. This process is not conducted thoroughly for every single improvement activity and Kaizen event, but the financial assumptions and validation still apply. Think of it as a detailed, skip-level financial audit of improvement activities and their actual benefits.

Deployment Planning

The MacroCharter and MicroCharter provide a useful repository of information for measuring the effectiveness of deployment planning. In Chapter 4 we discuss how these informational templates are typically used to support performance management. Some of the more effective deployment planning metrics include:

▲ Planned improvement activities by major improvement theme, responsible executive, business unit, core business process, functional area, key customer, product families, channels, and so on.

▲ Expected value contribution and timing from planned improvement activities and their alignment to higher improvement themes.

▲ Planned timeline of savings that can be budgeted into the operating plan.

In this area the executive core team and others are using these templates to ensure that the planned and teed-up improvement activities are direct hits to the larger improvement themes. The reference model encourages meticulous attention to planning and maximizing value contributions from limited resources. A Lean business is a precise systematic process; scattered improvement and demonstrations that give the impression of improvement are non-value-added activities.

Execution

The MacroCharter and MicroCharter provide a useful repository of information for measuring the effectiveness of execution. Some of the deployment planning metrics include:

▲ Planned versus actual improvement performance (i.e., performance to the deployment plan or schedule, money, and timing).

▲ Actual accumulated benefits achieved and validated by the financial organization.

▲ Actual improvements achieved by major improvement theme, responsible executive, business unit, core business process, functional area, key customer, product families, channels, and so on.

▲ Green-yellow-red execution grid.

▲ Executive core team peer reviews.

▲ Cumulative rate of improvement, aggregate and by other designated organizational and/or core process segments.

These metrics are validating the right results of a Lean Business System. The last metric is very interesting. In the beginning, the cumulate rate of improvement is higher because organizations are making the most obvious strategic and operating improvements. Over time it becomes more difficult to maintain or grow the cumulative rate of improvement without innovation and/or technology. Even in a Lean Business System, organizations must continue to think and rediscover new levels of improvement and superior performance.

Sustainability and Internalization

The MacroCharter and MicroCharter were deliberately designed to support performance measurement, and they are useful in this category. This is a challenging area because it is the measurement of Kata in a sense. Some of the more effective sustainability and internalization metrics include:

▲ Improvement saturation, measuring the level of engagement of executive sponsors, functional or core business process areas, or individual associates.

▲ Planned talent development schedule (what, who, when, why, where, how) and accomplishments.

▲ Planned and actual talent development offerings in the center of excellence.

▲ Formal periodic associate culture and climate surveys aimed at measuring changes over time compared with best-practice Kata goals.

▲ Level of self-directed improvement (Kaizen events) outside of the MicroCharter by core process, functional area, supervisor, and so forth.

▲ Structured 360 degree, peer review, town hall, communities of practice, and individual meetings.

This section has provided a new best practice: measuring the *process* by which organizations improve. We have not provided an all-inclusive list of metrics to measure a Lean Business System. Rather, we have provided a partial list to get organizations thinking about the best means of measuring their own Lean business infrastructure.

This *process* of improvement (especially in Western organizations) has remained the same for decades and has not worked very well in terms of achieving continuous systematic improvement and the associated behavioral patterns and other cultural attributes needed to sustain continuous progress. This traditional process became the accepted norm and was never really challenged as various improvement programs traveled through their respective birth-death cycles. A Lean Business System is dynamic. The reference model architecture is a *process* and group of *subprocesses* that are susceptible to the same casualties as any other process. This includes a variation of the traditional TPS wastes: defects, underproductivity, waiting and delays, non-value-added activities, movement between changing priorities, misused resources, unfocused activities, underutilized associates, security and lost opportunities, and an unenthusiastic workforce. The reference model provides a new process architecture for adaptive systematic improvement, and it also provides a means of measuring its effectiveness. If the architecture is not working effectively, the reference model encourages leadership interventions to readapt, change, modify, adjust, or take whatever actions are necessary to sustain a high-yielding Lean Business System. It is leadership's role to set up an environment for success; the architecture is the process or means by which to accomplish this ever-challenging role.

Balanced Scorecards Create Kata

A balanced scorecard is a performance measurement framework that integrates strategic, learning and development, and traditional financial metrics to provide a more balanced and holistic view of organizational performance. The balanced scorecard approach is very compatible with hoshin kanri and other best practices of the reference model. The balanced scorecard framework is a means of aligning strategy, deployment, and execution. It views performance from both an actionable activity and a behavioral and culture development perspective. The Lean Business System Reference Model stresses the importance of measuring the *visible* and *invisible* (Kata) attributes of performance. Figure 8.3 illustrates a generic balanced scorecard from the reference model, including a potential list of key metrics. This is a guide for provoking thinking about balanced scorecards; its actual design uses the strategy map or value creation diagram that we mention in Chapter 4. Organizations should choose the right metrics based on their strategic and operating objectives; they should also be prepared to modify or add their own appropriate metrics.

A balanced scorecard retains traditional financial measures of performance. This is a must-do: Executives are bound legally to shareholders, and this is not going away anytime soon. The other dilemma is that executive performance and rewards tilt the game toward short-term financial performance. Financial measures by themselves report on historical events, which is important in order for organizations to gauge their financial health and well-being and to plan for longer-term capital investments. Financial measures are not adequate for evaluating potential future value creation through customer relationships, associate talent development, and an integrated supply base. Additionally, financial metrics do not measure core business processes or value contributions from technology and innovation. A balanced scorecard displays a more complete and well-rounded view of performance by including these future value creation categories. It plays a critical role in translating business strategy into measurable actions, but it also develops the right behaviors and cultural standards of excellence to continue on the cycle of superior performance. Therefore, the challenge to balanced scorecard design is finding the *sweet spot* between short-term and long-term performance—and also visible business performance versus invisible behavioral and cultural performance. In a Lean Business System executives must learn how to achieve the total scorecard, and not focus on one category at the expense of the other categories.

	Objectives	Metrics	Goal	Actual	Improvement Initiatives
Customer Experience	Revenue Growth Sole Supplier to Top 20 Customers New Markets	Customer Share of Business Customer Retention Rate Customer Satisfaction Index Customer Complaints Market Share Conversion Rate Returns and Allowances			
Financial Management	Improve Profitability Improve Margins	Net Profit Net Profit Margin Gross Profit Margin Operating Profit Margin EBITDA Revenue Growth Rate Total Shareholder Return (TSR) Economic Value Added (EVA) Return on Investment (ROI) Return on Capital Employed (ROCE) Return on Assets (ROA) Return on Equity (ROE) Debt-to-Equity (D/E) Ratio Cash Conversion Cycle (CCC) Working Capital Ratio Operating Expense Ratio (OER) Capital Expenditures to Sales Ratio Price Earnings (P/E) Ratio			
Core Business Processes	Manufacturing Excellence Supply Chain Excellence Product Development Excellence Perfect Quality	M Performance to Schedule M Capacity Utilization M Revenue per Employee M Process Waste Level M Delivery in Full, On Time (DIFOT) Rate M Overall Equipment Effectiveness (OEE) M Process or Machine Downtime Level SC Order Fulfillment Cycle Time SC Inventory Performance SC Inventory Shrinkage Rate (ISR) SC Supplier/Contractor Performance Q First Pass Yield (FPY) Q Rework Level Q Cost of Quality Q Warranty Q Out-of-Box Quality NPD Time to Market NPD On Time % NPD On Cost % NPD On Budget % NPD Return on Development (ROD) Lean Cumulative Savings			
Learning and Development	Develop Technical Talent Develop Behaviors and Thinking Build an LBS Culture of Excellence	Human Capital Value Added (HCVA) Key Organizational Issues Behavior/Culture Surveys Employee Turnover Average Employee Tenure Absenteeism Talent Development ROI Coaching and Mentoring Statistics			

Figure 8.3   Lean Business System Reference Model Balanced Scorecard—Generic Template

A balanced scorecard is typically referred to as a management system rather than a measurement system. It is organized into four performance categories:

1. *Customer experience.* This involves moving beyond traditional customer focus and customer satisfaction and striving for customer intimacy and maximizing the total customer experience. These are leading metrics: unhappy customers have a low tolerance for poor performance in this area and will choose to conduct business with another supplier. This condition will negatively impact future revenues, while the current financials are in healthy shape.

2. *Financial management.* Timely and accurate financial reporting will always be a priority, and current practices can be improved by the addition of activity-based costing, improved program/project and resource costing, and risk and cost/benefit analysis capabilities. A balanced scorecard does not downplay the importance of financial metrics, but too much emphasis on financial performance leads to imbalances in other important performance categories.

3. *Core business processes.* This perspective addresses the effectiveness and efficiency of key internal business processes. This category of metrics enables organizations to gauge how well their business is functioning and is very specific to core business process performance.

4. *Learning and growth.* This perspective includes talent development, behavioral alignment, and cultural development related to both individual and corporate self-improvement. Organizations must deliberately keep their people in a continuous learning mode through structured education, coaching and mentoring, and constant exposure to a variety of workplace experiences. These metrics are the most related to Kata and create the right patterns of behavior in organizations.

In some organizations it might be useful to add another category for environmental, regulatory, and compliance issues. A balanced scorecard also uses a cascading approach with top-level metrics and additional tier metrics for business units, departments, improvement teams, and individuals. Organizations have constructed most balanced scorecards based on experience, intuition, and perceptions of what really matters to success. Although the measurements are more balanced than a pure financial perspective, there is the risk of measuring the wrong things. Not to sound like a broken record, but the danger is that the wrong metrics drive the wrong behaviors, choices, and actions and achieve the wrong results. Too many irrelevant metrics cause a loss of focus on the things that really matter.

Balancing the Scorecard

How does an organization know if its balanced scorecard management process is, in fact, balanced? Our friend *Monsieur Tallpole* can help us out. The answer is, "They don't know what they don't know"—it has not been balanced by analytical facts. This is not a criticism; it is another opportunity to add precision. A *fact* is a type of information, but all information is not factual. Analytics reveal that 80 percent of the results in organizations are best managed by 20 percent of their performance metrics. Another way of thinking about this is that resources are spending too much time on efforts that have an insignificant influence on fact-based and data-driven performance. One of the common transactional improvements is something that we have nicknamed *balancing the scorecard,* an analytical process of achieving perfectly correlated and aligned metrics. This involves an experimental design of sorts, attempting to understand the factors (the lower-tier metrics) that most influence the top-level scorecard metrics. Using several months of detailed financial and human resource data as a sample, the analytics includes predictive analytics, regression and correlation, probability, and modeling to determine the most influential metrics. The analysis also involves the use of variable timing offsets (i.e., this year's profitability significantly influences next year's capital budget; this month's inventory performance influences the next three months of delivery performance; etc.). Every analysis has revealed not only the most influential and leveraged metrics in top-level scorecard performance, but that organizations are measuring many activities that are insignificant to success. One must recognize that this is a statistical analysis and open to anomalies. But the analysis provides insight into the metrics where organizations should focus more and less of their efforts. For example, analyzing and understanding every detail about direct labor variances in a technology manufacturing organization with automated equipment and robotics will have no impact on profitability or revenue growth. In effect, it is non-value-added performance measurement.

Technology-Enabled Performance Management

Technology is definitely accelerating the transformation of organizations into a complex global network of interdependent transactional enterprises. The physical content of work is being replaced with professional and knowledge-based processes. As the shift in improvement occurs from the manufacturing floor to the transactional process areas, our ability to use our natural senses to solve problems diminishes greatly through traditional Lean performance practices. Additionally, the problems become much more complex and occur at a higher velocity. Even on the manufacturing floor, manually maintained magnetic production boards, pull systems, kanbans, and other principles are rapidly being replaced by technology. Manual cards, kanban labels, cell adjustments, and pull scheduling boards cannot be updated fast enough. When this happens, Lean slides backwards to the push and expedite, whack-a-mole free-for-all mode of production. For those who are dedicated TPS disciples hanging onto these decades, old manual principles, stop—because technology is coming at organizations like a freight train.

One of the future best practices in the Lean Business System Reference Model includes the seamless integration of improvement and technology. No longer can these roles be managed as separate silos. Technology is also morphing from add-on software applications to an integral part of future physical and business processes. Robotics, additive manufacturing, subtractive finishing, 3D modeling and printing, global virtual meetings, real-time digital performance dashboards, and real-time improvement (SIDAM) are but a few examples. Many organizations understand this shift in technology-enabled improvement and are using many technology capabilities in their Lean Business System and particularly in their performance measurement system. Following are a few examples.

▲ *Big data and data warehousing:* A central repository of data and information which is created by integrating data from multiple disparate sources. Data warehousing improves data quality and integrity by offering a repository of information that represents a single version of the truth. This is a must when you're attempting to improve complex, enterprisewide transactional processes. The real challenge here is harnessing and leveraging the right data because technology's ability to generate data is light-years beyond the capability of organizations to analyze and synthesize it correctly. No amount of technology can transform mediocre performance into great performance.

▲ *Business analytics:* The ability to analyze process performance in real time and make the right evidence-based adjustments. Business analytics enables us to execute what was once completed in a project in real time using a critical thinking cycle that we refer to as a SIDAM (sense, interpret, decide, act, monitor) and continue repeating the process, which is what we refer to as *preemptive improvement.* Business analytics provides that "sixth sense" needed for transactional process improvement because users and practitioners cannot sense problems before and during the point at which they happen, (i.e., feel an invoicing error, hear an incorrect shipment, touch new products that will be late to market or include field reliability issues, see premium freight, or smell a customer service or warranty problem). Business analytics enables organizations to bring their complex problems into focus with data. In the transactional space, most organizations learn about problems after the fact, and this is not the intent of Lean.

▲ *Digital performance dashboards:* These provide the ability to measure performance as it is occurring, almost like the stock market. Some of our clients have multilayered dashboards in manufacturing work cells where assemblers complete their work, wand the product bar code, and pass it on to the next associate in the cell. Productivity and quality are updated in real time at the cell and individual level. A second digital panel provides a Pareto analysis of problems experienced during prior builds and standard work instructions plus associate hints (from prior builds) to prevent these unexpected defects. Other organizations view real-time sales progress down to key global distributors; evaluate global supply versus demand positions in real time; monitor contractor and supplier quality performance; monitor distribution center and third-party logistics (3PL) performance around the globe—and take the right data-driven actions to minimize problems. These digital dashboards *pull* the right people together immediately—sometimes from different global locations—when there are problems. Well-designed digital performance dashboards encourage real-time engagement, empowerment, and self-management. Figure 8.4 is a photo of the cell we describe at the beginning of this paragraph. Note that it incorporates many design best practices which we provide later in this chapter.

Figure 8.4 Manufacturing Work Cell with Digital Performance Dashboard

▲ *Virtualization, mobility, cloud technology:* This allows for the ultimate management by walking around while being totally connected—anywhere and everywhere. Technology is rapidly placing the gemba at our fingertips on our iPads, iPhones, and other mobility devices—on a table at Starbucks, in a go-to-meeting session, in our automobiles and more often than not at our children's soccer games and baseball games, and everywhere else. We are connected 24/7 in our work and personal lives thanks to technology.

▲ *Data visualization:* This is related to technology and deals with the emerging science of displaying data and information to convey ideas and conclusions effectively, both in terms of aesthetic form and functionality. Data visualization attempts to achieve a balance between form and function, thereby reducing perceptions and opinions about different individuals' interpretations of the end result. This is an emerging science as practitioners and researchers create data visualizations that not only communicate information but reduce measurement system error by engaging people in the right single interpretation of the results and the right evidence-based corrective actions. Data-driven and fact-based decision making is very important. But how organizations choose to design, display, and communicate these facts is critical in order for groups of people to draw the right uniform conclusions and pursue the right improvement needs.

This is just the beginning! Wearable body-adapted electronics, screenless displays, brain-computer interfaces, Xbox-type video business architectures, cognitive computing, advanced virtual 3D conferencing and coaching, and the "fully integrated self" (connected continuously to data about everything in one's life) are on the near horizon. There is no doubt that technology is evolving faster than organizations can assimilate it successfully. If technology is integrated into a Lean Business System correctly, it will provide new breakthrough opportunities and far-reaching benefits. Technology is definitely a game changer for Lean and continuous improvement because it enables organizations to mine for and uncover their unknown opportunities. One of the largest threats to Lean and root-cause problem solving is that technology is pushing the immediacy and instant gratification factors of decision making. Today, many X and Y generation people who grew up in the digital and gaming age take this technology for granted. They send a text or e-mail—from anywhere, any time of the day or night—and expect an answer immediately. The window of critical thinking is shrinking—or maybe closing a bit. The new generation of workers is using technology in many cases as an *end* rather than a *means* (or enabler) to the end. Just because something shows up on a display does not mean that it is the *truth* or a *fact* or the *right data*. The other side of this is that data can often provide a conclusion that does not agree with expectations, but the facts are the facts. A major consideration of technology-enabled improvement that must not be overlooked is that the real intelligence still lies in the improvement practitioner and the user community in the form of human intelligence. There is no improvement intelligence software available that instructs and/or executes improvement automatically, and we cannot replace the tough work of improvement with some new mobile iPhone application—at least not yet!

The process of improvement still relies on human intelligence to define and segment the right root-cause information, analyze data with the right methodologies and tools, draw the right data-driven conclusions, take the right fact-based actions, close the loop with the right performance metrics, and continuously repeat this cycle. The bottom line is that if technology is placed into the hands of a user community that either does not know how to conduct true root-cause problem solving, doesn't have the time, or does not believe that all of this is necessary, the organization is reduced to "winging it" with new technology and achieving the wrong results. Regardless of what technology is available, people must not forget that they still need to *think* and go through the basics of interpreting and synthesizing information, drawing the right conclusions from fact-based information, making the right data-driven decisions, taking the right actions with technology, and making sure that technology is working well as an enabler of whatever they are trying to accomplish.

For the most part, traditional Lean manufacturing and the Toyota Production System as we know them are a commodity especially in their principles and tools state and their focus on production. Emerging technology such as business analytics, real-time digital performance dashboards, data visualization, and mobility are having an enormous positive impact on Lean and continuous improvement in general. These technologies are powerful in terms of increasing productivity and eliminating waste, but misuse of technology can introduce waste at much higher rates of speed. These technologies are limited not only to improving performance management, but they also improve the velocity, quality, and effectiveness of the larger Lean Business System architecture and all physical and transactional processes in organizations. The reference model does not include all technology possibilities because they are evolving every day. However, be assured that technology will continue to play a larger role in a Lean Business System.

Digital Performance Dashboards—Best Practices

Digital performance dashboards are having a positive impact on Lean initiatives in which developers think through the process of their design, display, interpretation, and responses. As we mentioned, many of these dashboards can easily incorporate an *Andon* feature to summon the right people to a performance issue. We share a few examples earlier in this chapter. Some organizations have not had good luck with technology. The largest reason is their failure to think through and map requirements and how the technology will be used. The reference model includes design guidance for digital performance dashboards and visualization. Below is a partial list of the most important design criteria:

1. *Design for communication.* The objective of performance dashboards is not to be pretty and colorful, but to communicate the right information with clarity and velocity to enable rapid but uniform fact-based decision making. There is a design concept called *augmented reality,* the science of transforming the vital signs of processes with graphics, metrics, visualization technology, and so on, in a way that results in uniform conclusions and uniform decisions. Take the time to think about and design the best visual display formats (e.g., simple data tables, pie charts, run charts, barometer charts, scatter plots, Pareto charts, etc.).

2. *Web-based architectures.* Manually maintained storyboards and performance charts are becoming dated because of evolving technology. Performance dashboards must be near real time, promoting instantaneous dialogue and quick responses to problems.

3. *The effective quick snapshot.* Areas should not have several different dashboards. There should be a single dashboard that displays the headlines of a process. It is acceptable to design referenceable layers in a single dashboard to fill in the answers to the five whys. Another design concept is *cognitive design,* or designing performance dashboards that are compatible with how the human brain visualizes and processes information. This concept enables quick conclusions, not more questions.

4. *A precise logical story.* Performance dashboards should be designed with a logical sequence in mind. For example, the first glance is the big news. Below that may be more detail to support the big news. Below that may be the corrective actions in process. Performance dashboards can have layers. If this is the design, then each layer should reveal deeper details. Performance dashboards should not be

autostereograms (i.e., posters that one must stare at long enough to see another 3D image emerge from within it) with a blurred picture of what is going on.

5. *Exception and alert Andons.* This design criterion contains two practices. First, the use of color selectively to highlight the most important information or problematic conditions. A section of a dashboard that changes colors (green, yellow, red) is a good practice. Second, performance dashboards can be integrated into mobility and other technologies to proactively signal and *pull* the right people together as necessary. A dashboard should never be a static information center waiting to be noticed and acted upon.

6. *Ease and simplicity.* Performance dashboards should be simple to understand and easy to maintain. Metrics should be readily available without excessive behind-the-scenes analysis and aligned with the balanced scorecard metrics. The last point facilitates ease and simplicity by automating standard countermeasure activity while reducing the Toyota 10-second rule to real time.

7. *Connectivity.* There must be a direct connection between the data displayed and how associates using the dashboard influence the numbers. The poorer performance dashboards leave people wondering how any of this information relates to what they are doing every day.

8. *Consistency and quality.* This is a no brainer. The data elements in performance dashboards must be timely and accurate. Timing differences in data can create disagreement about the real story and priorities. Performance data must include the right cascading balanced scorecard metrics that surface the right issues, drive the right behavior patterns, and achieve the right results. The goal is a single version of the truth.

9. *Design the total performance dashboard architecture.* This means a mapping of how data will be acquired, displayed, and distributed to the right people in the organization. Performance dashboards should be designed up front to integrate other technologies such as mobility, e-mail, texts, customized analytics, and so on. Performance dashboards include much more than developing and hanging up a flat screen display.

10. *Experimentation.* There is no single recommendation for designing a dashboard, what colors or fonts to use, which graphical techniques are best, or the best design for interpretation methodology. Technology groups should collaborate with users about design criteria. There are references on the Internet as well. The key here is customization to what works best in a particular organization and in a particular situation.

Bibliography

Eckerson, W. 2011. *Performance Dashboards: Measuring, Monitoring, and Managing Your Business.* John Wiley & Sons, Hoboken, New Jersey.

Few, S. 2009. *Now You See It: Simple Visualization Techniques for Quantitative Analysis.* Analytics Press, Oakland, California.

Few, S. 2013. *Information Dashboard Design: Displaying Data for At-A-Glance.* Analytics Press, Burlingame, California.

Kaplan, R., and Norton, D. 1996. *The Balanced Scorecard.* Harvard Business School Press, Cambridge, Massachusetts.

Kaplan, R., and Norton, D. 2004. *Strategy Maps.* Harvard Business School Press, Cambridge, Massachusetts.

Vorhauser-Smith, S. 2013. *Three Reasons Performance Management Will Change in 2013.* Forbes Magazine online. http://www.forbes.com/sites/sylviavorhausersmith/2012/12/16/the-new-face-of-performance-management-trading-annual-reviews-for-agile-management/.

CHAPTER 9

Adapting the Lean Business System Reference Model

This chapter provides guidance on how to adapt the reference model architecture, subprocesses, and other related critical success factors to an organization's operating environment. It is not possible to explain all the details of a complete build-out of a true Lean Business System. Remember that this effort is an evolutionary process and that the Lean Business System Reference Model™ is a guide or road map for the journey. We share some of the organization-centric retrofitting insights and best practices that are outside of the Toyota Production System (TPS) and that have been executed with great success. As a consultant I am blessed to be exposed to so many global learning opportunities. I have spent hundreds of weekends where our clients are located to observe and talk to people about culture and to learn more about culture and local customs. I also enjoy trying local cuisines and making the effort to adapt to local customs; it comes with the territory of 100 percent travel, and clients appreciate your interest in their language and way of life. All these experiences make one realize the importance of culture when introducing change.

Now a little fun: Think of the past and present state of Lean as a group of friends in the backyard grilling burgers. All those involved, including the grill masters, are limited to the recipe. Maybe they can add spices or sauces or cheeses, but the small group of people is content with burgers. Now elevate one's thinking to feeding a large, diverse group of people from 20 countries. The grill and burgers are irrelevant to the vegetarians, people who eat only fish, and others who have different dietary needs and expectations. The reference model is analogous to turning the burger grill masters into five-star Michelin master chefs who are skilled with a variety of kitchen equipment, utensils, and ingredients and are capable of quickly adapting and preparing a creative and delicious plate on demand for any appetite around the globe. The greatest difference between the two scenarios lies in the skills, knowledge, talent, creative and innovative thinking, no-fear attitude, and behaviors of doing whatever it takes in any situation to achieve success. This is the difference between a Lean manufacturing system and an enterprisewide Lean business system.

Adapt Yes, Copy No!

The Lean Business System Reference Model is just that—a reference model, with many proven real-world insights and best practices to create an organization-centric Lean Business System. The reference model is a pragmatic and useful guide that is always in a work-in-progress state and continuously under development. After interviewing a large cross-section of individuals and completing the Operations Excellence Due Diligence™, executives and practitioners are equipped with the business requirements, vital signs, cultural climate, and other related information necessary to adapt and architect their own enterprisewide Lean Business System. Some of what we discuss in this book is directly applicable; some features and functionality will require deeper thinking and design. Following the reference model enables organizations to define the requirements of *their own* Lean Business System and its subprocesses.

A word of caution is in order. Organizations are always overanxious to implement what they believe to be the next magic mantra of improvement. Like the Toyota Production System, it seems *quick and easy* to follow a hasty knockoff strategy, but organizations overlook the most important (invisible) behavioral and cultural development needs. A Lean Business System is not the next magic mantra or silver bullet, but the architecture, design, implementation, and sustainability *are* new to most organizations. A true Lean Business System is a never-ending journey to excellence and superior performance. Organizations have copied the visible principles and tools, but they must define and evolve their own *mojo* of improvement—their own Kata. This is a long and deliberate process of Adaptive Leadership, continuity of purpose, and a passion for human capital development. The reference model provides the means that will enable you to think through the requirements and challenges for success. It provides a framework for enterprisewide improvement and cultural excellence—and there are no shortcuts. Organizations must invest more time in the "invisible" Kata side of the house (behavioral and cultural development) to become great at adaptive systematic improvement with continuous "visible" benefits. Do not mimic or attempt to copy and paste the surface reference model, or the journey will be cut short very quickly. All industries have the capacity to improve beyond what is thought to be impossible or unreachable when they lead and engage the full potential of their organizations. *People* get organizations there, not tools.

Adapt to Industry Sectors

A Lean Business System must be adapted to a specific industry and its unique operating characteristics. For example, a Lean Business System will operate differently in a consumer goods, automotive, pharmaceutical, or aerospace and defense industry because of different market dynamics, customer expectations, operations (repetitive, job shop, process, and supply chain designs), performance criteria, and compliance and regulatory requirements. There is an even greater difference between manufacturing organizations and retail/wholesale distribution, healthcare, and financial service organizations. In the transactional process space, there tends to be more similarities than differences between organizations. My personal experiences with over 300 different clients globally is that the same holds true for Lean and continuous improvement in general. Exposure to this many organizations enables one to think of, and adapt possibilities that a practitioner with experience with only one or two organizations in the same industry may never think about. The important point is that the architecture of a Lean Business System integrates all the business requirements and cultural characteristics. In effect, the architecture addresses the, "Our business is different," or "We can't do this because," or, "We're regulated by law," or, "We don't assemble cars; we save lives" issues in organizations all of which build the *perception is reality* walls and have proven to be very real showstoppers of Lean and continuous improvement in the past. Adapting the architecture of a Lean Business System to specific industry requirements increases the rate of acceptance because it clarifies the objectives and *what-why-when-where-who-how* questions within a specific environment.

One area that could benefit from adaptive systematic improvement is Lean healthcare. Many practitioners have directly ported over the principles and tools of the Toyota Production System without giving deep thought to the significant differences in industry structures. For the industry as a whole it has been a Lean *false start*. A dozen or two hospitals really get it and have achieved significant benefits with their Lean initiatives. Many hospitals have not committed to Lean and continuous improvement for the long term because of their long cultural standard of external agency reimbursements to cover costs. Many practitioners have also been unsuccessful at taking advantage of the best opportunities for improvement in hospitals. As the population ages and other industry changes evolve, the game has changed drastically—with reimbursements shrinking while costs continue to increase at double-digit rates. Many hospitals are waiting for new legislation or filing lawsuits with their states to resolve their shrinking reimbursement dilemma. This is *not* adaptive systematic improvement with structured means and deliberate actions.

The administrative areas of hospitals have similarities in terms of transactional process improvement. However, the rest of a hospital environment is very different from an assembly line. Lean has not been explained and adapted properly as a way to help the clinical, laboratory, and primary care staff to make their lives easier. Additionally, Lean has missed the mark in terms of eliminating waste in the highest-impact areas of a hospital, namely the highest revenue-producing centers and highest cost drivers such as facility and operating expenses. Lean has been implemented in the *visual* lower-impact areas with the same focus on ported-over manufacturing principles and tools, while the strong clinically driven Kata has remained the same. I visited a large hospital as a patient recently and found myself in a nice conversation with a nurse about the hospital's Lean program. She said, "It started off with a lot of interest, lasted about six months, and we're finished with it now." I probed about some of the activities she was involved in, and she replied, "Mostly cleaning up and labeling supply rooms and medicine cabinets, mapping our processes, and stuff like that. Most of it is gone now; we're back to normal."

The largest opportunities in hospitals require a combination of transactional process improvement plus technology (i.e., real-time scheduling and logistics, real-time tracking with tighter quality controls on services and medications, digitally distributed full patient dashboards, etc.).

These resources within these areas must become heavily committed and engaged, and they must also understand that Lean is about removing *their* barriers to success. For example, many operating rooms and equipment labs are severely underutilized from a private industry perspective (like 10–30 percent). Supply chains are fragmented and create tremendous waste in different equipment, supplies, and maintenance contracts. It's just the institutionalized way that things have always worked in hospitals. We mentioned earlier that a small group of hospitals has achieved great success with Lean, but these institutions are the exceptions. Major innovations in scheduling and quick changeover thinking could increase the utilization rates and revenue-producing opportunities of expensive MRI equipment and operating rooms. This does not suggest that doctors and clinicians must work faster; it means finding a way to accommodate one to three additional operations per day or three to four patient appointments on key revenue-producing equipment by eliminating waste in the system. There are plenty of idle time and resources to implement these improvements, one additional surgery per day or an MRI or X-ray lab working at just 50 percent of capacity would make a tremendous difference. Consolidating spending through a single supply chain would also reduce significant waste. Again this requires engagement of the clinical and laboratory staff, and the incentive is their compensation. It also requires a new Kata that time is money, but not at the expense of the patient experience. These improvements can represent millions of dollars in incremental revenue for a single hospital.

As practitioners have found in manufacturing, reducing time and waste also improves quality at the same time. Lean practitioners have a moral obligation to win over physicians and other clinician and lab resources, help control double-digit cost increases, and find ways to offset reductions in revenue reimbursements. Labeling rituals and setting up a pull system for Jell-o and coffee creamer just aren't making a difference. The opportunities for improvement are enormous, but it requires a trip back to the drawing board and thinking about how to engage (rather than alienate) the right people. The hospital of the future will probably resemble a FedEx or Amazon, capable of moving people through a distributed network of service centers (maybe with no waiting rooms as inefficiency buffers) with even higher levels of quality and patient care, a much shorter length of stay, and a more positive total patient experience—and hopefully much more affordable.

Adapt to Business Requirements

At a specifics level, every organization has different strategic and operating challenges, planning systems, enterprise architectures, organizational structures, process inefficiencies and wastes, leadership challenges, levels and mix of talent development, and behavioral and cultural development needs. The purpose of the Operations Excellence Due Diligence in the reference model is to help organizations define and adapt their business requirements and cultural development needs to their Lean Business System. By now, it should be obvious that a tools-focused Lean *manufacturing* approach is not robust enough to significantly and positively influence these areas at an enterprisewide scale. Many of these tools-based initiatives have generated transparent improvements that do not impact customers or the organization's strategic and operating performance. Creating the capability of living, laser-targeted planning and deployment ensures continuous alignment between an organization's holistic improvement needs and what people are doing on a daily basis to fulfill these needs.

Adapt to Cultural Development Needs

Cultural development needs are the great missing link in Lean and continuous improvement initiatives, particularly in Western organizations. The living laser-targeted planning and deployment process and the balanced scorecard are two useful references for identifying gaps in this area. It takes structured means and deliberate actions to keep a Lean Business System aligned with behavioral and cultural development needs. Adaptive Leadership is a given to create the right environment, communicate expectations, reinforce behaviors and guiding principles, remove the barriers to success, and build a seamless teaming organization. The best approach is through the rigorous and widespread practice of coaching, mentoring, doing, and continuous learning. This is not an ad hoc practice that happens on its own. We use the *deliberate* word again because it requires the formal cycle of defining cultural weaknesses and needs, developing a plan to grow patterns of behavior and cultural attributes to higher standards of excellence, executing with the right actions and efforts, and measuring progress. In effect it is a complex PDCA for improving invisible behaviors, routines, and cultural attributes. There is so much unleashed power to improve by creating the right Kata and cultural standards of excellence.

There is a saying, "Let the cat out of the bag," a colloquialism meaning to reveal facts previously hidden. Organizations are just beginning to appreciate and accept this tremendous *under the radar* capability in the Toyota Production System. Now it is time for all organizations globally to "let their own Kata out of the bag." The future of Lean is an enterprisewide business system, an adaptive systematic process of improvement that is highly leveraged by the skills, knowledge, talent, and full potential of people in organizations. This has been a superficial topic of discussion for decades; the secret is doing it for real—putting the tools aside and developing people—and evolving the right patterns of behavior and cultural attributes that exist at Toyota and within several other great organizations. Leadership cannot delegate behavioral and cultural development to internal change agents or the human resources department. Eventually these efforts become thorns in the side of change management. As we always say, "The *soft stuff* is the *tough stuff*," but also the *greatest stuff* for continuous improvement and superior operating performance.

Adapt to Technology Architectures

The cloud, big data, mobility, additive manufacturing, business analytics, virtualization, advanced robotics, artificial intelligence, neuromorphic technologies, and distributed manufacturing models have arrived. Drone logistics and doorstep delivery is not far behind. In the future more organizations will resemble the business models of Amazon and Google that provide almost every product to the marketplace within 1–3 days. These organizations are the cybermalls of the future. The combined technologies enable these and many other big box organizations to work as a large transparent manufacturer and distributor of everything, contracting with a large network of suppliers and taking advantage of drop shipments and other logistics strategies as close to the customer as possible. Another growing trend is a rise of private labeling, custom bundling and packaging, and other specialty requirements by large technology-enabled organizations which add cost and cut into the margins of retailers and their supply base. Organizations need a higher order paradigm of Lean to address these complex emerging technology-enabled innovations in business models.

The best time to make decisions about how to integrate improvement and technology is when an organization designs its Lean Business System architecture. A best practice in the reference model is to map the architecture and subprocesses and then think about the technology requirements to further enable the system's efficiency and effectiveness. This is a good time to recruit an IT resource that can create a parallel technology road map to support a Lean Business System. This includes the identification of system requirements from an IT perspective and then identifying and recommending alternative technologies such as business analytics, cloud and mobility applications, digital performance dashboards, virtualization technologies, and other emerging technological solutions. The objective is not to turn this into a two-year IT development project but to efficiently phase in the right technology solutions with the right priorities and the highest payoffs.

Another need in this area is that Lean practitioners become more familiar with technology options. Relying solely on an IT resource is not recommended. Executives, IT resources, and Lean practitioners must all work together to find workable technology solutions that enable a Lean Business System's ultimate success. In a Lean Business System, people enabled with technology are much more important than the standard collection of improvement tools.

Add Local Cultures to the Architecture

Local cultural norms must be considered when implementing a Lean Business System. Choosing to downplay the cross-cultural encounters in a global Lean Business System sets up major barriers to success. There are major cultural differences, for example, among behaviors in the United States and Europe and South America and the Far East. On a microlevel, there are even subtle cultural differences between people and organizations in Cambridge, Massachusetts; Hackettstown, New Jersey; Columbus, Ohio; St. Louis, Missouri; Milwaukee, Wisconsin; Cupertino, California; Houston, Texas; Atlanta, Georgia; Knoxville, Tennessee; Germantown, Maryland; and Melville, New York. Culture is the foundation of adaptive systematic improvement; failure to recognize and integrate local behavioral patterns of work and culture is likely to take down the house of a Lean Business System. For large multinationals, a global Lean Business System requires a deep understanding of the cultural ramifications of introducing an enterprisewide systematic process of improvement. Culture change is an evolutionary journey that strongly influences behaviors, trust, collaboration, and cooperation as well as the Kata elements of a Lean Business System. Organizations cannot simply transplant the cultural standards intact from one country to another and expect success. Executives must begin with their local behavioral and cultural realities and build continuity of purpose and trust before they begin changing patterns of behaviors and building a renewed culture of excellence. Practitioners with global implementation responsibilities must also appreciate and play by the local cultural norms. Some of the global cultural idiosyncrasies of the reference model are provided in Table 9.1, Select Global Cultures. These cultural references must be part of the Lean Business System design in a particular geographical location. Table 9.1 provides a starting point for appreciating and understanding the *different but okay* attributes of culture around the world. This is a simple guide for thinking through the various elements of the reference model and how best to architect and implement each element with local culture in mind.

In the Lean Business System Reference Model, the purpose and objectives of the architecture are almost universal because the continuing need for improvement is universal. In fact, the architecture and its subprocess structure are universal in concept. It is the *what-where-when-why-who-how* questions that introduce differences in leadership, planning, communication, execution, and sustaining a culturally centered Lean Business System. Some of the answers to these questions may also be universal, such as people engagement, talent development, and strong coaching and mentoring, although there might be small idiosyncrasies in daily practice. The largest challenge of implementation lies in finding the delicate balance between the standard architecture and the *how* of implementation across different cultural environments. A quick study of Table 9.1 will stimulate thinking about how to better adapt systematic improvement in various parts of the globe. Implementing a Lean Business System in Germany, the United Kingdom, Spain, China, or Peoria, Illinois, requires different behavioral and cultural considerations in the architecture. These considerations are also important in cross-collaboration efforts around the globe. This requires an appreciation for local cultural attributes and accepted codes of conduct in different cultures around the globe. This appreciation goes beyond a Lean Business System. When someone from a large multinational corporation looks at Table 9.1 in greater detail, for example, it is not surprising to learn why there are global supply chain or global software development complexity issues. Whether it is an issue of religion,

Cultural Attribute	Description	United States	Great Britain	France
Autocratic vs. Participatory Leadership	Is power an autocratic hierarchy or a participative, consultive process?	Authority is respected, but most work gets done through informal networks, participation, and consultive learning.	Open collaboration, not influenced by hierarchical status; prefer wealth of lateral experiences working with others vs. climbing corporate ladder.	Prevailing formal autocratic hierarchy where adherence to rules, titles, formality is important.
Individualism vs. Collectivism	Do people identify with themselves (all about "me") or with a group (all about "we")?	Extreme individualism and self-reliance, freedom to make choices; connect and recognize individuals as heroes vs. teams.	Individualism, people and organizations have loose relationships; people get as much as they can out of a situation and move on.	Enjoy freedom and autonomy but stick to the rules and their duties; smooth relationships depend upon everyone doing what they are supposed to do.
Masculine vs. Feminine	Is culture more competitive or cooperative?	Objective, rational, numbers-driven, in it to win it, work/life imbalance.	Long work hours, skipping meals, must be a tough contender in business.	French value their career, but value their quality of life higher, tilted toward feminine.
Tolerance for Uncertainty	What is the cultural attitude toward uncertainty?	Extreme tolerance; cultures of innovation, creativity, new ideas; spontaneous, reactionary.	At ease and comfortable with uncertain and unpredictable situations.	Low; prefer security through rules, structure, formality; react openly and challenge change; may ignore if it does not work well.
Long-Term or Short-Term Focus	Is culture focused more on long-term or immediate results?	Quarterly performance now; instant gratification; performance and rewards drive these behaviors.	Quarterly performance and quick profits today; live in the present.	More long term than other European countries; executives are expected to also achieve short-term gains.
High or Low Context	Is culture open or closed to information exchange and informal communication?	Get to the point, time is money; frustrated by indirect and slower communication of other cultures.	Words over emotion, keep communication minimal, controlled, and on their terms; at times manage disruptions by not responding to communication.	Mask emotions and thoughts, play by the rules; difficult to read non-verbal signs; suppressed emotions and masked behaviors.

Table 9.1   Select Global Cultures

Germany	Spain	India	China
Consultive; hierarchy respected but opportunity to debate and discuss alternatives is encouraged; leaders receptive to employees, knowledge, skills, and insights.	New generation is shifting from hierarchy to participative leadership.	Autocratic, respect for hierarchy, power, and status; unquestioned disparity between management and employees.	Hierarchy present, managers act more as mentors and coaches; for employees, harmony is more important than voicing ideas and opinions; shift beginning with new generation of managers.
Middle ground; need professional space and respect invasions; open to collaboration about areas of interest; quiet listeners and analyzers about unfamiliar topics.	Enjoy individualism but embrace group activity and collectivist learning; shifting to more collaborative and social cultures.	High; a cultural trait to be loyal to family and community, for protection, security, and happiness is carried over into organizational life.	High collaboration and collectivism; complex system of etiquette to facilitate trust-building.
Masculine; most competitive culture in Europe, strong importance on work, strive to be the best.	Work is an arena of competitiveness, but value personal time and family; personal life holds slightly higher value over work life.	Balanced; the culture places high priority on success and power, and spiritual values drive for harmony.	Extremely success-driven culture, long hours, sacrifice family and leisure time over work; competition most obvious between teams (vs. individuals) and displayed through decisiveness and earned achievement.
Middle-of-road aversion to risk expressed in their extreme regiment, attention to detail, and disciplined approaches.	Stronger security orientation through rules and predictability; can be improvisational to risk and uncertainty at times.	Very tolerant and receptive to risk, uncertainty, and change; adapting employees to process changes may require little "change management"; excellent change laboratory environment.	Tolerant to uncertainty and comfortable with ambiguity; the spirit of Confucius is vague and adaptable to situations, pragmatism guides actions.
Mid-to short-term disciplined planners; prefer to know what they will be doing at a specific time on a specific day.	Intense short-term focus due to insecure future; a high degree of spontaneity, but progressing toward a better balance.	Leaning toward longer term; religious beliefs are more long-term focused; building relationships is more important than immediate profit.	Emotionally invested in long term; more important than short-term profits.
Low, rely on exchanging information in great detail to build understanding.	High; place high value on relationships and encourage high interpersonal communication; can sometimes be emotional, implicit, nebulous to outsiders.	High; communication is full of cultural nuances which are easily misunderstood; people work in close groups and avoid conflicts; face-to-face relationship-building is important.	Communication cannot take place outside of relationships and trust; communication can be ambiguous and conflict-avoiding; small group discussions more effective than one-on-one phone calls.

gender roles, dress standards, diet, or any other dimension, it is important to always realize that culture is deep seated in every person's sense of self. Passing judgment is destructive and builds barriers to change; understanding other cultures as different and okay rather than better or worse opens new global opportunities for breakthrough improvement.

The Polarization of Culture Change

There is a plus side to the complexities of different cultures. My prediction is that two common threads will significantly influence the polarization of Lean and culture change: people and technology. Actually it is 50 percent observation and 50 percent prediction. Today it is a common daily practice for people to regularly collaborate with different people in different time zones and geographical areas. Cross-cultural collaboration and innovation work environments can help build trust—the currency of collaboration—among coworkers, between employees and managers, and between customers, suppliers, and other stakeholders. Establishing trust is the foundation of Kata and can be accomplished by studying the local cultural traits that outwardly manifest themselves in the workplace.

Technology is homogenizing many elements of culture through virtual mobile and video-based collaboration, teaming, coaching, and cross-cultural learning. Twenty years from now it is predicted that 50 percent of the workforce will be operating in a virtual mode. Think about the impact on Lean. IBM, SAP, and a few other organizations are there now. Twenty years ago, thousands of employees came to work at IBM's headquarters; today on any given day, it is a ghost town, but the employees are accessible through technology. People are working from a customer's site, their homes, automobiles, Starbucks, or a son's soccer game. People are also connected to work much longer than they were 20 years ago. Working two days a week from home is rapidly becoming the new norm.

All gains have some trade-offs. For example, technology is creating the loss of interpersonal and social content at the office. This is too important to be just another trade-off. There is extensive research being conducted at MIT on advanced cybertechnology to improve these interpersonal and social losses resulting from technology. IBM and MIT have been developing simulated cyberconference capabilities in which participants can digitally regain the human interaction element of communication. It is a cybergemba environment. Developers are forecasting the future and discussing the ability to meet and collaborate with associates and translate different languages in real time. Early signs of this evolving capability demonstrate that people will be able to meet face to face in cyberspace regardless of geography, language, and other constraints. Imagine six people in a cybermeeting, all talking in their native language; everyone can interact with each other, share exhibits and other documents, and fully understand the conversation. This continued evolution of technology changes not only the way people work but also the way people live. However, it will never homogenize global culture into a single universal model. Despite the advances in technology, understanding different cultures is critical for architecting a Lean Business System and larger global success.

Culture Matters

The Lean Business System Reference Model promotes the importance of developing the right behavioral patterns and cultural attributes as well as appreciating cross-cultural differences in designing an organization-centric Lean Business System. As the heading states, culture matters; it is the foundation and ongoing underpinnings of a Lean Business System. Executives and Lean Business System practitioners cannot overlook the fact that culture is the organization's civilization and social control system. This is a universal principle in all organizations and in all cultures. Within an organization, Kata is not possible unless executives and managers deliberately promote and reinforce the right thinking and behaviors—and sanction the wrong thinking and behaviors. They must also engage, empower, and develop their people to be a primary part of the solution. The goal is to create norms of behavioral patterns through coaching, collaboration, learning and development, or consequences if necessary. As culture evolves to a higher state, it becomes a business immune system, preventing waste and inefficient practices from creeping in and taking hold of progress.

What works well within one organization is not a universal solution. This is the purpose of providing Table 9.1 as a starting point. "We're all different," and this is fine as long as it is recognized and built into a Lean Business System. Organizations cannot impose their culture on others just as organizations cannot directly copy and paste the culture of other organizations. Toyota's culture incorporates all the principles and behavioral ingredients needed for successful continuous improvement. No one could argue about these principles and behavioral ingredients, but the real challenge is adapting them to a culturally acceptable approach. The only option for success is to evolve an organization's own local culture and characteristics to a higher state of excellence.

A universal principle about culture is that people become outstanding contributors when they are engaged, empowered correctly, and encouraged to participate in open dialogue without fear. They also improve with planned and *deliberate* behavioral and talent development. I lost count a long time ago of the clever ideas that cell operators, stockroom clerks, machine shop workers, maintenance mechanics, quality control technicians, welders, electricians, buyers, planners, customer service representatives, material sweepers, and others have come up with to save the day. It's not just a Toyota thing; all organizations have the opportunity to engage their people and benefit significantly from the results.

Adapt New Methodologies and Approaches

Complex transactional processing environments have introduced new challenges for the improvement practitioner. Many Lean initiatives have missed the mark in these areas because of limited thinking concerning the principles and tools of the Toyota Production System. Once again, this is not a criticism; improving new product innovation or global supplier management or advertising effectiveness requires a much more robust level of problem solving. On several occasions we have found ourselves in severe turnaround circumstances where leadership needed to correct situations now and could not wait for the usual analytical and graphical approaches. In other complex situations we have found ourselves and our client resources totally overwhelmed, trying to pinpoint the right root causes and develop the right corrective actions. Nothing in the standard toolbox of Lean, Six Sigma, theory of constraints, and other methodologies filled the bill. This is a time to remember that even Frederick Taylor did not start out with a list of defined principles and standard improvement tools; he was clever enough to develop them along the way for particular improvement scenarios.

These are situations in which it is best to put all the tools aside and freelance map the problem situation and its cause-and-effect relationships. Lean practitioners worth their salt should be creative enough to *engineer* themselves and a team through a complex challenge. Many of these types of challenges have *reflexivity*—circular relationships, interaction properties, and interconnectivity between causes and effects. In essence, causes and effects are multidirectional and influence each another, so neither can be easily assigned as causes or effects. Furthermore, causes and effects are relative at any moment. These situations require deeper and broader skills and a designed experimental analytics approach (not design of experiments or DOE). Basically this involves designing and adapting a nonstandard analytical problem-solving methodology for this unique situation. Throwing the standard TPS tools at these complex situations creates nothing but an *improvement ricochet effect*. The following material provides several examples from the reference model.

Abstraction Factor Analysis

Abstraction factor analysis is a fact-based approach to understanding and evaluating the utilization of shared resources on new product development projects. The abstraction factor itself is a measurement of the number of steps a resource is away from the executive development program manager responsible for the successful completion of a project. An abstraction factor of 1 represents a team resource that is a direct report; an abstraction factor of 9 represents a team resource that is several functions, business units, and site locations away from the executive development program manager. The higher the abstraction factor, the more likely a resource will receive *invisible* direction(s) and shifts in priorities from others in the abstraction chain. In other words, the many managers and supervisors closest to their resources involved in cross-functional teams can inadvertently throw large development efforts off course by interjecting with a pressing immediate need in their own areas. This is not limited to new product development; this invisible disruption occurs in all transactional processes in many organizations in multiple sites, and/or people involved in teaming efforts.

Now we discuss how to conduct the analysis. To initialize the analysis, templates for the portfolio of gate-approved projects are created with a list of team members and the resources involved in each project. In effect, a matrix for each live project with its organizational mapping origins resembles the matrix set shown in Figure 9.1.

Figure 9.1 Abstraction Factor Analysis Matrices
Copyright © 2015, The Center for Excellence in Operations, Inc.

Next each project matrix is compared to the organization chart and an abstraction factor is calculated for each person for each project. Each template includes other critical project data (stage/gate status, budget, actual time reported by individual by project, development complexity, etc.) in the abstraction factor baseline matrix. Now there is a baseline of quantifiable data that enables the evaluation of project status and resource utilization, and the calculation of the costs and lost opportunities associated with disruptions to the development process. These costs and lost opportunities do not exist on the financial statements because they are "hidden." This analysis provides the ability to *see the unknown* and draw valuable conclusions when correlating abstraction factors and actual versus planned resource utilization with project status and potential lost revenue.

The analysis is not complete yet. It still requires further investigation to quantify the "why-why-why" around these issues. Abstraction factor analysis plus the development time reporting system provide the ability to drill down to specific projects and individuals and measure actual versus planned allocated time spent on projects or if the best resources are assigned to the highest-risk programs. The big difference is that people are sitting in meetings armed with hard, Minitab-generated analytics and facts and not wasting time with attribute-based explanations. Using this approach, it is not unusual to find that actual development time spent might be as much as 30 percent or more below planned development time at any given point, meaning that resources are pulled away from what they are scheduled to be working on. The opposite may be true where a project is resource overloaded at the expense of all other projects in the portfolio. Another common occurrence is a single resource being so overloaded that the associates working on the project cannot possibly get anything completed effectively and on time. These people are creative enough to find shortcuts and work-arounds to meet deadlines, but there are more serious consequences further downstream in the development process. All these situations create significant project delays, design process and quality issues, budget overruns, and late time to market.

The first step of the analysis is to design a sampling plan, a matrix of data elements that will help to describe and solve our problem. Abstraction factor analysis is a type of transaction stream mapping. Sample data are collected every time a process breakdown or disruption to a project schedule is detected. This sampling process is not a witch hunt; rather it is an objective effort to understand the organizational dynamics at play behind the formal system. Sample points are based on individual activities skipped, incomplete, incorrect, or late in each development project and are identified during and in between the weekly program manager's review meetings. For each incident, the following six questions need to be answered to better understand the individual disruption sample points:

▲ Who caused the disruption (name and reason) and on what project?

▲ What caused the disruption to happen?

▲ Where in the organizational network did the disruption occur (individual, manager, organization)?

▲ When did the disruption occur?

▲ Why did the disruption happen, and what was the real root cause of the disruption?

▲ How could this disruption have been prevented?

Since samples are collected across all gate-approved projects over time, they are a good indicator of how the overall development process is working. Using simple Pareto analysis, scatter plots, regression analysis, and other simple graphical and tabular analytics, abstraction factor analysis quantifies the surface-level hidden waste in the development process resulting from shared resource issues such as:

▲ Projects that are the furthest behind schedule that are causing the highest lost revenue potential because they have high complexity and high abstraction factors.

▲ Data patterns that provide a quantitative means to identify the resources and the management chains causing the most disruptions to projects (e.g., resources with highest recurring abstraction factors, common managers in the disruption chains, workload impact on abstraction factors, etc.).

▲ Resources working less than the planned allocated time on development projects because they are being directed to work on other things by other executives and managers in the abstraction factor chain.

▲ An assessment of the best resources with the right skills who are often not aligned with the specific needs of projects. The best resources are also spread so thin across multiple activities that they cannot be effective at any single effort.

▲ Resources working hard but not together. The harder people work, the more they fall behind because they are working and competing against each other's resources, not in a synchronous program flow mode based on the facts.

▲ The actual and projected compression times for the latter phases of development which set off more shortcuts and work-arounds, and certain quality, reliability, and performance problems after final release to market.

Abstraction factor analysis enables program managers to collaborate and smooth out project flows, and prevent much larger problems from occurring downstream in the development process. Abstraction factor analysis also provides a residual input into future resource planning and talent development. By the way, these typical findings are not a slam at executives, program managers, and resources who are usually working 120 percent to bring projects to market. Programs are never late because people are not working hard or because they are intentionally inefficient. It is a limitation of the development process and our inability to *clearly see* and identify the root causes of problems with our normal senses and traditional approaches to improvement. This discussion has focused on new product development, but the analysis is applicable to any complex transactional process (i.e., global supply chain, software development, packaging design, etc.) with many shared resources, touch points, and multiple organizational involvement.

Accelerated Value Stream Mapping

Value stream mapping (VSM) has produced mixed value in organizations, and in some it has become a "VSM gone wild" exercise. The traditional Lean textbook VSM approach tends to be more about producing a large diagram of the entire process and then attempting to improve the whole. In far too many cases it becomes a world hunger exercise in practice, particularly in the professional, knowledge-based transactional process space. It uses a static snapshot of descriptive data and includes very little analytics to pinpoint major detractor root causes. It also does not enable people and teams to really understand the various analytical input/output variables and their relative influence on longer-term process performance. It pushes people to chase symptomatic problems rather than true root causes of performance. And, because it deals with a static picture of the process at a single point in time and space, it has a short "shelf life" of usefulness. A VSM that takes six months to create is about as useful as a single six-month summary of delivery performance—nice to know, but nonactionable.

One example that comes to mind is an organization that hired a Lean consultant to help with VSM. The consultant led an internal team through a year-long exercise, and the only thing the organization had to show for its efforts is walls covered with massive VSMs that were incorrect, incomplete, or had changed since the original work. I visited this organization where the team leader began explaining the VSM while she described all of the nonstandardized practices, procedures, and work-arounds not shown on the map. As we talked further she was removing, writing on, and repositioning sticky notes and saying, "This doesn't really work like that," and "These data are incorrect." Then she showed me the team's improvement punch list which included purchasing more printers and fax machines, turning up the office heat, eliminating the distribution of a few document copies, buying more comfortable chairs, better communication, more raises, flexible work hours, new report requests from IT, and many other changes unrelated to the massive processes hanging on the walls.

During another meeting team members made comments like, "Management will not let us stop this effort," or, "It is a complete waste of time," or, "We followed our consultant's advice right over the cliff—even he doesn't know what we should do next." How do you think the Lean Kata has been influenced in this organization? The typical VSM process is primarily attribute- and snapshot-based and consumes months of time, resources, and money. By the time people realize the limited use of this approach, the organization cannot reverse the cost of its huge waste exercise. This does not happen 100 percent of the time, and several organizations have generated impressive successes from the correct application of VSM. However, the wallpaper syndrome happens in far too many instances, and a better way is needed in this fast and furious economy—to *improve the speed and value from value stream mapping.*

We have learned through hundreds of client experiences that value stream mapping works best as a living diagnostic and corrective action process instead of a discrete, broad-brush application of another single point improvement tool. This is particularly true in the transactional process improvement arena. There are an unlimited number of new and undiscovered improvement opportunities in the broader and more complex interconnected network of professional knowledge-based transactional processes. Here is the big differentiator: The visible and invisible complexity of improvement increases with the level of globalization and the human professional and technology content of processes, but so does the incremental value contribution of improvement. A more responsive and reconstructive forensics approach to VSM is required in these invisible transactional processes.

Rather than beginning the VSM process with the objective of mapping the organization's entire universe of processes, much quicker and higher value creation can be achieved with a more focused building-block approach. The objective of accelerated value stream mapping is many smaller hits in the right process pain points that achieve breakthrough results. This process aligns limited improvement resources with the highest impact improvement opportunities and promotes a more robust approach to improvement. Over time a broader VSM evolves from the smaller elements. In some cases tandem efforts are encouraged to suspect areas. As some critics have claimed, VSM does in fact view the end-to-end process, but the corrective actions are targeted to the highest-impact segments of the process. The proof is in the quicker and better results for the resources invested in mapping. Traditional VSM can often end up as a dead-end, solve-world-hunger exercise. The largest difference between the traditional and accelerataed VSM is that the mapping process becomes a more streamlined, continuous living reference to architect, reengineer, or improve enterprisewide business processes. This requires the integration of VSM with other improvement methodologies and tools and at a basic level the integration of Lean thinking (elimination of wastes) and the most basic Six Sigma problem-solving analytics.

Accelerated value stream mapping is more of a laser-targeted, rapid deployment and rapid results process that leverages the organization's current knowledge and tall pole (Pareto) thinking. This approach is more of a surgical peeling back of the onion by several means (e.g., focus group sessions, preanalytics, evaluation of customer and internal operating data, other diagnostic activities) before any specific VSM activities begin. Here is a simple overview of the accelerated process:

▲ *Conducting the accelerated value stream diagnostic.* For the process under study, the practitioner and the team develop the *SIPOC+ Diagram* (SIPOC/P/C/TGW/D for supplier, input, process, output, customers, performance metric, controls to maintain quality and standardization, things that typically go wrong, and supporting data) for the process under investigation (usually 6–12 steps, 1–2 pages max), and complete the remainder of the template.

▼ Next, an *extended dialogue CED (cause-and-effect diagram)* is developed following the processes identified above, and the team brainstorms potential root causes of the process problem within each step. It is wise to use the white space to free-form other related issues such as barriers, broader summary root causes, interrelationships, data needs, and so on.

▼ The next step is to validate root-cause information with hard data and then eliminate the perceived causals that do not stand the test of truth.

▼ Finally, conduct a designed force ranking analysis of the remaining root causes using frequency, severity, improvement impact, and controllability, borrowed from FMEA (failure mode and efficiency analysis) logic.

Look at the top 20 percent of the force ranked root-cause scores and note which step of the process they occur in. This analysis always points to a particular step or subprocess and isolates the highest influence detractors. It focuses resources on the most important detractors within a segment of the process. This is where the remaining focus of improvement efforts are pointed.

▲ *More detailed implementation.* The purpose is to analyze the highest-ranked *problem process segment* in more detail, integrating the traditional and more detailed VSM approaches with other simpler analytics (Pareto analysis, run charts, defects analysis, sampling plans, Cp and Cpk analysis, MultiVari, etc.) and other less structured tools (e.g., A3, mind mapping, affinity diagrams, worth factor analysis, etc).

▼ The analytics lead to developing, calibrating, and recommending opportunities for improvement, and developing the detailed implementation plans and control plans.

▼ Next, the team implements the improvements and monitors process performance.

For those who have difficulty with constructing a large map, remember that this is an iterative process where the puzzle pieces eventually come together as a whole. The largest benefit to accelerated value stream mapping is that organizations are dealing with real problems in the real process in real time.

Note that accelerated value stream mapping is not created in a single lengthy task with one tool. Such an approach usually ends up as wasteful fishing expeditions. Accelerated value stream mapping is many smaller cycles of "map-calibrate-prioritize-improve-validate," combined with broader and more robust analytics. The objective is not to issue a vague directive to create a map and see where the problem areas lie. An incorrect, out-of-date, big picture VSM of the entire organization is not very useful to support continuous improvement efforts. The objective is to improve problem areas that are well recognized by the people who work within the process every day. This rapid deployment approach leverages associate knowledge and experience, directly engaging people where they work in the improvement process, and validating opportunities with data and facts. We are creating detailed segments based on highest-impact opportunities. The size of the segment is relative to the interconnectivity of the process segment under investigation (manageable "chunks" for rapid improvement), but it is never a megadocumentation exercise of every process in the entire organization. Accelerated value stream mapping involves deep diving into the largest detractor process segments and understanding the factors that really make the overall process tick. Over a relatively short period of time, the process segments can be pieced together to present a larger picture of the organization. Another reminder: In this scenario VSM is but a single tool in the broader improvement toolbox and a living process of *improving how you improve.*

Transactional Enterprise Improvement

Transactional process improvement represents the missed mark of Lean in many organizations that continue to operate with excess hidden wastes, costs, time delays, quality problems, and major customer issues. Despite the

Lean and general continuous improvement (CI) investments of the past, organizations certainly deserve and can achieve significant value contribution in transactional process improvement. In fact, transactional process improvement represents the highest hidden area of opportunity in many organizations that continue to work with their institutionalized IT architectures and related business processes.

Why should organizations be all over the topic of transactional process improvement? The benefits of transactional process improvement are enormous—larger than Lean *manufacturing*—because they often involve fixing problems that are the root cause of manufacturing issues, fixing problems that the organization does not know about yet, or fixing problems that as stand-alone efforts can easily run to tens of millions of dollars in new value. Think about the cost of excess/obsolete inventory, returns and allowances, late time-market, poor outsourcing decisions, or ineffectual innovation, just to name a few. The following is a partial list of transactional process improvement initiatives where our clients have achieved significant benefits:

▲ Strategic planning and business alignment

▲ Customer and market research

▲ Product and market strategy

▲ Product management and SKU rationalization

▲ New product innovation and concept engineering

▲ New product development and time-to-market

▲ Global commercialization, packaging, literature

▲ Warranty, returns, and allowances

▲ Invoicing and billing errors

▲ Excess/obsolete inventory reduction and reserves

▲ Requests for quotations (RFQs)

▲ Customer service, repair, spares management

▲ Global sourcing and outsourcing

▲ Financial adjustment, variance, close reduction

▲ Outsourcing rationalization

▲ Advertising, marketing, and promotions

▲ Sales and operations planning (S&OP)

▲ Supply chain execution and control

▲ Distribution, transportation, and logistics

▲ Supplier development and management

▲ Selling and account/channel management

▲ Organizational development and human resources management

▲ Global real estate and space management

▲ Strategic maintenance and facilities management

▲ Performance measurement processes

▲ Information technology effectiveness and ROI

▲ Acquisition and integration process

The remainder of this chapter provides guidance about how to rethink and how to adapt a Lean Business System to the interconnected global networks of complex, professional knowledge-based transactional processes and achieve renewed breakthroughs in operating performance.

Understand the Challenge of Transactional Processes

The first step to success is to understand and appreciate the nature of transactional processes. Manufacturing, from which many Lean and general process improvement techniques evolved, represents a declining percentage of the end-to-end economic and strategic process activities in organizations. Sure, manufacturing is still part of the value chain, but a very small component in terms of the fully loaded process costs of doing business globally. Many organizations have morphed themselves from geographically and country-specific physical sites to a global network of complex, knowledge-based transactional processes. Yet their Lean resources are dated in attempting to port over the approaches that worked well on the production floor and thinking about eliminating rather than integrating information technology. The operating environments in organizations have changed faster than the capacity and capabilities of their resources to improve it. Walking off the production floor and into the offices of very talented professionals with the same narrow, tools-based Lean thinking is a prescription for disaster. Success is highly dependent upon a paradigm shift to nimble and efficient strategy and opportunity alignment processes, supply chain processes, time-to-market processes, cash-to-cash processes, engineering processes, customer service processes, sales and marketing processes, and many other "people plus technology" processes in organizations. As the number of professional knowledge workers and technology content increase, the complexity of transactional processes increases, the degree of difficulty of improvement and change increases, and the usefulness of the Lean manufacturing tool-set thinking decreases.

By comparison, Lean manufacturing is simple. Even the most commoditized tool-set approaches to Lean manufacturing produce temporary results. Transactional processes are much more complicated because of their interconnected, convoluted, and cross-enterprise processes, lack of standardization, unsighted activities, velocity and touch points, and of course the human element of originality and work-arounds in daily operations. So why has Lean failed to deliver in these strategic and mission-critical business processes? Because transactional processes require a higher order of improvement with an integrated approach. The Lean principles and tools that produced success on the production floor are success limiting in human-dependent transactional process environments. As we mentioned previously, transactional improvement cannot rely upon normal senses to identify issues and new opportunities for improvement that is possible on the production floor. One can observe physical bottlenecks, measure defects, view excess inventory, listen to equipment vibration, detect odor from poor ventilation systems, and the like. Transactional process opportunities are hidden in the human and information architectures of organizations. One cannot see an IT transaction or observe a human thinking bottleneck, or sniff end-of-month general-ledger adjustments—

or readily define and measure defects and root causes. In the absence of hard data and facts, transactional processes are managed via opinions, perceptions, cursory explanations, and political deflections that lead to quick symptomatic responses.

We also mentioned value stream mapping earlier in this chapter. Lean practitioners have relied too heavily on a canned, single-point methodology in the transactional process space. For example, many organizations have spent months conducting blind value stream mapping exercises of the entire company with no purpose or specific problem in mind ("Field of Dreams" improvement—if you map the process, the problems and solutions will automatically happen). Value stream mapping is one of the most useful improvement tools, but it needs to be adapted to the megahertz transactional process environment. Transactional process improvement also requires a much deeper view of Lean thinking, approach, analysis, information, and measurement systems. It requires a broader blend of improvement thinking, methodologies, and technologies. In the absence of a proactive, well-planned and well-executed transactional improvement effort, organizations cannot manage and prevent problems. Instead, they are forced into a mode of detecting and reacting to problems after the fact—and that is too late (e.g., disconnects in supply and demand, returns and allowances, supplier delivery and quality issues, late new product development tasks, buried financial variances, excess/obsolete inventory, write-offs and adjustments, billing errors, customer complaints, etc.). This is not acceptable because these wastes are assignable and correctable. Organizations that are willing to launch an all-out aggressive campaign against transactional process waste with the right holistic approaches will find *new money*—millions of dollars of new and previously unknown opportunities for improvement. It requires putting the Lean keys down for a minute and rethinking the journey with the right competencies, resources, and approach.

Adapt Lean to Transactional Process Opportunities

One thing is for certain: The philosophy and mindset of Lean are directly applicable to complex transactional processes, but the planning and execution are very different. Adapting Lean to the complex realities of transactional processes is not straightforward. Success involves putting away the traditional bag of Lean principles and tools and thinking outside the box.

Here are a few points to consider when adapting Lean to a more robust Lean Business System environment:

1. First, improvement practitioners and other resources must develop a deep understanding of how to adapt Lean to extremely nonconventional and highly complex processes and environments. Simply attempting to overlay the commoditized Lean tools that worked well in manufacturing is dead wrong and doomed to failure.

2. Second, improvement practitioners and other resources must develop a deeper understanding of the organization's complete information architecture and the specific knowledge-based "people plus technology" core business processes that are embedded within the overall architecture (e.g., ERP, BOMs, financial systems and G/L, inventory management and accountability, receiving, sales systems and account management, HR systems, warranty and returns, invoicing and collections, order fulfillment, patient admitting and scheduling, and other system architecture applications). The right team composition is a mandate for success.

3. Third, this transactional process improvement requires a high degree of creativity and innovation. The objectives may be the same (e.g., eliminate waste, improve process quality, align with customer requirements, velocity, asset and human capital optimization, etc.), but the execution is typically created to achieve a specific purpose. There are no invoicing error or inventory variance or failed design verification or incorrect behavior and culture deficiency Lean tools. Transactional processes require experimental re-creations, replications, and simulations of problems using the combined knowledge, wisdom, experiences, and data of highly competent professionals that *live* the process every day. Tracking down and eliminating the root causes of waste is often analogous to an accident or crime scene investigation.

4. Fourth, transactional process improvement requires measurement system analysis (MSA) and other analytics in parallel with process analysis. Many issues in transactional processes can be directly pegged to the mechanics of how performance is measured—and not measured. Transactional processes have root causes embedded in both the measurement system and the process itself.

One might argue that this is overkill. It definitely is not, and the over-simplification and underestimation of transactional process complexity is why organizations have not achieved the benefits that they deserve through a traditional Lean *manufacturing* tool-set approach. Fact is, all of these "people plus technology" transactional processes are interconnected and interdependent professional processes. Silo-based improvements will actually create more waste and inefficiencies in the business. The right cross-functional improvements will produce both direct and residual benefits throughout the business. Transactional processes are much more dynamic and subject to change than a machine on the production floor. They require true continuous monitoring and improvement to keep the waste from returning.

Transactional Process Improvement Requires Lean Forensic Skills

Over the years we have referred to transactional process improvement as *transactional forensics*. No, the evidence may not be used in a court of law (although we have been involved in expert testimony work in the past), but the process of digging out the truth about what really happened is very similar. Complex transactional processes include a lot of unpredictability, professional judgments versus hard data, a high degree of informal activities underlying a formal process, and fuzzy cause and effects in space and time. In this example judgment is not a casual opinion—it is verifiable and sufficient *cause of clue data.* Lean forensics entails bringing scientific order to the ways and means that one manipulates and tests the speculative causes and effects in transactional processes, which opens up the door to improvement and greatly reduces the risk of drawing false conclusions. Too many executives and professionals view transactional processes as "the way it is" and are not motivated to change them. They fail to see the enormous benefits of data mining, analytics, and transformation. The seasoned improvement expert uses the organization's integrated enterprise architecture and other applications to trace and defrag the transaction trail like a forensic detective reconstructing and processing a crime scene to identify root causes and other existing conditions during the actual event. In practice, the differences between root causes and outcomes are often fuzzy (the *reflexivity factors*), and the challenge becomes one of identifying and isolating the right, most severe detractor segments of these transactional processes with facts. Success requires a deep understanding of both improvement and key business processes.

This is how and why we developed accelerated value stream mapping. Organizations can map the end-to-end transactional processes, but they cannot improve them end to end because causes and effects are overlapping and relative in time and space. What is meant by this statement? Here is an example: Ask managers and associates in the sales, S&OP, manufacturing, engineering, purchasing, quality control, distribution, and finance organizations why there is so much obsolete inventory, and you will receive at a minimum, eight different answers—most likely dozens of conflicting and finger-pointing opinions and perceptions. The real story and root causes are buried and unknown to the organization. By the way, how do organizations normally "fix" this problem? They allocate financial reserves for future write-offs. Does that address and eliminate root causes? What happens next year and the year after that? Does obsolete inventory go away? Absolutely not! The seasoned improvement is able to mine and construct the real story and root causes, and in the majority of cases they are totally different from everyone's perceptions and opinions. Trying to improve an end-to-end transactional process often turns into symptomatic problem solving. These transactional issues are complex. Often these situations require deeper skills and approaches than a team has that is introduced to VSM and being coached to follow the recipe and standard symbols verbatim. It comes back to the axiom, *You don't know what you don't know.* This is not your traditional Lean or Six Sigma practitioner at work; it's a bit analogous to how one might expect a Henry Lee and Michael Baden to conduct an improvement initiative.

Technology and Improvement Are Inseparable

Currently there exists another huge missing link between human Lean talent development and the evolving technologies such as cloud computing, event-driven performance dashboards, business analytics, and data visualization. Many Lean practitioners remain in the Stone Age holding onto their magnetic scheduling systems, manual production boards, and other manually maintained Lean practices. Some continue to see technology architectures as inhibitors rather than enablers of Lean, especially in an enterprisewide Lean Business System. Others have a comfortable, fixed focus on Lean *manufacturing*. On the IT side of the house practitioners implement the technology first and then come back to business process improvement at a later date. Improvement can be viewed as an impediment to quick technology spending and implementation. The game has changed for everyone in every organization. Technology-enabled improvement plays a key role in transactional process improvement. Transactional improvement is transparent and composed of key business processes, information flows, knowledge-based employees, and complex, contradictory decisions. There are literally hundreds of professional and knowledge resources managing thousands of dynamic process touch points, a continuous churn in changing requirements, specific country needs, time constraints, communications issues, and exponentially greater opportunities for waste, variation, human risk, and bad decisions. Technology enables the sophisticated Lean practitioner to *see* these wastes and the true root causes through a virtual reconstruction of the processes and conditions that create the wastes. Particularly in the transactional process improvement space, one finds several consistently recurring situations:

▲ Different executives, managers, and associates have different perspectives and ideas about the problem and its root causes, and in most cases nobody including the Lean expert knows the real problem ("You don't know what you don't know").

▲ Often, what was thought to be the problem is not a problem at all, but symptomatic of deeper waste activities buried in the complex transactional process network.

▲ In almost every case, what was thought to be the root cause of a transactional process problem is incorrect, and turns out to be a totally different and unknown root cause once the onion is peeled back and the transactional process is stripped butt naked.

▲ All improvements require a combination of analytical methodologies, and all improvements typically include a combination of people, process, and technology (e.g., training and education, process improvement, technology-enabled enhancements).

Technology is a huge game changer in a transactional process-intense Lean Business System environment because it is transforming the whole discipline of improvement and how organizations *improve how they improve.* Technology is also simplifying the design, focus, maintenance, and measurement of the entire Lean Business System architecture.

Do Not Be Fooled by the Existing Lean Presence

As we say throughout the book, if an organization has a Lean initiative in place, chances are that it is missing the mark on the total opportunities of transactional process improvement. Forget about thinking failure. Many of these new and unknown opportunities exist because the world has changed. If your organization is one of the success stories, then congratulations! If your organization is in the majority segment of organizations that are underperforming in the Lean transactional improvement space, there may be many reasons for this but they are irrelevant when compared to the enormous opportunities for improvement and competitiveness that exist. Several organizations have their Lean Business System in name only; it is really a success-limiting *production* system with a broader label. It requires a lot more than a 5S exercise, A3 templates, and a modified production board to uncover and harvest these complex opportunities. There should be absolutely no question at this point about the differences between a Lean Production System and a real, enterprisewide Lean Business System— and the significant differences in upside potential for value contribution.

The Lean Business System Reference Model is the guide to a new and much larger beginning with Lean. Improvement via innovative thinking and enabling technology often results in total process and business model reinvention. Transactional process improvement is undiscovered territory for Lean and represents tens or even hundreds of millions of dollars in new value contribution for many organizations. Think about the short-term P&L impact and the longer-term competitiveness of:

▲ Reducing returns and allowances by $30 million.

▲ Improving time to market by 80 percent and being number one in the market.

▲ Adding three or four gross margin points to the P&L through less planned financial reserves.

- ▲ Reducing supply chain time, complexity, and costs by $100 million.

- ▲ Gaining hundreds of millions of revenue growth, cost reduction, profitability, and competitive market position from developing new products on time, on budget, without post-release quality, reliability, or performance problems.

- ▲ Reducing the financial close and all related G/L clerical adjustments and clerical resource needs by 75 percent.

- ▲ Reducing engineering changes by 50 percent.

- ▲ Hitting new product features/functions out of the park with customers—like the emotional Apple, Porsche, and Harley Davidson customer experiences.

- ▲ Reducing travel expenses by $6 million and reducing the need for limited resources to travel internationally to put out fires.

- ▲ Improving advertising and promotion effectiveness by 100 percent.

- ▲ Reducing operating supplies and facility costs by $10 million.

These are actual transactional process improvements achieved in organizations. The challenges are much greater, but so too are the opportunities for improvement. Beyond the numbers, transactional process improvement provides an extremely challenging and professionally rewarding leadership and general business growth experience. Organizations can really accelerate talent and organizational development by engaging people in a variety of experiences in different functional areas. Over time this builds knowledge and an appreciation of other people's roles in the organization, increases the broader core business process thinking, and helps to create the right behavioral patterns and cultural attributes for enterprisewide success.

Bibliography

Burton, T. 2010. *Accelerating Lean Six Sigma Results: How to Achieve Improvement Excellence in the New Economy.* J. Ross Publishing, Boca Raton, Florida.

Burton, T. 2013. *Abstraction Factor Analysis: A New Approach to Improve New Product and Software Development.* CEO Executive White Paper series. http://ceobreakthrough.com/wp/wp-content/uploads/2013/03/Abstraction-Factor-Analysis.pdf.

Burton, T. 2013. "Faster Value Stream Mapping," *Industrial Engineering Magazine*, June 2014. Norcross, Georgia.

Burton, T. 2013. *Lean Six Sigma in Healthcare.* CEO Executive White Paper series. http://ceobreakthrough.com/wp/wp-content/uploads/2013/03/Lean-Six-Sigma-in-Healthcare-.pdf.

Burton, T., and Filipiak, E. 2011. *Improvement Excellence in the Federal Government: Addressing the Urgent Need to Reduce Waste and Deficit Spending, and Improve Service Delivery.* CEO White Paper Series. http://ceobreakthrough.com/wp/wp-content/uploads/2013/03/CEO-Website-Government-Waste-White-Paper-Part-1.pdf.

Navarro, P., and Autry, G. 2011. *Death by China: Confronting the Dragon—A Global Call to Action.* Pearson Education, Prentice Hall, Upper Saddle River, New Jersey.

Steelcase. 2012. "Culture Code: Leveraging the Workplace to Meet Today's Global Challenges," *Steelcase 360 Magazine*, iss. 65.

CHAPTER 10

A New Beginning

This is the last chapter in this book. It represents a new beginning with evolving Lean to a much higher standard of enterprisewide improvement. Think about all the new possibilities available to organizations with a holistic Lean Business System. This is the most exciting time for improvement in the entire history of improvement! As practitioners we must lead this new evolution of Lean and continuous improvement and not let it pass us by. We cannot wait and rely on executive leadership—executives are overloaded by a continuous stream of larger challenges, and most are not up-to-date with the new requirements and possibilities for Lean and where it is headed. And for certain, we cannot give the future of Lean up to technology which is coming at organizations like a freight train. Running around with iPads, iPhones, and other mobile devices, interpreting data on charts—any charts—blasting out hundreds of e-mails and text messages, and other technology influencing behaviors are not Lean. In several situations these taken-for-granted practices are actually undermining Lean and root-cause problem solving. On the positive side, there are a great many new and hidden opportunities for improvement through the marriage of a Lean Business System and technology. This is the future of Lean—and it has already arrived in many forward-thinking organizations.

We have provided a detailed discussion of the Lean Business System Reference Model™, its architecture and subprocess functions, best practices, and real-world examples. Adaptive Leadership is the engine of a Lean Business System; it creates the vision, behaviors, and cultural attributes of success (Kata). The intent of the reference model is to help organizations *improve how they improve* through a more robust architecture, a new focus on behavioral alignment and cultural development (Kata), and an expanded enterprisewide scope. A continued focus on a narrow set of manufacturing principles and tools in the absence of Kata equals just another fad improvement road trip with illusive benefits. There is no such thing as maintaining Lean or limiting oneself to Lean manufacturing: Both are forms of passive regression. Every organization can and deserves to do better than this.

Follow the Lean Business System Reference Model

The urgent need to evolve Lean *manufacturing* to an enterprisewide Lean Business System is evident. This is not a replacement for the Toyota Production System (TPS) but is a major enhancement for most organizations that are following the TPS as their Lean approach. Throughout the book we discuss the limitations not of the TPS itself, but of a continued narrow focus on Lean manufacturing. As I mention several times, I admire Toyota and have been a practitioner of the Toyota Production System for decades and under many labels. I admire executives who have stepped up and made Lean and continuous improvement a nonnegotiable mandate in their organizations. I admire the creative practitioners and teams that give it their all every day, often going unnoticed by their management. The situation that needs to change swiftly is how organizations and practitioners have attempted to mimic and implement only the visible, non-Kata parts of the TPS. Lean manufacturing is still important in the totality of adaptive systematic improvement. Organizations still need to achieve higher levels of excellence to justify and grow our existing domestic manufacturing. They can also benefit from revisiting and rationalizing previous outsourcing decisions based on total cost of ownership, which may justify reversing outsourcing decisions and reshoring manufacturing. This is transactional improvement. Organizations will still need to adapt their TPS or Lean manufacturing initiative to new technology developments that are changing the landscape of manufacturing like 3D printing, robotics, additive manufacturing, and other technology game changers.

Organizations continue to be challenged by the dynamics of the global economy, yet the fundamental principles, tools, and practice of the Toyota Production System or Lean manufacturing have remained the same for decades. Think about it: just-in-time (JIT), single minute exchange of die (SMED), work cells, kanban, pull systems, quick response manufacturing (QRM), continuous flow manufacturing (CFM), mixed model scheduling, manufacturing excellence, total preventive maintenance (TPM), demand flow technology (DFT), factory physics, mass customization, variety reduction, Six Sigma, Lean Six Sigma, and on and on. For the most part Lean manufacturing has remained intact for years while the world has changed drastically. Most organizations are long overdue for a rediscovery of Lean in this chronic disruption economy. Lean requires an injection of disruptive innovation, a *Lean moon shot* that takes it to a higher order and higher-yielding and technology-enabled adaptive systematic process of improvement.

A *moon shot?* Yes, according to Google's definition. A true holistic Lean Business System addresses a huge problem with innovative thinking and solutions, integrating the latest technologies. Remember that this is an ambitious but empty statement without fully engaged and empowered people, constant talent development, and developing the right improvement Kata through structured means and deliberate actions. Organizations begin this breakthrough journey by defining their specific business requirements and cultural development needs and then integrate technology as a key enabler of success. The primary purpose of the Lean Business System Reference Model is to provide the guidance to evolve Lean to its next level of potential: a holistic, enterprisewide, adaptive, systematic, culturally grounded, and technology-enabled Lean Business System. The reference model adds significant sociotechnical clarity to this moon shot mission. We have provided examples of organizations other than Toyota that are well on their journey to a *for-real* Lean Business System. The majority of organizations can benefit significantly by joining this new journey. The reference model is a pragmatic and useful guide that is always in a work-in-progress state and continuously under development. Don't attempt to mimic or treat the Lean Business System Reference Model as the next magic diet or you will never get *Lean*.

Act Now! Waste Is the Organic Enemy

Waste is like a living organism. Waste is an organic phenomenon in organizations that grows without deliberate attention and proactive countermeasures. Waste can be prevented by constant attention to its presence. As soon as organizations stop paying attention to waste, it grows. Waste can halt progress. Waste can grow until it becomes a much larger problem, or it can continue to grow under the radar (hidden) until it creates a catastrophic event with far-reaching consequences. Every executive knows this intuitively, but often leads the organization down a different road, a road that reinforces the wrong patterns of behavior and cultural codes (Kata).

Lean and continuous improvement have not always been the most enticing topic for executives because they require commitment and a disciplined effort. They also reveal waste and root causes and establish accountability and metrics for progress. Like it or not, the need for continuous improvement and eliminating waste never goes away. Yet there are always excuses for postponing continuous improvement that, when one thinks about *postponing improvement,* are silly choices. The following is a list of authentic excuses heard on the street:

- ▲ "There's no money in the budget for improvement."

- ▲ "The time is not quite right for improvement."

- ▲ "Improvement is not in my goals and objectives."

- ▲ "We finished our Lean program years ago."

- ▲ "We stopped our Lean program. It did not work for us; we're different."

- ▲ "We don't have the time and resources to improve and do our regular jobs."

- ▲ "We're good at fixing this customer problem every time it comes up."

- ▲ "If I had more time, I would have found a better way."

Rationalizations for not improving are a tragic testimony to executive leadership, who are usually focused solely on short-term financial performance and thereby inadvertently create *bad Kata.* Their organizations desperately need to break out of their mode of thinking and working. In this challenging global economy, many organizations are running out of time and need to discover a paradigm shift in strategic and operating improvement. The purpose of the Lean Business System Reference Model is to help these organizations rise up and face their business and cultural issues with a superior approach with structured means and deliberate actions. Look at your own current state of improvement with objective judgment and conviction. Accept the humility, it's temporary and healthy; no executive or organization is perfect. Then recognize the gaps in performance as new opportunities, not failure. Innovative thinking, evolving technology, and the right improvement-enabling behaviors and cultural attributes (Kata) significantly reduce the takt time of Toyota's 70-year history of continuous evolving success. But organizations must begin this new journey today. Not tomorrow or next week or next month—*today!*

While writing this book, we learned about several customer issues with Ahrens, Flextronics, Lincoln Electric, Avery Dennison, General Cable, Audi, GE, Harley Davidson, Bosch, Motorola, IBM, BMW, Deere, Lockheed Martin, Raytheon, Dana, Boeing, Porsche, Johnson Controls, Visteon, Honda, Daimler Benz, Emerson Electric, Caterpillar, Honeywell, and dozens of other great global organizations—including Toyota. No matter how much an organization tries, it is never perfect 100 percent of the time. What sets these organizations apart is that they strive for perfection 100 percent of the time, and they achieve perfection most of the time. They also strive for perfection in the responsible and responsive resolution of their occasional unanticipated quality problems and other customer issues. Their batting average is superior to competitors in their industry, and when they do hit an occasional bump in the road, their recovery is fast and impressive.

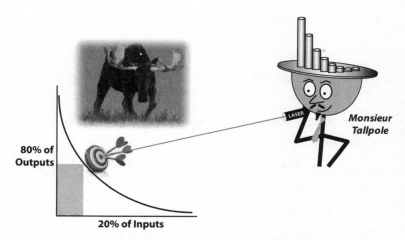

Figure 10.1   Monsieur Tallpole and the 80/20 Principle

Think Pareto—Focus on the Right Tall Poles

Throughout the Lean Business System Reference Model there is a built-in awareness to identify problems correctly, understand the underlying root causes, and then focus on the 20 percent of the problem that will yield 80 percent of the opportunities as quickly as possible. This does not mean that you leave the remaining 20 percent under the table because the remaining 20 percent might well influence other issues in the interconnected network of transactional processes. This is the practice side of things. As organizations and practitioners go forward with architecting their own Lean Business System, it is important to observe and always be aware of the tall pole perspectives of improvement. This takes many different iterations to arrive at the facts behind an improvement opportunity, and the data mix within each of these iterations may be very different. I like to explain this analysis as if the results were printed on glass panes, and then stacked in a rack. If you were to look through the stacked panes, you notice different groupings of commonality that can be extracted for further analytical and calibration activities. For example:

▲ 80 percent of products are sold in 20 percent of the world.

▲ 80 percent of revenues are derived from 20 percent of products.

▲ 80 percent of gross margins are derived from 20 percent of products.

▲ 80 percent of gross margins are derived from 20 percent of customers.

▲ 80 percent of products are sold through 20 percent of dealer channels.

▲ 80 percent of inventory accuracy problems are caused by 20 percent of possible causes.

▲ 80 percent of maintenance resources are consumed on 20 percent of unplanned downtime occurrences.

▲ 80 percent of product development cycle time is consumed by 20 percent of development activities.

▲ 80 percent of time-to-market issues are created by 20 percent of resources.

▲ 80 percent of operating supplies are composed of 20 percent of line item transactions.

▲ 80 percent of the monthly financial close is completed with 20 percent of the miscellaneous transaction and trial balance adjustments.

▲ 80 percent of revenues are generated by 20 percent of sales activities.

▲ 80 percent of yield problems are created by 20 percent of possible root causes.

▲ 80 percent of hospital patient time is spent waiting (actually higher).

We could go on, and on, but the message here is to always try to focus limited improvement resources on the highest-impact opportunities.

The leadership side of tall pole thinking is to *put the moose on the table*. Like major business challenges, a moose is huge, intimidating, aggressive, ugly, and not so pleasant to the senses. The analogy encourages people to address major challenges and opportunities as openly, honestly, and as aggressively as if they were confronting an 1,800-pound bull moose. Great organizations operate in a *no fear* mode, from the executive suite to the design engineering functions to the receiving dock. Organizations that have the confidence and passion to overcome any obstacle make significant progress with improvement when the *no fear* emotion is part of their Kata portfolio of behavioral patterns. They are usually the best performers in their industry.

Personalize the Journey

Throughout this book we have used the Lean Business System Reference Model and Lean Business System for discussion and clarification purposes. This new journey requires deeper divergent thinking and an expanded definition of Lean by several measures: adaptive, systematic, enterprisewide scope, a higher and more deliberate focus on the invisible Kata side of improvement, a creative and expanded set of improvement methodologies, better balanced performance, and integration of evolving technology. An organization-centric Lean Business System goes way beyond a *manufacturing* or *production* journey. However, these terms and their perceived meanings are well entrenched in people's minds from previous improvement initiatives. This journey is new and very different in terms of how we have presented it in the Lean Business System Reference Model. We have used the word Lean in the reference model because it is a generic framework that must be continually adapted to a particular organization based on *its* business requirements and cultural development needs. The reference model represents a new generation of improvement that includes Lean as we have known it plus many other critical success factors. Organizations must adapt the reference model to their own organization-centric Lean Business System. We encourage organizations to think through and personalize their journey, including establishing a broader identity such as *The XYZ Company Business System* or other name that does not insinuate a particular production or tool-set approach from the past.

Understand the Deeper Implications of Global Kata

How do executives and organizations understand the deeper implications of global Kata? The first step is to take a deep breath, stand back, and *observe* what they have been doing with Lean and several other continuous improvement programs of the past. Many organizations have been unintentionally developing *bad Kata*. It's often painful for executives to come to the realization that what they have been doing with Lean and continuous improvement isn't working anymore. The entire organization shares this pain. Customers, suppliers, and other stakeholders share this pain. The pain increases the longer executives and their organizations remain in this situation. Staying the same course allows all of the operational detractors and their associated wastes to multiply exponentially and destroy strategic improvement initiatives. It is time to go back to Toyota and other great organizations and take a closer look at and embrace the importance of the cultural underpinnings of their adaptive systematic process of improvement. The key to a successful Lean Business System is turning *bad Kata* into *great Kata* through the continuous development, nurturing, and reinforcement of how people think and work.

Kata is so much more than a production worker and a coach in a Toyota factory. Kata is not limited to the Toyota Production System. At Toyota, Kata is an enterprisewide cultural standard of excellence and perfection in everything that it does as a global corporation. This fact is not recognized to the extent that it should be when one limits the discussion of Kata to the Toyota Production System or Lean *manufacturing* system. One might think that the TPS principles and tools represent all the *keys* to success—but if organizations do not know how to think about a new destination and what automobiles (architecture and processes) they will be driving to get there, the keys are irrelevant.

Global Kata is a far-reaching adaptive systematic process of how organizations think, learn, and execute throughout the interconnected web of activities in the total enterprise. This is a continuous process based on structured means and deliberate actions, with each cycle raising the bar of behavioral and cultural excellence. We discussed Adaptive Leadership and best practice leadership behaviors as the primary drivers of Kata, but one must understand the deeper dynamics of what is going on. Leadership injects, nurtures, and reinforces a vision and the positive emotions that align patterns of behavior with cultural attributes. Now it is the executive's, practitioner's, and reader's turn to do the same thing in their own organizations. This is the invisible foundation of a Lean Business System, and all the improvement tools in the world cannot create it. (See Figure 10.2.)

Figure 10.2   Lean Tools Tradesperson

Find the Kata in the Self

One of my goals throughout the book is to create the right positive emotions with the readers so that they recognize the need, understand the new unknown opportunities, and go for their own culturally grounded Lean Business System. Transforming the Lean Business System Reference Model into a custom-designed and architected powerhouse Lean Business System within an organization begins with vision, knowledge, passion, discipline, and conscience—and all the related positive emotions provided in

Chapter 3. Go back and revisit these positive emotions, and then recognize that every individual has the capacity to step up and influence positive change. People are not born with these positive emotions; they learn them not only from great leaders and mentors, but through their own initiative and experience in several Kata events in their lives. There is no standard improvement principle or tool that compares with courage, conviction, creativity and innovation, passion, divergent thinking, collaboration and dialogue, emotional engagement and empowerment, inspiration, interest, awe, and pride. Nothing can beat the strong and persistent presence of these emotions. Nothing can stop people who are set on the right course with the *fire in the belly* of these emotions. Nothing can stop the progress of learning, developing, and doing when people have these emotions on full throttle. But experiencing these emotions requires an attitude of exploration into the wilderness of the unknown which can be challenging, fearful, and often humbling. Change is always accompanied by anxiety, fear, and many unknowns. At the same time the ability to change (and keep up with change) is an individual's and organization's only security in this economy. The victory of turning the unknown into new knowledge and personal growth far outweighs the (perceived) risks of change. It is this very attitude that launches people and organizations into new levels of professional and personal success. These emotions exist in the souls of all people who want to learn, grow, and experience a happy and healthy career and life. Remember that *your limit is your limit*: People's limit is the self-imposed limits that they choose to place on themselves. In other words, the sky is the limit!

Turning Lean Tradespeople into Enlightened Problem Solvers

Lean is at a crossroads. We discuss this in Chapter 6. There is a fundamental difference between how Toyota has implemented and continues to implement Lean, and how Western organizations have chosen to implement Lean and a long list of other previous programs. Taiichi Ohno recognized that continuous improvement was an integrated sociotechnical process and a lifelong commitment for Toyota. His inspiration and vision for what he wanted to create at Toyota came from reading about American supermarkets. Ohno did not mimic the American supermarket model; he adapted the idea and used basic industrial and systems engineering principles and tools as the means. He also evolved the discipline of industrial engineering into a new paradigm. Ohno was a brilliant, enlightened problem solver. Genichi Taguchi, Masaaki Imai, Kauru Ishikawa, Shigeo Shingo, Seiichi Nakajima, and others expanded the body of knowledge and were also enlightened problem solvers. Western organizations, on the other hand, have implemented continuous improvement with more of a *preferred tools tradesperson* approach. This approach was based on what these organizations could *see* (visible changes and tools) which appeared simple and easy to copy. Additionally, these approaches have been highly influenced by the preferred approach of the moment: 5S, value stream mapping, Kaizen, gemba walks, Lean tools, or Six Sigma analytics. These are very different approaches—a scientific, disciplined process of higher-order problem solving combined with developing the right sustaining patterns of behaviors and cultural characteristics to sustain success as opposed to a tradesperson putting up another copy of a spec home (a prespecified home) of choice. Not a criticism but a fact: Many Lean practitioners are functioning in the tools tradesperson category. Many executives are also endorsing this *canned, check-the-box* approach, and nobody is winning. It takes a lot more than memorizing principles and terminology or mimicking tools to become the next global Toyota organization. One of the objectives of this book has been to convince the Lean manufacturing zealots to rethink their belief system and approaches in light of a rapidly changing world with new requirements and possibilities, and to develop into more highly skilled, influential, valuable, and recognized business improvement professionals throughout their enterprise and extended enterprise.

Think about this. In the absence of improvement, any process controlled by humans eventually finds its comfort zone. Associates pay less attention to what is going on around them because they *know how to* do their work. The same holds true for Lean practitioners and change agents who are involved in a steady-state *process* of improvement. Over time people and processes settle into comfortable routines and standard practices of work, including how practitioners implement and sustain Lean, TPS, or continuous improvement in general. Consider this scenario: If one leaves a process alone and sticks to the same routine, does it improve? *Continuous* improvement is not possible without improving the process, scope, and content of how improvement is implemented and achieved. This is what is meant by *improving how we improve*—constantly. The TPS principles and tools by themselves are very limiting in a true Lean Business

System. *Continuous* improvement requires the process of *improving how we improve* through new divergent thinking, exploration, creativity, more analytics, a tinkering mindset, no fear, new and diverse approaches, preemptive actions, deeper coaching and mentoring skills, more emphasis on people and cultural development, the integration of technology, and a raising-the-bar mindset.

Executives, managers, and supervisors need to rethink leadership behaviors, choices, and actions—and how to positively influence new patterns of behavior and cultural attributes required in a Lean Business System. They need to step back and understand what a real Lean Business System is all about and what it takes to achieve lasting success. Lean manufacturing practitioners and TPS disciples need to develop and grow beyond what they have been doing and into sophisticated, enterprisewide problem-solving experts. They also must learn how to nurture the right associate behaviors and create a culture of excellence. This is a bold commitment and a bold venture that develops over time. But it is absolutely necessary to be a value-contributing owner, leader, practitioner, and coach as well as a value recipient of a Lean Business System. See Figure 10.3.

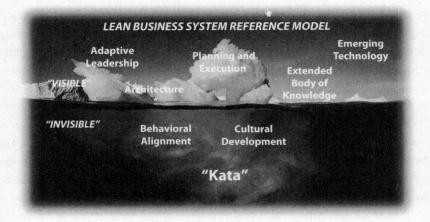

Figure 10.3 Turning Lean Tools' Tradespeople into Creative Problem Solvers

Graduating to "Learning to Observe"

In 1999 D. Jones, Mike Rother, John Shook, and J. Womack wrote *Learning to See*. The authors introduced a new genre of Lean books that invited the reader to follow along and actually *do* for themselves. People in organizations had been mapping out process flows for decades prior to the publication of this book, using everything from rolls of meat paper, yarn, push pins, actual documents, sketches and data on D- and E-sized drafting paper, standard IT process flow charting templates, and so on. *Learning to See* introduced value stream mapping into the everyday vernacular of Lean, complete with standard symbols, logic, and terminology that made it easy for teams to grasp the process, construct standard value stream maps, and discuss the findings with a broader community. In 1999 this was a breakthrough book because it provided a simple but robust methodology for breaking down, analyzing, and understanding a larger process and its component parts.

Back then, the focus of Lean was more about what people could visibly *see*; culture change was given lip service or avoided totally. Organizations made respectable progress in manufacturing based on what they could see. There is absolutely no doubt that organizations have benefited from value stream mapping. However, there is a dilemma with value stream mapping and all other improvement tools that develops over time, and it has nothing to do with the book. As methodologies become more commoditized and easy to learn, they also reach an abusive state where practitioners blindly follow the recipe without thinking. When practitioners become so obsessed with memorizing the principles, tools, and terminology that they can see, they become exponentially less observant. They create a situation in which the answer comes before the real problem and root causes are known. Many Lean practitioners are in such a deep principles and tools routine that they can no longer see anything different (never mind observe). They have molded their thinking into an *I already know how to improve* mode. The true purpose of Lean decomposes into blind faith rituals of symbolic storyboards, beautification exercises, filling in templates, and other non-value-added work.

Today, value stream mapping has gone viral in several organizations and is producing more waste than value. Many organizations are struggling with getting any value out of their value stream mapping efforts. We have discussed the reasons why and an alternative (accelerated value stream mapping) in Chapter 9. *Learning to See* is a great Lean classic book, but learning to *see* has run its course because we cannot see the invisible Kata aspects of improvement. In a Lean Business System, the new requirement is *learning to observe* (the visible and invisible factors) which goes beyond learning to see.

What is the difference between seeing and observing? Taiichi Ohno taught himself the rigid discipline of observation on a regular and almost superhuman basis. Coincidently all the early Western time-and-motion study books also cover *principles of observation* in depth—including patience, finding the right observation points, quantitative analysis, and multiple observations. Ohno was always observing and always in touch with his factory processes. Most people are not that aware of what is going on around them. The human senses (vision, touch, hearing, smell, taste) are powerful observation forces. Often our sixth sense and our collection of experiences also provide insights to observations. Most people have a sharp set of senses but tend to use seeing and squander the rest. Seeing is instant, attribute-based, and requires the least interpretation. People have a tendency to see with their eyes on autopilot, focused full speed ahead to the destination and become irritated at the slightest disruption. It is this behavior mode that causes people to miss a wealth of valuable information that might have significantly altered the course of their decision making. Technology is enabling deeper visibility into processes and root-cause relationships.

Observation is a self-taught discipline. Police and firefighters, rock climbers, detectives and forensic scientists, martial arts competitors, and extreme hikers are masters of observation because they know that a wrong move could produce severe consequences or end their lives. They are all equipped with the right tools; the difference is that they are looking beyond the physical evidence of what they can see. They are observing behaviors, playing back and verifying current conditions, checking for more clues and missing puzzle pieces, continuously clarifying and validating situations, testing and evaluating unknown conditions, anticipating and preventing disasters, thinking outside of the box, scenario planning, and following up on leads, to name a few behavioral patterns. There is no secret to observing other than time, effort, and awareness. *Observing* is the disciplined practice of using all normal senses, taking note of what is going on around you, and how and why it might affect your thinking. It will not make you an expert extreme hiker or a criminal investigator, but it will make a huge difference in behaviors, decision making, and actions. This may sound contradictory to the discussion of transactional process improvement where we talk about the inability to calibrate problems with normal senses. Technology provides the means for mining for hidden opportunities and expanding our senses. Observing involves the intersection of all of one's senses plus other capabilities with one's mind. Being mindful means being aware of one's environment and its potential interactions with thinking and decision making.

Organizations must learn to see beyond the obvious, to think about the questions that lead to a higher state of learning and innovation, and to correctly interpret and act upon what they observe. *Observing* in a Lean Business System requires thinking that is deeply invested in situational scanning, analytics, hypotheses, predictability, creativity, and synthesis. Observation is the first crucial step in acquiring new knowledge. Observation is the process of collecting information; it still requires reflection and synthesis of the data to put things into proper *perceived* perspective, and analytics to validate the results of observation. The outcome of true observation is learning and new knowledge. Observation requires the right patterns of behaviors and cultural disciplines. The widespread development of these behavioral patterns and cultural disciplines is a function of leadership Kata, which creates the organizational and individual Kata. Organizations can never develop the right patterns of behaviors and cultural disciplines when constancy of purpose is absent, and all of their people are running around with their hair on fire.

Hitozukuri: Speeding to Kata Harada

The concept of Kata is rapidly evolving. A process called *hitozukuri* is being integrated into the culture of Toyota and other Japanese companies. Hitozukuri is a form of shaping people's thinking toward pride and excellence in craftsmanship through continuous improvement. This craftsmanship element is called *monozukuri*, which is the art form of and deep thinking needed to create superior products. Hitozukuri goes far beyond education; it is a continuous talent development process that enables people to mature along with their art (or work) to achieve superior success in their skills and areas of expertise. Hitozukuri is a way in which people inside and outside of the organization train and mentor the employees to learn new skills, master current jobs and mentor others, rotate jobs and grow personally and professionally, develop a higher sense of self-confidence and self-belief that leads to a higher order of improvement.

A high school teacher in Japan, Takashi Harada, developed what is now known as the Harada method, which provides a disciplined process for developing the hitozukuri attribute in culture. The Harada method is used in high schools and grade schools to teach basic fundamental thinking (not tools) of continuous improvement, but it is evolving to a standard teaching process within industry. Think about the competitive advantage of grade school children eventually entering the workforce with these advanced continuous improvement disciplines and mindsets. The Harada method also deals with the invisible human side of Lean and improves the success of individual employees by identifying and embracing a goal or task that helps them move forward. The Harada method was designed for use in schools but can be adapted for businesses with the view of teaching employees to be great leaders and also great coaches capable of building a winning team. This method falls in line with Lean Six Sigma and other methods and tools that drive continuous improvement. The essence of the Harada method is building self-reliance, confidence, and the ability of employees to develop their skills to the extent that they become virtually irreplaceable. This self-confidence enables employees to be truly empowered; to use their skills for their own improvement as well as that of the organization. Employees are developed to where they set their own goals so that there is no question about ambiguity or ownership. They can be trusted to execute and make correct, well-informed decisions.

This is yet another example of the speed of change and the increasing need to discover new approaches to Lean to keep up with the pace. This is the idea behind *improving how we improve* used throughout the book. The Lean Business System Reference Model provides many processes *and* practices to accelerate improvement and enhance patterns of behavior and cultural excellence. But as we have mentioned, it is continuously under development. An organization's adapted and custom-architected Lean Business System should also be a continuous work in progress as new challenges, requirements, and solution needs arise in the business.

Chronic Disruption Is the New Norm

All organizations compete in a global economy best characterized by chronic disruption. This includes persistent, unplanned, and unanticipated events that degrade and disrupt any normalcy in daily operations and key core processes. The source of these events is from both external and internal factors, with most coming out of the complex network of global transactional process issues. What makes these situations so challenging is that, because of interconnectivity, disruptions can quickly yield widely divergent interaction effects across the enterprise. Chronic disruption does not totally inhibit functioning of the business (although it might temporarily), but it introduces disruptions that require more than the traditional remedies and fixes. Chronic disruption often requires a new combination of science, engineering, art, mathematics—and sometimes a little magic. The usual response to chronic disruption is rapid breakthrough improvement followed by incremental improvements over time.

The Lean Business System Reference Model includes provisions for handling chronic disruption by its very adaptive systematic nature and its focus on adapting Lean to transactional enterprise environments. This topic is being discussed more and more in Lean Business Systems because the challenges are often more complex and unknown. Executives are seeking business model, new product, and new value proposition innovations that will change the competitive landscape and industry structure and place their organizations in a market leadership role. Executives are also interested in a *bigger bang for the buck* version of Lean for continuous improvement. The frustration for them is that the traditional principles and tools approaches of Lean *manufacturing* are not yielding enough value in the right places and fast enough—and Lean and continuous improvement in general have slipped to a lower strategic priority. Executives are not interested in slow, high-overhead, hamster-on-a-treadmill, continuous improvement. Yet they cannot disband improvement altogether. How do executives and their organizations turn this situation around? The answer is a holistic Lean Business System, one that integrates the best practices of Adaptive Leadership, architectural design, behavioral alignment and cultural development, planning and execution, an extended Lean body of knowledge, and emerging technology. But it goes beyond creating a system and then using it in a steady-state mode.

Chronic disruptions require a creative and innovative response. This is what the principles of adaptive systematic improvement are all about. We have discussed the need to adapt improvement and go as far as creating new analytical approaches and leveraging technology. We talked about the combinations of these topics plus Kata development as a means of sustaining improvement. This warp speed economy is unforgiving to organizations that choose not to keep up with change. In the future the concept of sustaining improvement in a Lean Business System will become sustainability, then disruptive creativity and innovation, then a higher order of sustainability, then more disruptive creativity and innovation, followed by an even higher order of sustainability. From an organizational and resource deployment perspective, this means leaving the traditional and rigid chain-of-command, span-of-control structure of organizations behind and developing the capability to morph into several different value stream organization configurations on demand. Pretty scary stuff—but very doable with *the right stuff*.

A Lean business is heavily reliant on technology and in particular the business analytics and real-time digital performance dashboard functionality. The Lean Business System Reference Model provides the framework for building a more nimble, organization-centric and culturally grounded Lean Business System to respond to new business requirements and cultural development needs. At the same time the reference model provides guidance for aligning and laser-targeting the highest-impact opportunities for improvement, while accelerating and producing double-digit bottom-line gains. Chronic disruption creates chaos; an adaptive systematic means is necessary to restore order. Chronic disruption creates continuous cycles of chaos followed by order. The adjectives *disruptive* and *adaptive* are expected norms in a Lean Business System and a very positive means of keeping organizations healthy and on top of their game. These conditions are handled systematically through a systematic architecture, and systematic behavioral and cultural development. Without both of these systematic competencies, *disruptive* creates catastrophic events and *adaptive* just does not work. When organizations build these strong systematic competencies, then *disruptive* and *adaptive* are no longer a big deal. Organizations that live through and benefit from these continuous chronic disorder cycles build a very bold and resilient improvement Kata.

Rethinking Lean Organizations

In Chapter 3 we mentioned that most Western leadership and organizational designs are based on a combination of military organizational theory, principles of scientific management, and short-term financial performance. There have been many variations on these same themes over time and from organization to organization. Recently, many innovative organizations are evolving themselves into more innovative organizational models where nimble structures and cultural development are center stage. In essence, it is creating the ideal organizational structures and talent streams in harmony with customer, business, and cultural development needs—a perfect fit for a true Lean Business System, a true adaptive systematic process of improvement.

In 1995 I coauthored a book called *The Future Focused Organization*. The book presented ideas and a few examples of evolving traditional functional or "silo-based" organization structures into more free-flowing pods of virtual super-teams who are engaged to respond to major improvement needs. "Virtual" meant that a specific organizational unit (pod) evolved, performed, achieved success, morphed itself away, and then repeated the process into new pod activities. Virtual super-teams was the staffing model within a pod. We used the analogy of a 1960s lava lamp where the substance rises to the surface creating a shape, falling back down to the bottom of the lamp, and then rising to the top again in a different shape. We incorporated principles of thermodynamics and fractal science to describe the dynamic, *chaos-to-order* birth-death dynamics of virtual super-teams. We talked about the formal structured organization remaining in the background for the benefit of bankers, private equity firms, and other funding sources that, when raising capital, may not warm up to the idea of lava lamps, pods, virtual super-teams, and morphing organizations. The future-focused organization was a nimbling of the traditional rigid chain-of-command, span-of-control organizational models with a goal of taking cross-functional teaming to a higher level in daily work. The book sold well but was ahead of the times in terms of implementation. We are talking about the early days of Just in Time (JIT) and Total Quality Management (TQM), where organizations were struggling through the emotions of allowing their people to participate on teams, reconfiguring departments of equipment into work cells, or taking local ownership for quality without relying on a small army of in-process inspection and rework resources.

Today there is a new organizational model emerging in popularity at organizations such as Zappos, David Allen Company, Precision Nutrition, Adscale Laboratories, and others. These operating structures are based on a holacracy organizational model. Holacracy-powered organizations are based on extant and requisite structures that are actually operating in real-time, day-to-day activities. Extant structures (aka pods, virtual super-teams) become the expected cultural norm and unconscious way that things are done. Requisite structures (a morphing and continuous reconfiguration and realignment of pods) are multiple extant structures that are the most natural and best suited structure to the current work at hand and purpose of the organization.

It does not matter when or who invented the idea. Fact is, this organizational model is the Lean Business System (and total enterprise) model of the future. Holacracy organizational models are a natural fit with adaptive systematic improvement and the sheer velocity of change coming at organizations in today's global competitive environment. Holacracy models also increase focus, alignment, engagement, empowerment, innovation, and creativity in organizations. In parallel with a for-real XYZ Business System, organizations must continuously think about how best to structure and deploy the right resources at the right time to get everything done. At the same time, organizations must use their organizational model as a continuous developer of talent, individual behaviors, and the nurturing of the right cultural standards of excellence (Kata).

Preparation Makes the Journey Successful

Many organizations have been on a path of improvement that is fascinated with colored belts, sensei certificates, rebranded fad programs, mimicking the Toyota Production System, and tools and more tools. These approaches have produced temporary success but have failed to create the much needed, autonomous and continuous systematic way of thinking about improvement. Benchmarking and *adapting* the TPS to one's specific business requirements and cultural development needs are perfectly acceptable. Many organizations have flatlined with their Lean initiatives because of their focus on manufacturing and tools and their disregard for behavioral and cultural development. At the same time, the world has changed dramatically. If organizations remain on the same "mimic the tools of TPS," they will achieve the same (or less) results. Additionally, they will never become a great enterprisewide, adaptive systematic improvement organization like Toyota. The Lean Business System Reference Model is certainly not the cure-all and end-all for an organization's total competitive challenges. However, the improvement Kata side of a Lean Business

System has a tremendous, positive cultural impact on the entire scope of enterprise strategy, execution, and superior market performance.

A major objective of this book has been to guide organizations away from the superficial mimicking of the Toyota way and to think, innovate, expand boundaries, develop the right improvement Kata culture, and become the next global Toyota organization *in their own way*. The book is not a criticism of the past, but an effort to evolve Lean to a higher-order adaptive systematic process and capitalize on new and much greater opportunities in a rapidly changing global economy. *All* global organizations deserve more than they are getting out of their Lean and continuous improvement initiatives, and *all* global organizations have the capacity to evolve their current state of Lean into much higher-order and higher-yielding XYZ business systems.

Think about China's industrial development for a moment. China has accomplished more in its industrial revolution of the past 15 years than the Western world has accomplished in its 150-year industrial revolution. In terms of a Lean Business System the world is challenged to catch up to the progress of Toyota's 70-year track record of success within the next 5–10 years. A different Lean paradigm is needed to achieve new breakthroughs in improvement and superior performance. A very different and superior Lean paradigm—because organizations do not have 70 years to catch up to Toyota—and they will never catch up to anyone with a superficial copying and pasting of manufacturing principles and tools without any regard for culture. This different paradigm is the Lean Business System Reference Model. It incorporates all of the best practices to lead, design, architect, implement, and benefit significantly from an enterprisewide Lean Business System. The reference model also incorporates the most critical success factors above the water (visible) and below the water (invisible Kata). The reference model is the ticket and road map to a new evolution and higher order of Lean—a holistic, enterprisewide Lean Business System. Take the journey and lead new breakthroughs in improvement and avoid becoming a casualty of your competitors' breakthroughs in improvement.

Regardless of an organization's strategic improvement progress, it is time to stop, observe, and shift direction to a higher ground. The 20 percenters do this all the time which is why they are 20 percenters and market leaders. Toyota improves *continuously*. The majority of other organizations can *improve how they improve* by a factor of 10 to 100 times or more, given the new and unknown opportunities in their markets. Improvement will always remain in a temporary and suboptimized state unless organizations place much more attention on developing the right improvement Kata. It has always been easy for executives to skirt culture change—it takes too long, the process is too slow, it does not fit their culture, let's get human resources involved, and so on. These are no longer convenient excuses because Kata is the long-lost foundation of Lean and continuous improvement. Kata is not some new magic mantra, it is the puzzle piece that executives have conveniently kicked under the rug in hopes that it will go away or develop on its own. Kata is a very simple concept: The right nurtured and reinforced behavioral patterns and cultural attributes are the foundation of Lean.

As we mention earlier, global Kata is a far-reaching adaptive systematic process of how organizations think, learn, and execute throughout the interconnected web of activities in the total enterprise. This is a continuous process based on structured means and deliberate actions, with each cycle raising the bar of behavioral and cultural excellence. The Lean Business System Reference Model provides guidance and prepares organizations for this exciting journey to a true Lean Business System. This journey is simplified when one follows the reference model, but it is not necessarily an easy journey. Even with the reference model, there are many company-specific unknowns that must be thought through and integrated into what ends up as *your* XYZ business system. Find, apply, and learn from the Kata in your own soul: Continuous learning outside of the comfort zone and in the wilderness of your intuition is what really develops one into a respected Lean expert and practitioner. The reference model is *our* guidance system for a new beginning—the actual journey to a higher level of enterprise excellence and superior performance is now dependent upon *your* structured means and deliberate actions—and evolving to a higher-order XYZ business system *in your own way*.

Bibliography

Burton, T., and Moran, J. 1995. *The Future Focused Organization: Complete Organizational Alignment for Breakthrough Results.* Prentice Hall, Upper Saddle River, New Jersey.

Burton, T. October 8, 2014. "Millennium Enterprise Excellence," *Industry Week,* http://www.industryweek.com/lean-six-sigma/millennial-enterprise-excellence.

Christensen, C. 2011. *Disruptive Innovation: The Christensen Collection (The Innovator's Dilemma, The Innovator's Solution, The Innovator's DNA, and Harvard Business Review article "How Will You Measure Your Life?").* Harvard Business School Press, Boston, Massachusetts.

Harada, T., Bodek, N., Simone, B., and Hutchens, Will. 2012. *The Harada Method: The Spirit of Self Reliance.* Publisher Communications Systems, Margate, Florida.

Jones, D., Rother, M., Shook, J., and Womack, J. 1999. *Learning to See.* Lean Enterprise Institute, Brookline, Massachusetts.

Laloux, F. 2014. *Reinventing Organizations: A Guide to Creating Organizations Inspired by the Next Stage of Human Consciousness.* Nelson Parker, Brussels, Belgium.

Tobias, R. 2003. *Put the Moose on the Table: Lessons in Leadership from a CEO's Journey Through Business and Life.* Indiana University Press, Bloomington, Indiana.

APPENDIX

Lean Transactional Process Improvement Examples

This appendix provides a partial selection of mini case studies of transactional process improvement and the dramatic improvements that were realized by real organizations. The intent is to encourage new thinking and new possibilities for improvement in a Lean Business System. Please keep in mind that these examples, although impressive, represent but a handful of the hundreds of transactional process improvement opportunities that exist in most organizations. Additionally, there are many unique, industry sector-specific opportunities that can be added to the list (e.g., healthcare, public utilities, airlines, oil and gas, financial services, insurance, retail, government, etc.).

Sales and Operations Planning

A $900 million business unit adapted a segmented approach to sales and operations planning (S&OP). It changed its one-size-fits-all process to a highly customer-centric process considering customer and distributor requirements, product logistics and movement, supply and demand patterns, selling geography and channels, and other differentiating attributes. It designed a hybrid S&OP process based on specific demand and supply stream characteristics and also revised its policies and planning parameters to accommodate the different demand/supply scenarios. Total inventory was reduced by 16 percent and on-time delivery increased from 78 to 96 percent within six months. Incremental revenues from prime customers who were previously searching for secondary suppliers also increased by $48 million. S&OP resources are now spending the majority of their time on the activities that matter the most to revenue success.

Supply Chain

Supply chain is definitely worth mentioning here, and there are hundreds of Lean supply chain improvement opportunities to reduce time, waste, cost, and complexity. Many organizations have ongoing Lean supply chain initiatives underway in the areas of supplier management (e.g., sourcing, evaluation, selection, development, performance management), global planning and logistics, distribution and warehousing, transportation and premium freight, engagement of third-party logistics (3PL) resources, inventory management and performance, analytical flex fencing policies, packaging and shipping container optimization, vendor-managed and consigned inventory strategies, complexity reduction (process simplification), outsourcing versus reshoring, quick response and hedge strategies, service level planning and analytics, branding and packaging configurations, collaborative marketing and supply chain ventures, and the like. Sales and operations planning is the best place to start; this area is always under conflicting pressures from sales, operations, finance, and engineering and is ripe for improvement. Additionally, many improvements in this area have a very positive downstream supply chain impact. Group discussions with supply chain management, accelerated value stream mapping, and other analytics are very helpful at carving out the highest impact opportunities for improvement. Another piece of advice is to carry Pareto around on your shoulder; it is easy to become swallowed up in the universe of issues in the supply chain and other complex core business processes.

Product Rationalization

An $850 million organization in a shrinking industry pressured its sales organization to get whatever orders it could, no matter what it had to do. The sales organization decided to promote a mass customization strategy, giving customers a choice of their own color and other features without even showing them the current product line. This seemed to make sense because once it landed new business, the company would be the sole source supplier for repeat business. The sales organization also allowed customers to order products in much smaller lot sizes without any regard to the implications this would have on the business. This organization was set up to run large lot sizes because the equipment was large and capital intensive. So the dilemma unfolded: The more sales sold of its 3,800 mass-customized

SKUs, the less capable manufacturing became at delivery performance. Warehouses began to overflow with raw materials and the wrong mix of finished product. As always, the first strategy was to scream at manufacturing which was already running 24/7 in four locations. An improvement initiative was kicked off to solve the problem. The team came up with a few recommendations to reduce scrap and set-up times, but not nearly enough to fix the problem. The real problem was product proliferation. The company found itself involved in so many new low-volume products that it was in effect wrapping hundred dollar bills around them with every order. Over 90 percent of revenues and profitability was derived from just 118 products. Worse yet, servicing these customers became a severe drain on the company's ability to take care of its premier customers and markets. The standard offerings were offered at competitive prices with smaller lot quantities. The custom products were offered at premium prices with larger minimum quantity lot sizes. The number of SKUs was reduced by almost 36 percent and profitability increased by over $40 million in the first year of the changes. There were also residual improvements from improved forecast accuracy, higher yields, and major reductions in premium freight.

Inventory Management

One organization had serious excess and obsolete inventory issues and severe inventory financial variances. All these issues are surprise killers to profitability and cash flow. The company initiated several transactional process improvement activities:

▲ The root causes of excess raw material were determined to be an informal and reactionary "over-planning" process, equal treatment of A, B, and C items, and outdated planning parameters (e.g., lead times, safety stocks, minimum order quantities, and unit of measure and bill-of-material errors, etc.). Pareto analysis and other simple analytics were used to identify the right corrective actions, and excess inventory was reduced by over 90 percent within three months. New planning policies and updated parameters were established for A, B, and C items and ERP filters were developed to dampen planning noise caused by changing schedules.

▲ The root causes of obsolete inventory were pegged to specific products and customers. In one case the team found that an obsolete problem was actually a customer installation problem which was eliminated through additional installation training. Preventive measures were put into place for obsolete inventory, and the company reduced its reserve rate by four points (4 percent), an instant positive hit to profitability.

▲ The root causes of inventory variances were also pegged to a variety of detractors such as poor stockroom disciplines, rework and inadequate scrap reporting, incorrect master data standards, supplier short ships, BOM (bill of material) errors, incorrect ERP planning parameters, unreported material cannibalization, engineering change effectiveness dates, and pricing and applied discount issues. A "Paretoized" corrective action program reduced inventory variances by 50 percent.

New Product Development

A $500 million organization was experiencing many challenges in its new product development process. Products were always released late and were over budget. They also required significant engineering resources and time to resolve quality and manufacturability issues after product release. Several specific improvement projects were identified: specification and scope creep, design for manufacturability, design validation, and postrelease improvement.

▲ The documented hidden cost of specification changes amounted to millions of dollars in engineering time, material, and capital costs. Several new product identification templates outlining the required information needed to develop a *complete* specification were implemented, reducing months of non-value-added engineering development time. The number and magnitude of specification changes was not totally eliminated, but the changes were tamed to the tune of $4 million in benefits. These changes increased the capacity of engineering resources available to reduce time-to-market.

▲ There were multiple design verifications (DV) spins and redesign activity in the typical project. The cost of DV spin was documented to be $24,000 to $86,000 depending on what was involved. The DV spin rate was somewhere between 1.7 and 3.9 DVs during the product development cycle, representing millions of dollars in waste. The root causes of DV spins were quantified through an activity-based approach. Surprisingly, this revealed several recurring root causes of DVs traceable to specific failure categories and design engineers. Changes upstream in product design were implemented to reduce the number of downstream DV spins. The benefits of this project were the elimination of over $3.2 million in non-value-added development costs and an improvement in time-to-market.

▲ Another problem included the high engineering support content of ECNs (engineering change notices) after release of products to manufacturing. Most organizations have this process in place, but they have no idea how much cost and waste is involved with ECNs. An improvement team reconstructed the last five new product releases as a representative sample of the process. Team members analyzed the type and level of engineering support for various ECNs after release and grouped activities into categories (e.g., electrical, mechanical, software, test, vendor, etc.). The team identified specific root causes and quantified the "cost of development after release." For the five releases, these hidden costs ranged from $24,000 to $364,000. Again, this is the equivalent of not having time to do things right, but finding time to do things over. Beyond the costs, the disruptions, and customer confidence, these activities take away valuable engineering time for developing new products and stretch out the development cycle or squish the development cycle into the remaining time causing more ECN issues. The team developed and implemented recommendations upstream in the development process, and the amount of ECN activity after release was reduced dramatically. The benefits of this project were estimated to be over $2.6 million per year.

The combined benefits of these five initial product development improvement teams yielded around $13 million in benefits at a time when they were just getting warmed up with Lean Six Sigma.

Time-to-Market

Another organization constantly experienced new products that were late to market, over budget, and often missing critical customer functionality. We discuss this organization earlier in this book. It implemented a highly structured and disciplined formal stage-gate process with an automated system of digital performance dashboards displaying the status and hold-up point of each open development project (green, yellow, and red digital flags, instantaneous resolution). The stage-gate process was flexible, allowing for different levels of discipline for different types of projects. The stage-gate process work elements were arranged in the right routing sequence to facilitate standardization while preventing work-arounds and rework swirls in the process. The process incorporated strict design and phase reviews and a go/no go discipline if something was missing or incorrect. There was no more of the typical engineering attitude of, "We'll deal with that later." A good example of this is packaging which is often an afterthought. The development process encouraged a deliberate "do the right things right the first time" environment with built-in peer pressure from other engineers whose performance was dependent upon the performance of activities further upstream in the development cycle. Time-to-market was reduced by over 55 percent, and revenue from new products doubled over the next year.

Supplier Management

There are dozens of improvement opportunities with the supply base to reduce spend, improve and streamline procurement and supply management processes and practices, and other activities to improve efficiencies and performance, minimize transactions, eliminate wasteful activities, reduce total cost, satisfy stakeholders, and work with the best possible suppliers who meet requirements and performance expectations. One global procurement organization contracted with an offshore supplier to fill the requirements of eight different divisions. Each division placed its demands on the supplier, and the supplier began having serious delivery, past due, and quality performance problems. Each division began overstating its requirements in the hope of receiving what was needed. Each also had daily conference calls to status and reset *its* priorities. Nobody was paying attention to the larger consolidated picture which grew to generate millions of dollars in hidden waste.

An emergency collaborative improvement effort was launched to turn this situation around. The analysis quickly pointed out that the supplier was missing the latest revision level of drawings, critical specifications were incorrect, and the aggregate demand from the eight divisions was overstated by over 50 percent. Many of the past due orders were no longer needed. The supplier's factory was clogged with partially built late orders where there was no longer a demand. An intense four-week improvement effort was implemented that included cancelling open orders without customer demands, removing planning *fluff* in each of the division's ERP systems, purging the factory floor of partially built product that was no longer needed, cleaning up drawings and specifications, and leveling the loading process based on actual supplier capacity. Within six to eight weeks there was a complete turnaround in supplier performance.

Outsourcing Rationalization

Reshoring versus outsourcing is a very hot topic these days, and many organizations are revisiting their strategy. Many of their outsourcing decisions were based on a flimsy foundation, driven by a cursory spreadsheet analysis that focused on labor and other visible profit-and-loss elements of costs. These costs are often irrelevant in the total scheme of outsourcing. Some organizations, moreover, blindly followed the outsourcing paths taken by other companies. Several executives even mandated that "X levels of outsourcing be achieved by Y date" without any analysis at all. Along the way, companies became confused about the difference between price and total landed cost, and they failed to consider *all* of the cost factors associated with outsourcing. Those overlooked factors—the hidden costs and risks of outsourcing—were not considered or even recognized in the outsourcing strategies of most organizations. However, they are very real costs that can represent anywhere from 14 percent to as much as two to three times of total production cost. Beyond cost, there are strategic intellectual property and customer satisfaction implications of outsourcing solely based on cost. You can't outsource making a baby in a month to nine women in China or India. On top of this, many of the economics of outsourcing have changed dramatically such as oil prices, natural gas rates, transportation and freight costs, rising wage rates, lost opportunity because of knock-off products, coordination and third-party costs, environmental, safety, and brand risks because of the unknown substitution of toxic or substandard raw materials, and so on.

We have been involved in several Lean outsourcing rationalization initiatives to revisit outsourcing decisions equipped with more accurate, complete, and up-to-date information. There are many positive movements to repatriate manufacturing back to the United States and to rebuild the U.S. manufacturing base. In other cases, the basic sourcing strategy might remain unchanged, but with significant wastes and costs eliminated in the total supply chain. Think about the airline and other travel expenses involved in doing business with China contractors—especially those with severe quality and delivery issues. One approach to improvement is to rationalize outsourcing decisions of the past, using a total cost of owner-ship (TCO) model that captures both visible accounting costs and the huge hidden supply chain costs and risks such as professional time and travel for coordination, scrap, warranty and returns, currency exchange issues, excess and obsolete inventory, cash-to-cash implications, lack of flexibility and responsiveness to market shifts, premium freight, technology pirating and intellectual property theft, and on and on. The Lean Business System Reference Model™ includes a TCO guide for defining and evaluating all visible and hidden costs. In many cases, this analysis by itself points the needle of outsourcing strategy in a *home* direction. In other situations it is financially feasible, despite the updated TCO assumptions. What we are saying is that some products will never be financially justified as reshoring candidates.

One company with a 100 percent content of its high-complexity/low-volume manufacturing in China experienced a catastrophic situation. A supplier of one of its products called one day and said that it was no longer in business. All of the tooling, specifications, and manufacturing know-how disappeared with the supplier. A disaster recovery team looked for alternate suppliers and decided how best to proceed. When the total cost of ownership including the opportunity loss was calculated, the answer was a no-brainer. The team learned that 80 percent of the world demand was in the Midwest and greater Los Angeles area, and the parent corpora-tion was located in Indiana. The team created subteams of engineers that quickly reverse-engineered and improved the design of the product and eliminated the need for most of the tooling. Then the decision was made to manufacture a new and improved version of the product in Indiana. The company was up and running in three months. The decision was very stressful but produced a 26 percent lower-cost design and $70 million in incremental revenue. The cash-to-cash cycle for this product was reduced from 150 days to 30 days.

For the record: Throughout the book we have provided proven and objective guidance. The following discussion is not intended to be a China bashing session but to reveal the facts of today's global outsourcing game. On the subject of outsourcing, we remain objective and neutral; however, we believe that organizations must look beyond the financials and consider the ethical and moral questions of their outsourcing decisions. Below we have provided social and political policy facts about outsourcing that should be considered in any outsourcing rationalization initiative.

Over 15 percent of what is manufactured in China is counterfeit products. This is a fact. That is tens of billions of dollars in lost sales to companies that outsource business to China. Name a brand, any brand. Name a product, any product. From dirt bikes to fashion clothing and accessories to electronics to sporting goods to Harry Potter books to integrated circuit reclamation are being counterfeited in illegal shops. The United States provides employment so Chinese citizens can spend wages paid by American companies on counterfeit American products sold out of a large facility owned by the Chinese government in Shanghai. China also exports the counterfeit products back to the United States and other countries.

We have discussed the impact of technology in this book. Now consider technology's impact on outsourcing. Companies outsource products to China. They provide material and specifications and tooling. Copies are counterfeited with technology (modeling and CAD) and end up with a distant cousin, grandfather, brother, or other family relative. It takes seven to ten days to reverse engineer an American product and have it available for sale in China and other parts of the world. Lower-specified-quality materials are substituted and purchased from the same suppliers. Shops are set up in some back alley in Shanghai or surrounding township. They are masters at copying. When toys, electronics, performance footwear, fashion merchandise, office furniture, or golf clubs are counterfeited, organizations lose revenue and tarnish their brand. When defective knock-offs with a company's logo on it are returned, who gets stuck dealing with the customer to resolve the problem? These are all costs not included in our reference model TCO (total cost of ownership) analysis, and definitely not factored into outsourcing decisions by organizations.

Why do organizations not consider these factors when making outsourcing decisions? As if that is not enough, consider the following in rationalizing outsourcing decisions:

▲ Chinese currency is grossly undervalued. For every $1 of product that China sells to the U.S. market, Chinese exporters only have to charge the equivalent of 60 cents—a huge subsidy. For every dollar of U.S. product sold to China, there is the equivalent of a 30 cent tariff. Do the math: a 70 cent per $1 spend advantage. This is not free trade.

▲ Whom do you think the United States is borrowing money from to fund its trillions of dollars of debt? Our current administration continues to turn a deaf ear to unfair trade actions as long as China continues to buy our bonds. This process is not stimulating anything; it is increasing U.S. dependence on China as an unfair trading partner at the expense of the U.S. economy. This situation is also nonpartisan and has been allowed to fester for decades.

▲ Cyber warfare is the next cold war. China employs over 100,000 documented agents or informants, and another 50,000 amateur cyber cops and hackers who conduct intelligence and espionage activities on industries, academia, and government agencies to steal valuable financial, industrial, technology, military, and political information. What is the cost of these "hacktions"?

▲ Strategic markets are smaller than optimistic projections suggest. The grand illusion among U.S. executives is that they are selling high volumes of expensive U.S. products to 1.3 billion Chinese consumers, many of whom are dirt poor. Furthermore, the next protectionism countermeasures (e.g., minority ownership, forced technology transfer, and forced export of western R&D facilities to China) are the equivalent of self-destruction for American companies that continue to play this stacked, zero-sum game.

The outsourcing dilemma extends beyond corporations to government policies and tax legislation that has actually encouraged outsourcing for the wrong reasons. This discussion is not a plea for or against outsourcing or reshoring; it has been included to get people to wake up and think about outsourcing from a holistic Lean Business System perspective.

Returns and Allowances

A large retail apparel organization became interested in Lean to improve financial performance and develop its people's problem-solving skills. This organization outsourced all of its manufacturing: It was a highly efficient sales, fashion merchandising and design, and supply chain organization. Upon reviewing the financials, the returns (millions of dollars) jumped off the page. When we asked the executive team members about the returns, they replied, "We just benchmarked ourselves against our competition, and we're actually better than all but one of our competitors. It's the cost of being in this business." Further discussions convinced them to open the door because most of the returns were assignable and correctable workmanship issues. Furthermore, major improvements in this area would offer breakthrough customer service and competitive advantage.

Several teams were set up to resolve returns problems across the entire business. Many of the root causes were attributable to simple fixes such as wrong size, wrong SKU, wrong color, different from catalog picture, embroidery errors, wrong quantity, catalog color never available for sale, wrong mix, truncation of Internet order data at warehouse (not enough character spaces on Internet order form). The teams collectively identified and reduced the returns rate by over $18 million annually.

Advertising and Promotion

The advertising group in one organization was in constant pressure-cooker mode with the design and distribution of its product catalogs. A team was tasked to improve the catalog development process. The company sent out product catalogs two times per year. During the design of a catalog, the pages were displayed on the walls in a large room. The CEO (who was previously senior vice president of sales) and any sales or marketing executive could walk in the room at any time and suggest changes to wording, text type, graphics, and general layout. There was no structured process with defined steps. The catalogs were never late, but the process was painful and costly; the company paid excessive premiums at the printer and mail house for last-minute production and distribution. A few designers and graphic artists told the team that they were wasting their time because this was just a fact of their creative process. The team created a simple value stream map of the process including all of the rework loops, elapsed time, and quantified costs of changes. It was an unbelievable site, a complicated spaghetti diagram. When they presented to management that the company consumes the time, cost, and resources of 2.6 catalogs to produce a single sales catalog, it got managers' attention. The team redesigned the process with a designated approval team and rigid approval gates. Other additions such as new catalog design standards for text and graphics were developed, and segments of the process were reconfigured into a continuous flow publishing model. The company decided to invest the savings from this initiative in incremental advertising. Without any increase in budget, it produced and distributed three catalogs per year, plus several smaller catalog mailings for targeted products and special offers. Revenues grew by over 24 percent annually over the next two years. During the same time period the advertising budget was reduced by 4 percent through further productivity improvements.

Acquisition and Integration

Acquisitions are usually not a repetitive process, and the process itself tends to be nonstandardized. Sure, banks and investors require certain financial information and exhibits. We are talking about the process of identifying, evaluating, purchasing, and integrating new acquisitions. The standard financial due diligence is a very rigorous process. However, the standard due diligence process does not go deep enough into operations and the possibilities for improvement. Nor does it look deep into the present patterns of behavior and cultural attributes and address these elements in enough detail to ensure a smooth purchase and integration process.

We have participated in a number of these initiatives with private equity and venture capital firms and with public and private corporations. The reference model includes several templates designed to create a standardized approach to acquisition evaluation and integration beyond the normal due diligence process. These are not checklists but a more open-ended analysis of the critical integration success factors excluded from the typical due diligence process. The Operations Excellence Due Diligence discussed earlier in this book is a deep analysis of operations and business improvement opportunities, with a detailed plan for implementing the improvements and realizing the benefits. The typical operations due diligence used in acquisition evaluations provides a very cursory and subjective view of the true shape, improvement opportunities, implementation barriers, and cultural considerations of an organization.

Maintenance and Facilities Management

Maintenance and facilities management is another huge opportunity for improvement in most organizations. This includes a wide variety of topics such as total preventive maintenance, unplanned downtime, utilities and fuels consumption, heating and air-conditioning, trash and recycling, scrap reclamation, facility repairs and maintenance, and major equipment maintenance. In hospitals, oil refineries, paper mills, large-scale repair depots, airlines, and other highly capital-intensive operations, improvement activities in the transactional processes of how these services are planned and delivered can save millions of dollars annually.

We have provided a few examples of transactional process improvement. A fact about these examples and all other professional knowledge-based transactional processes is that the major detractors of performance are assignable and correctable with the right facts and the right Lean improvement-enabling actions. These "right Lean improvement-enabling actions" include a broader, integrated set of principles, methodologies, and tools discussed in Chapter 6. Since most of these transactional processes have not been analyzed and defragged to the extent we suggest, the results are usually breakthroughs in operating performance. Transactional forensics is a very appropriate name for this approach to Lean and transactional process improvement. It involves setting up deliberate process experiments for transactional stream mapping and classification to either discover the deep root causes and magnitudes of problems and/or to verify that problems have been eliminated through the right data-driven improvements and corrective actions. In most cases, what was perceived to be the problem is not the problem at all; it is something different, often several interdependent multiple root cause-and-effect issues buried in the complex transactional network. Solving this complex reflexivity puzzle is what creates the breakthrough magnitude of improvements in organizations.

The Last Word

The appendix includes a small, diverse sample of transactional challenges and nonstandard, higher-order solution requirements. The Lean Business System Reference Model provides a guide for architecting an adaptive systematic process and how organizations think, learn, and execute throughout the interconnected web of activities in the total enterprise.

These examples strengthen the premise that a true Lean Business System is organization-centric and culturally grounded. The design, architecture, and implementation focus is always driven by industry-specific business requirements and cultural development needs. The foundation for success is always great improvement Kata: courage, conviction, creativity and innovation, passion, divergent thinking, collaboration and dialogue, emotional engagement and empowerment, inspiration, interest, awe, pride, and other positive improvement-enabling cultural attributes. Because many of these opportunities are hidden or unknown, this holistic combination of requirements, design factors, and patterns of behavior usually generate breakthrough results.

INDEX

About the Author

Terence T. Burton is president and chief executive officer of The Center for Excellence in Operations, Inc. (CEO), a management consulting firm headquartered in Bedford, New Hampshire, with offices in Munich, Germany. Terry has over 30 years of diversified industry experience in executive leadership, manufacturing, quality control, engineering, supply chain management, distribution and logistics, maintenance and repair, customer service, finance, information technology, and sales/marketing. Terry is best known for his innovative but "hands-on" approach to consulting and his executive leadership savvy in mentoring executive teams through major change. He and his firm have a long and dedicated track record of leading organizations through complex challenges to best-in-class practices and superior industry performance.

Prior to his consulting career, Terry held several senior executive and line management positions at Wang Laboratories, Polaroid, and Atlantic Richfield. In addition, he held practice leadership positions with two premier international consulting firms—KPMG Peat Marwick and Pittiglio, Rabin, Todd, & McGrath (PRTM). Terry has extensive and diversified Lean, Six Sigma, technology, and general continuous improvement experience through consulting for over 300 clients in the Americas and Europe—ranging from large multinational Fortune 500 corporations to small and midsized companies, financial services organizations, and hospitals.

Terry holds BS and MS degrees in industrial engineering from the University of New Haven, and an MBA from Boston University. He is a certified Six Sigma black belt and has been an active member of APICS, AME, ISM, CSCMP, ISSSP, ASQ, and PDMA. He is also a member of L.E.K. Consulting's Expert Network. Terry is an internationally recognized thought leader, implementation expert, distinguished keynote speaker, and webinar presenter at many industry and professional associations and has written hundreds of articles on business strategic and operations improvement for various magazines and trade publications. In addition to this current book, he is the author of eight other books on Lean, Six Sigma, continuous improvement, executive leadership, and change management.

For additional information, contact the author directly at burton@ceobreakthrough.com.